IMAGES
of America

BRENHAM

ON THE COVER: Brenham loves parades. Seen here in the early 1930s, people line the street as a marching band prepares to make the turn from Main Street and head north on Park Street. A banner hanging above the courthouse lawn welcomes visitors, for good reason. Thousands of residents from neighboring counties and towns came to Brenham for the annual Maifest celebration when this photograph was taken. (Brenham Heritage Museum.)

IMAGES
of America

BRENHAM

Mike Vance

ARCADIA
PUBLISHING

ISBN 978-1-4671-0862-1

Published by Arcadia Publishing
Charleston, South Carolina

Printed in the United States of America

Library of Congress Control Number: 2022937202

For all general information, please contact Arcadia Publishing:
Telephone 843-853-2070
Fax 843-853-0044
E-mail sales@arcadiapublishing.com
For customer service and orders:
Toll-Free 1-888-313-2665

Visit us on the Internet at www.arcadiapublishing.com

To the board, staff, and volunteers of the Brenham Heritage Museum and all who love Washington County history.

Contents

ACKNOWLEDGMENTS

When gathering photographs and information for a book such as this, one requires many hands. Some have shared photographs, and several have loaned their expertise in local history. Among those on the list of people to thank is Carl Schlottmann, a fine man who has studied Brenham history so long that the city routinely consults him. A score of others are right there with him. Gloria Nix, Stanley Sommer, Natearah Austin, Cheryl Dabera, Susan Myers, Bob Grabarschick, Janel Jefferson, Seth McMeans, Tina Henderson, Lowell Herzog, Beth Rothermel, Robert Mueller, Faye Williams, Atwood Kenjura, John Barnhill, Dave Hubbard, Ben Seeker, Brian Scheffer, Teddy Boehm, Nancy Low, and the late—and greatly missed—Eddie Harrison were there to fill a newcomer in on local history when he asked. Finally, none of this book would have happened without the full support of the Brenham Heritage Museum, where I am lucky enough to be executive director. The board of directors, volunteers, and fellow staff members are, like all longtime residents, passionate about the history of Brenham and Washington County.

Unless otherwise noted, all images appear courtesy of the Brenham Heritage Museum.

Introduction

Brenham, and by extension the neighboring areas of Washington County, is filled with hidden stories. For a small town, it casts a long shadow in Texas history. Even before a totally nascent city became the county seat in 1844, the surrounding area was home to determined American immigrants to Austin's Colony in the Mexican state of Coahuila y Texas. The communities of Independence, and then Washington, were small but notable parts of what Stephen Austin called "the foreign settlements" within the Mexican Republic.

After victory at San Jacinto, a new Republic of Texas was born, having been declared in Washington County. Though that republic lived its entire short life mired in deep bankruptcy, turmoil, and uncertainty, the dreams of its citizens were often grandiose. Some business-minded early Texans even imagined growing wealthy in a thriving metropolis on the frontier. Early Brenham was lucky enough to be home to a few such people who could tell a good enough story to attract the capital needed to outpace its rivals. Growth for the city began as the supply center for a rich agricultural area, but when leaders in Brenham and Chappell Hill secured a railroad spur just prior to the Civil War, progress was all but assured. As the terminus to the line, Brenham added transportation hub to its resume.

Thanks to the first railroad, which became the Houston & Texas Central, and the addition of the Gulf, Colorado & Santa Fe in 1880, Brenham businesses of the late 19th and early 20th centuries shipped out not only agricultural products but also goods manufactured by local light industry. Plows, buggies, mattresses, cottonseed oil, and small industrial engines were made locally and exported regionally. The railroad economy meant the rise of other Washington County towns such as Burton, and the demise of places like Washington, which spurned the new technology, choosing instead to double down on steamboat traffic along the fickle Brazos River.

African Americans, families who had been brought as enslaved workers, made up almost half of the population in Washington County for a century, and those numbers held strong in the city of Brenham as well. Following emancipation, black-owned businesses prospered in Freedom Colonies such as Camptown and Watrousville and in downtown Brenham along Alamo and Commerce Streets. It was a parallel economy that existed in response to smothering segregation.

From the 1840s through the 1880s, European immigrants, primarily German, flooded into Brenham and Washington County. Slow to assimilate, German clubs and churches thrived. Classes in the language were a staple in all levels of local schools, and it was common to hear leading citizens conversing in German on the streets of downtown Brenham. Smaller enclaves in the county brought Polish and Czech immigrants into the ethnic mix. Jewish merchants arrived and played an oversized role in the town's retail and wholesale trade, owning the city's top dry goods stores and cementing a spot as leading citizens.

Among the traditions imported from Germany was a spring festival. Begun by a German club and handed off to the Brenham Fire Department, Maifest was a sensation from the get-go. Crowds flocked to Brenham from surrounding counties to enjoy the finery and festivities. Longtime families eagerly awaited word of the chosen royalty, and coronations and parades were the social events of the year. The Washington County Fair, the oldest in the state, is another Brenham tradition with roots that stretch back a century and a half. Juneteenth can also make that claim. Black Texans from outside the county traveled to enjoy the parades and games. Let no one ever charge that Brenham does not enjoy a good celebration.

Education has been valued greatly over the years. The influx of religious institutions was a factor, as was the preponderance of German immigrants who had a record of promoting education that far surpassed their English American counterparts. Though Texas was painfully slow to embrace taxpayer-funded schools, the citizens of Brenham were quick to respond when the current state constitution offered the chance. The Brenham Independent School District is the oldest district that exists under the current framework, a law that dates to 1875. Graduates of Brenham schools remain fiercely proud of that fact, and grandstands still fill at local games, especially for Friday night football and for baseball, where the high school's legacy runs deep.

Higher education also enjoys an illustrious past. Some of the earliest colleges in Texas, for both men and women, started in Washington County in the towns of Independence and Chappell Hill. A teacher's college for African Americans did well over 100 years ago. Those schools are gone, but Blinn College on the west side of Brenham has grown into one of the top-rated community colleges in Texas. It began as a German Methodist institution, but became nonsectarian in the 1920s. By 1937, it was the first county-owned junior college in the state. Today, it has multiple campuses and is a leader at transferring successful students to four-year universities.

All denominations in Brenham can point to churches that date to the 19th century. Many still utilize buildings over a century old. With such a strong history of German Lutheranism, Washington County is currently one of only two among the 254 counties of Texas whose largest denomination is neither Catholic nor Baptist.

Even folks outside of the Lone Star State have heard of Brenham thanks to the marketing campaign of hometown business Blue Bell Creameries. The ice cream favorites are shipped to almost half of the United States, but the local economy enjoys much more diverse contributions. Tourism prospers in Brenham, and much of it is due to the embrace of historic preservation. Dozens of Victorian-era homes have been restored, and some neighborhoods can claim pristine mid-century architecture. It is the wonderfully preserved downtown that draws most people to Brenham, however. Defying trends in many other parts of small-town America, city leaders have turned the past into a bright future, and Brenham is now on the wish lists of many Texans seeking a better place to live.

One

DOWNTOWN

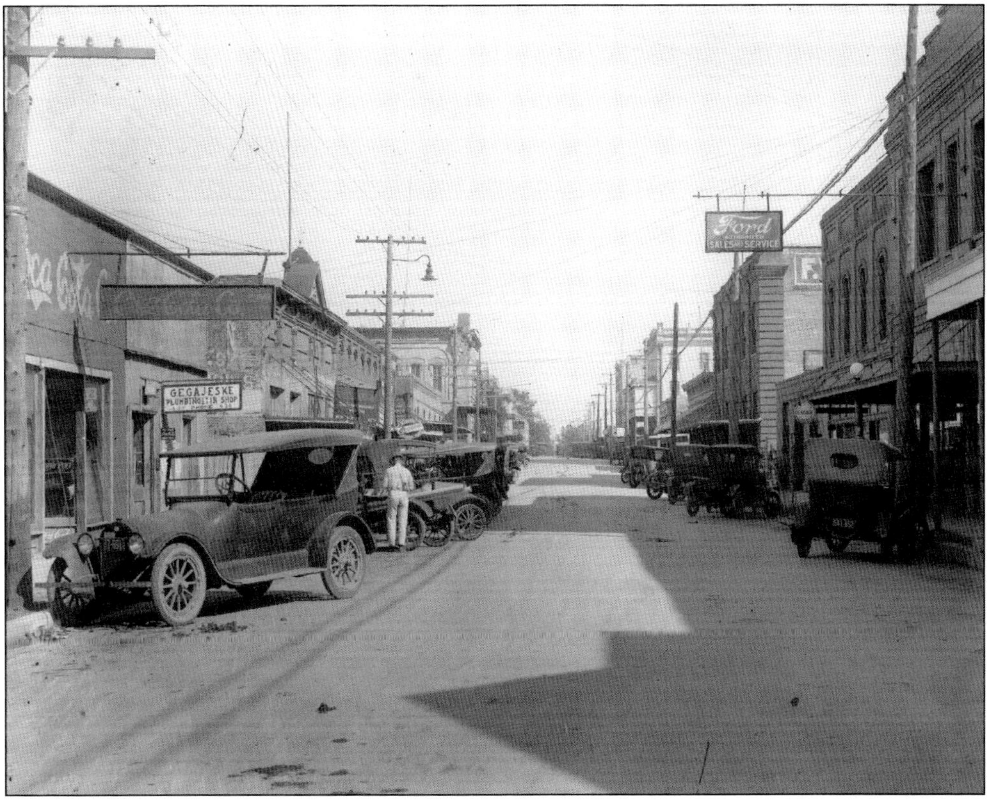

Here is Alamo Street looking east, almost from South Austin Street, in the early 1920s. Gus Gajeske operated the plumbing business in the left foreground. In 1928, his brother Albert opened a mattress factory, which was run out of the same building. The Brenham Mattress Factory invited customers to drop by and view the "up-to-date machinery" that would fashion their custom mattress.

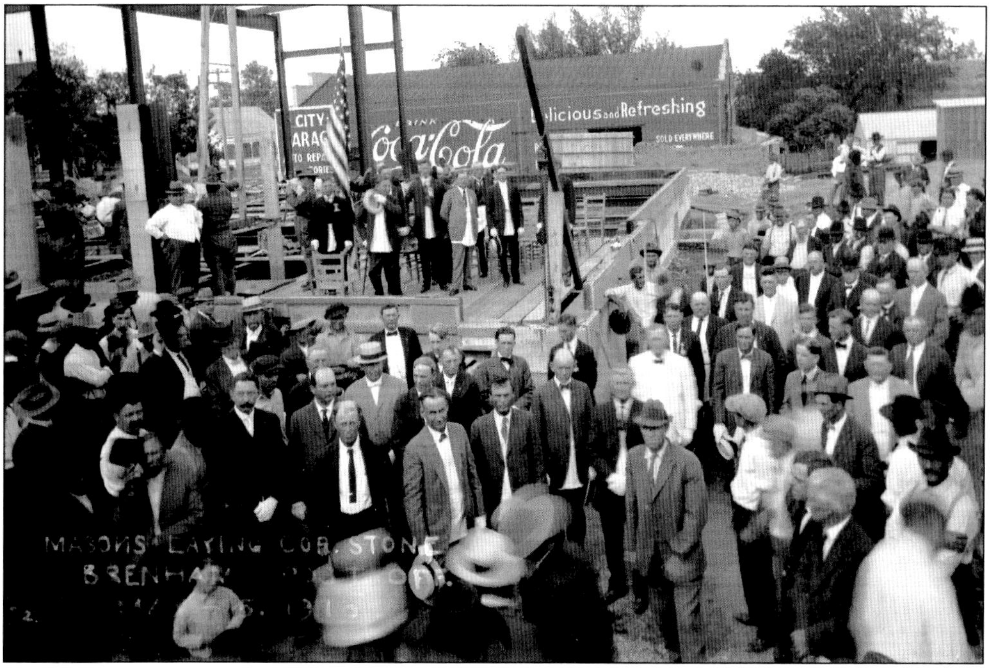

Members of the local Graham Masonic Lodge No. 20 took part in laying the cornerstone for the new Brenham Post Office in 1916. The masons' request that the cornerstone be moved from the southwest to the northeast corner of the building to conform to their tradition was denied.

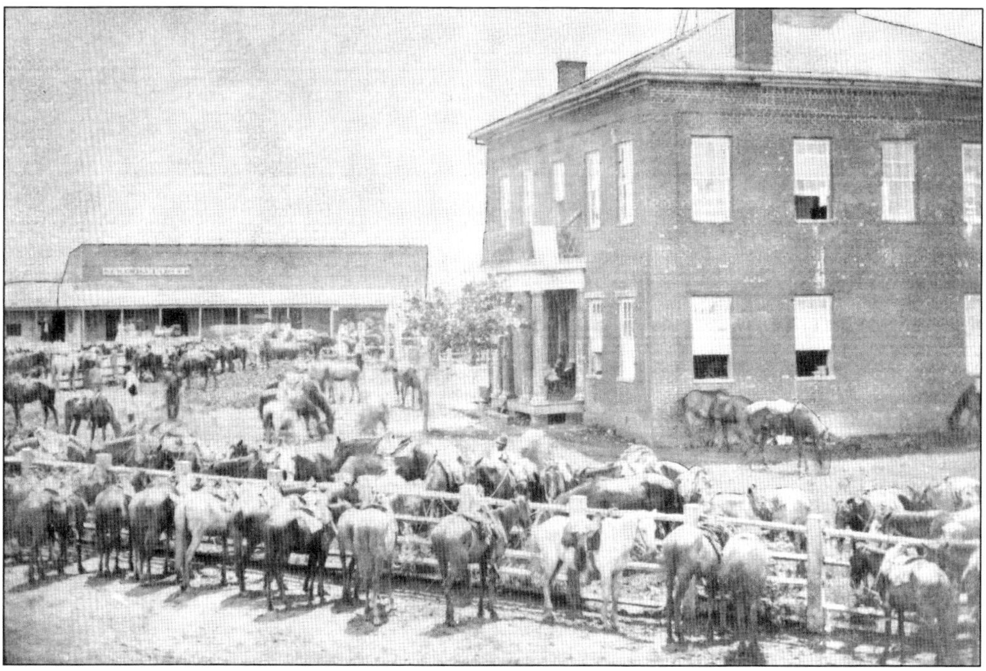

The second building to occupy Brenham's courthouse square rose in 1852. It was a square Greek Revival building constructed by the firm of John Stamps. It used locally made brick, as did many other buildings in the new town. That brick proved to be very brittle over time; however, some downtown buildings with Brenham brick veneer still stand.

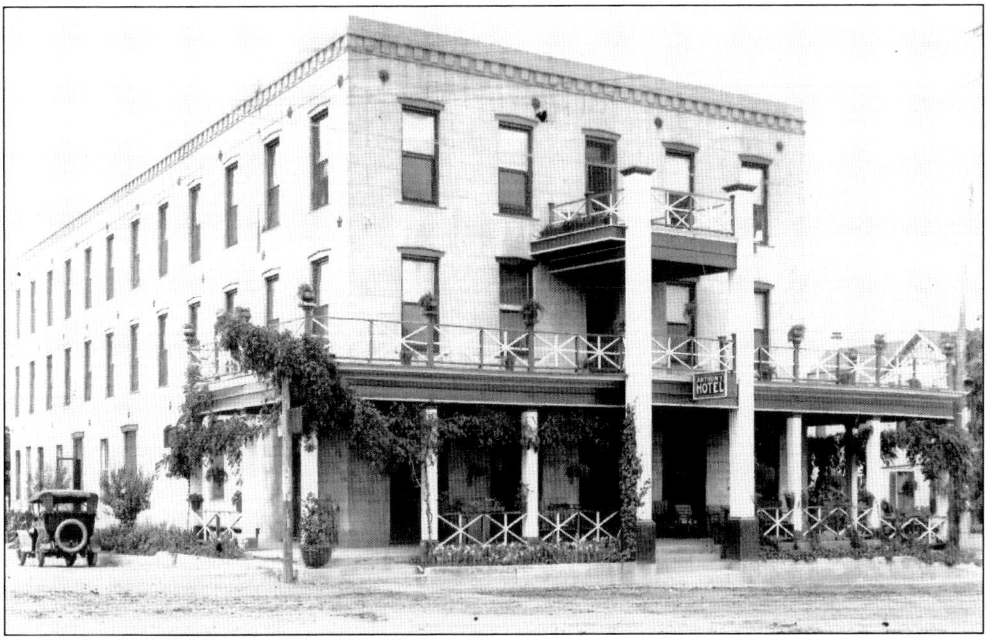

The Anthony, which became the St. Anthony Hotel in 1914, offered Brenham's finest lodgings for almost a century. It had opened as the Exchange Hotel in the 1870s and was run for 40 years by George Wilson, who moved from Houston for that reason. In the mid-20th century, Mrs. E.R. Hacker operated the hostelry, which had been rebuilt in the 1920s.

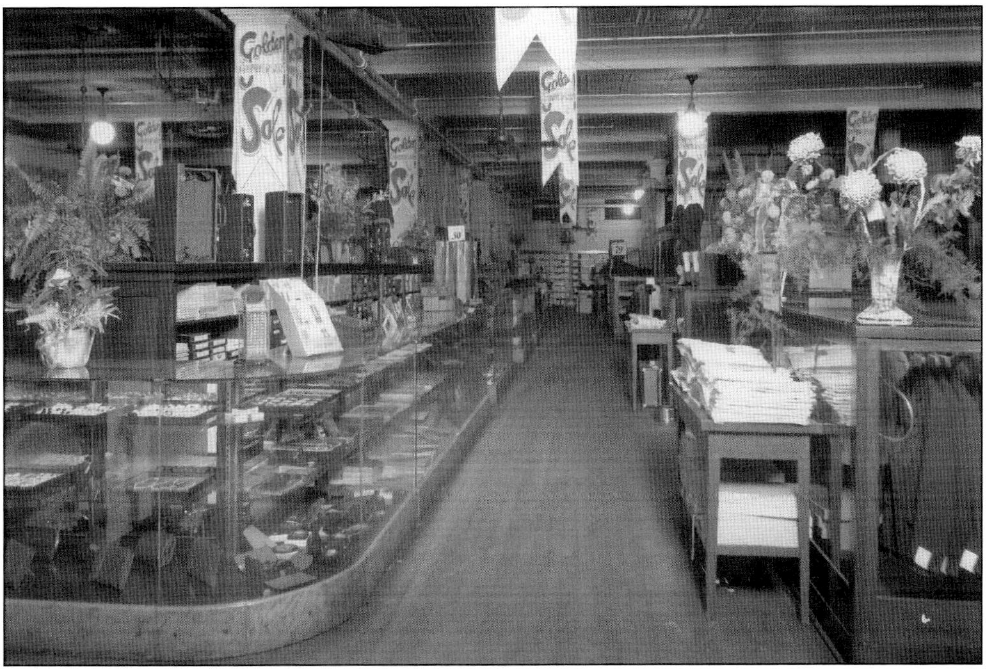

The main floor of Hohlt's Department Store was gussied up for its 50th anniversary in 1934. The store started selling dry goods and clothing under the name of Brockschmidt & Hohlt, but it was reorganized into the H.F. Hohlt Company in 1902. The family-run business added a large grocery and a feed department as well. People still fondly recall the wire basket payment conveyor system.

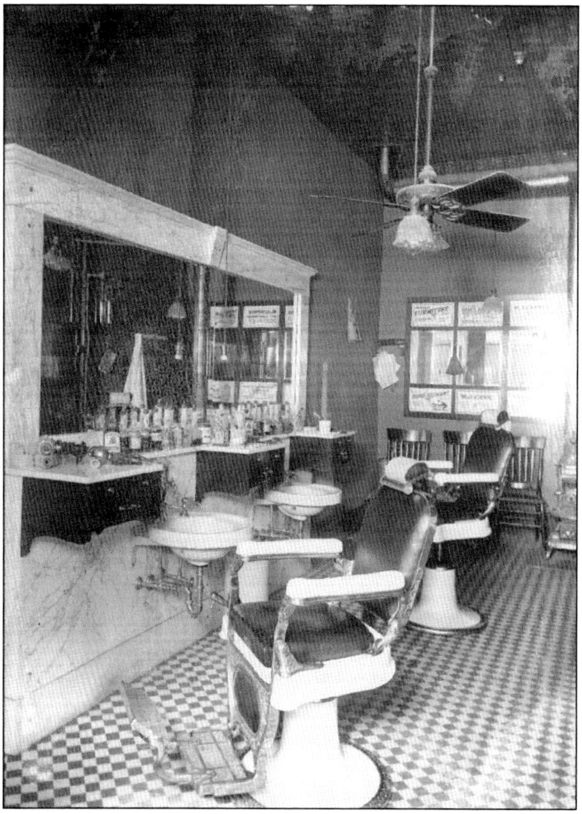

Charlie Stokes owned the Elite Barbershop on the west side of the square in the early 1900s and employed several other barbers over the decades. In the late 1930s, a shave ran a quarter, and a haircut would set a customer back 35¢. The adventurous man could add an "oil steam shampoo" and an electric scalp massage with tonic for a dollar more.

The well-dressed staff of Robertson Grocery at 200 St. Charles Street show off their wares through the painted plateglass. Among the young men starting there was Rudolph Wintz, who soon moved to the Nu-Way grocery operation at Hohlt's Department Store on Main Street. Wintz remained there for over 45 years.

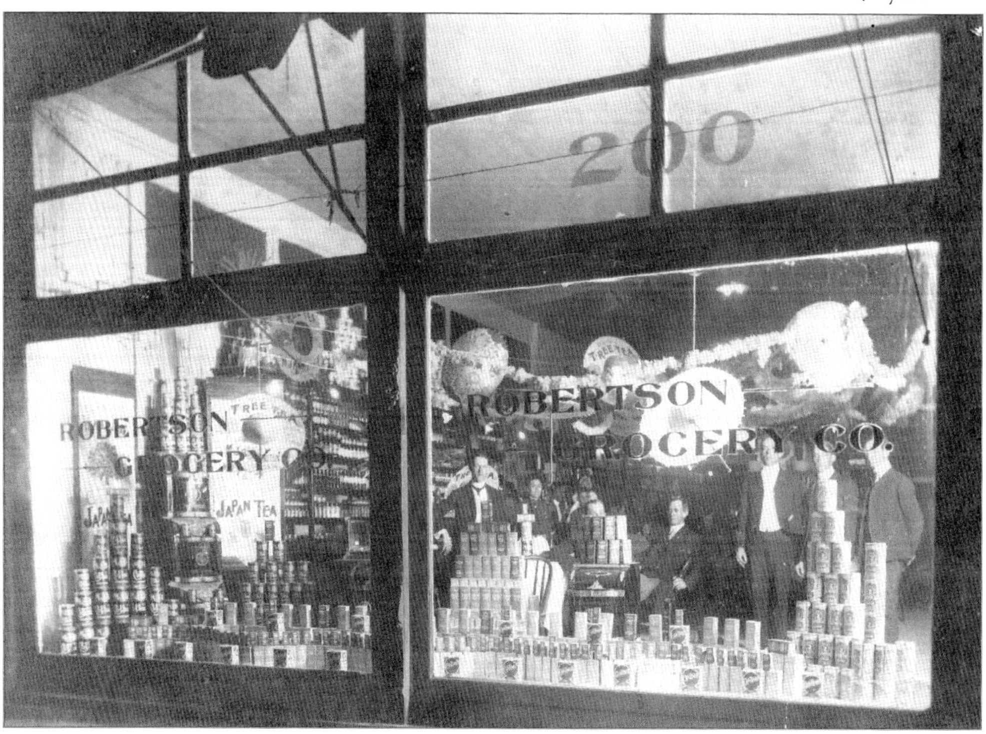

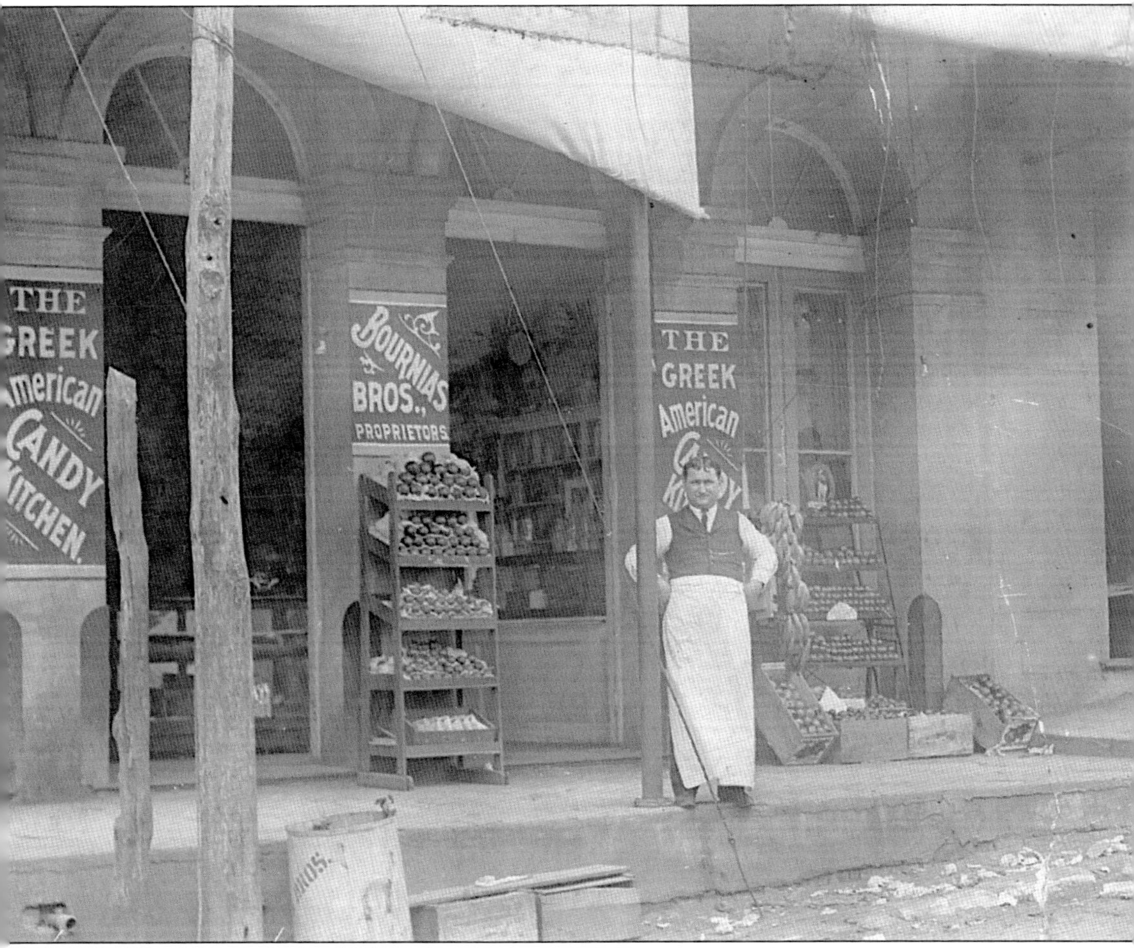

The Bournias brothers owned the Candy Kitchen at Alamo and St. Charles Streets in the first decade of the 20th century. In 1910, the 38-year-old George and his younger brothers Peter, James, and Nick were all living together, as was a nephew who was also born in Greece. All five were either confectioners or candy salesmen, and had come to America less than eight years earlier. Brenham was never home to any sort of Greek immigrant enclave, but the family from Koroni, Greece, became popular members of the community. In addition to sweets and frozen items in the summer, cold weather brought hot chocolate, beef tea, and bullions of chicken, tomato, oysters, or clam. A fine line of picture postcards, a craze of the day, was also available. Today, a mural memorializes this image on the east exterior wall of the building.

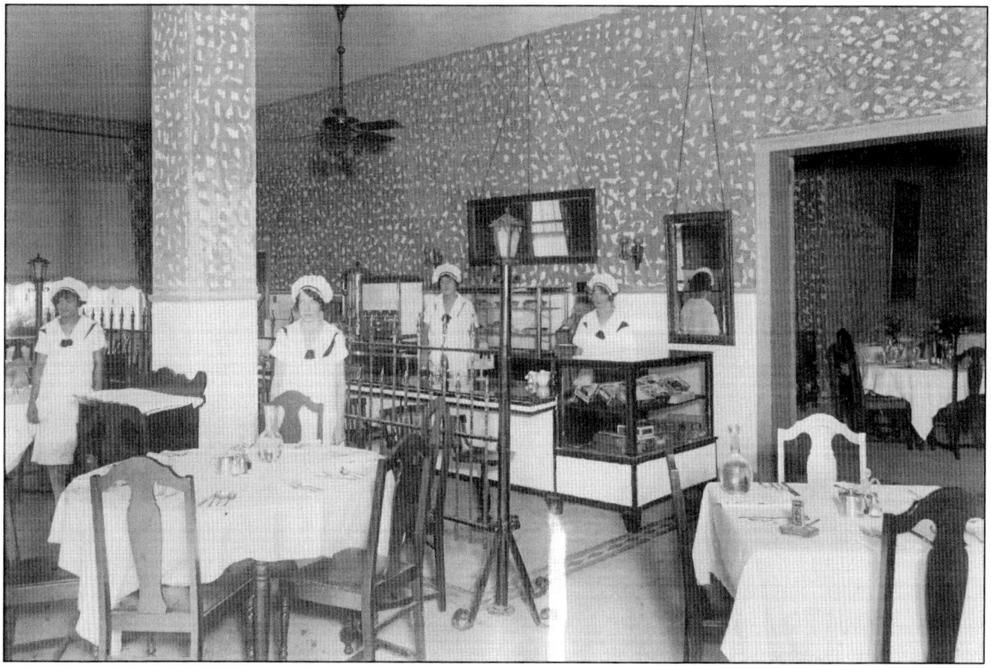

The café inside the St. Anthony Hotel was a bit upscale. In the 1920s, it offered a daily Merchant's Lunch for 50¢. It also responded to special events, such as staying open until 2:00 a.m. to feed sandwiches, salads, and cake to revelers at the 1927 Elks Lodge dance. The hotel gave this café configuration an updating in 1930.

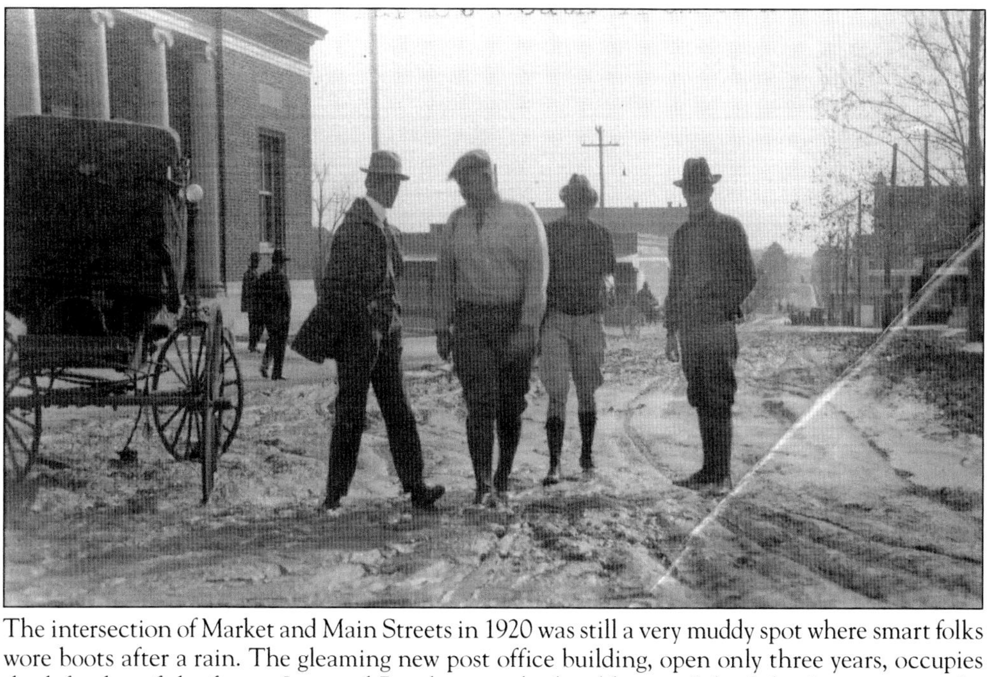

The intersection of Market and Main Streets in 1920 was still a very muddy spot where smart folks wore boots after a rain. The gleaming new post office building, open only three years, occupies the left edge of the frame. It served Brenham as the local home of the federal government for another half century. (Texas Department of Transportation.)

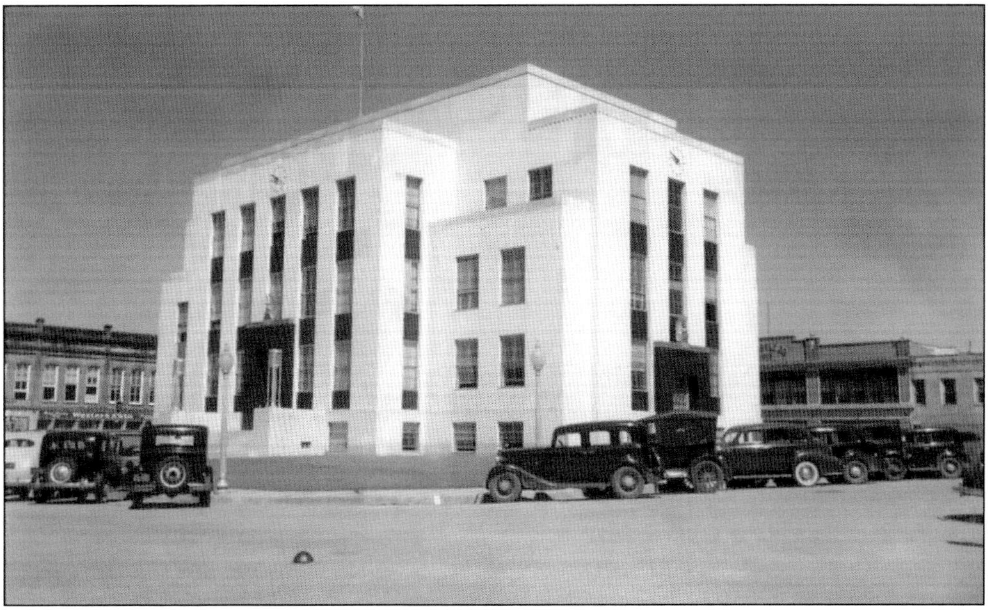

The new Washington County Courthouse, viewed from the intersection of Alamo and Baylor Streets, was an Art Moderne design by Travis Broesche that opened in 1939. Built of white limestone, using funds from the federal government's Public Works Administration, it was completed under the tenure of county judge Sam Low. C.L. Browning was the contractor, bringing the project in for about $200,000. (Texas Department of Transportation.)

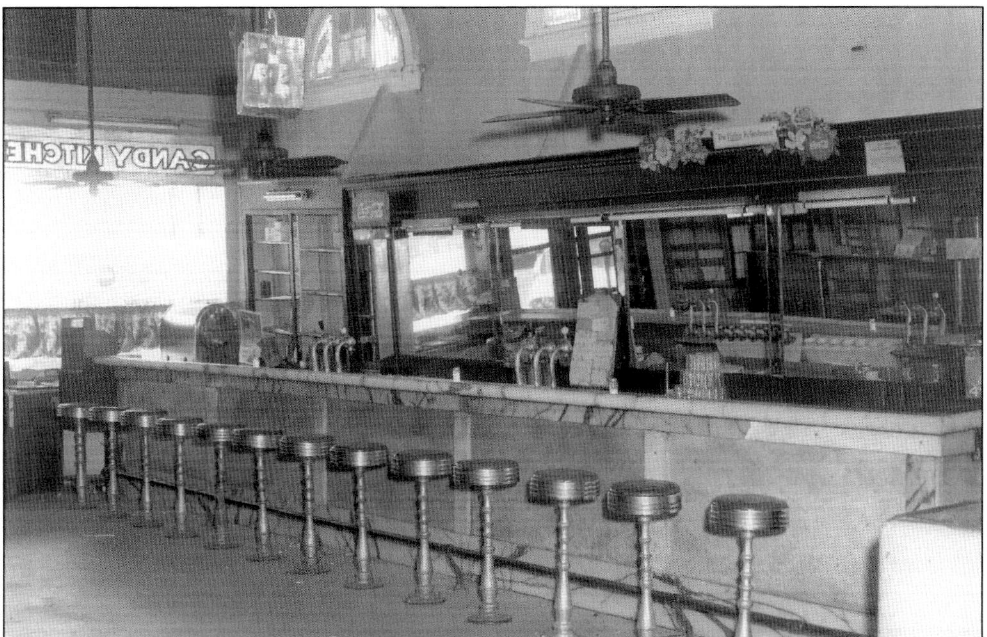

The counter at Candy Kitchen was a popular place. In 1933, it advertised a double dip ice cream cone for a nickel and a special on banana splits for only a dime. As the name suggests, they also made candy, and there was a soda fountain. The marble counter and white tile floor provided the sugar fix for two generations of Washington County kids.

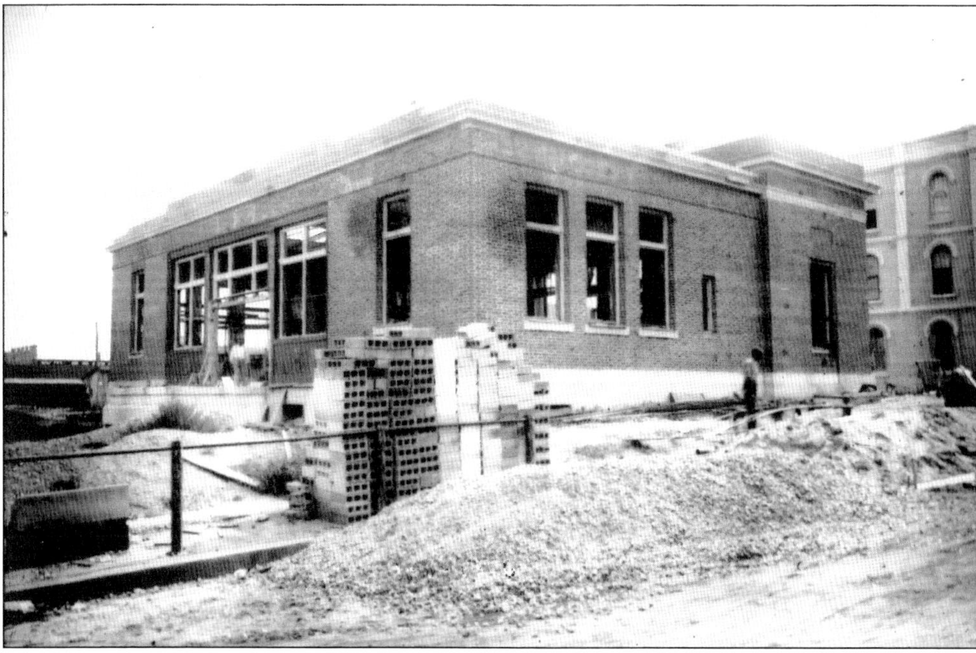

On the eve of World War I, Brenham received a grand new post office. The facility put many community postmasters out of work since six new rural routes radiated out from Brenham. Construction was delayed for some time as crews waited for structural steel while limestone blocks piled at the site and the completed basement, waterproofed with two heavy coats of coal tar, sat idle.

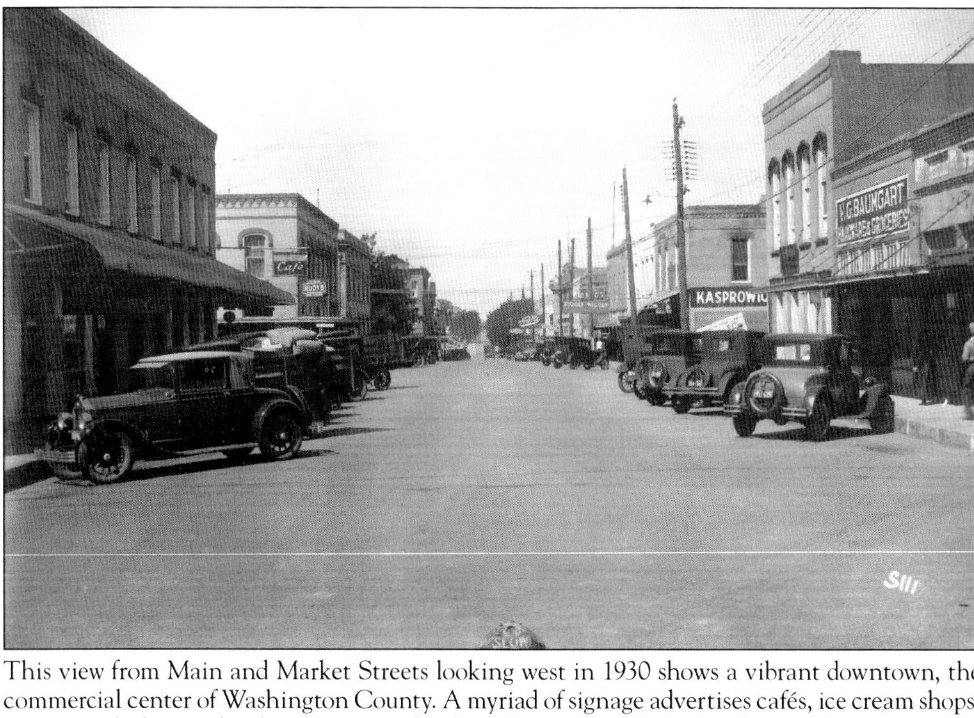

This view from Main and Market Streets looking west in 1930 shows a vibrant downtown, the commercial center of Washington County. A myriad of signage advertises cafés, ice cream shops, groceries, clothes, and a place to get cars fixed. Large iron "buttons" at each intersection reminded motorists to keep their speed to a slow, safe pace through town.

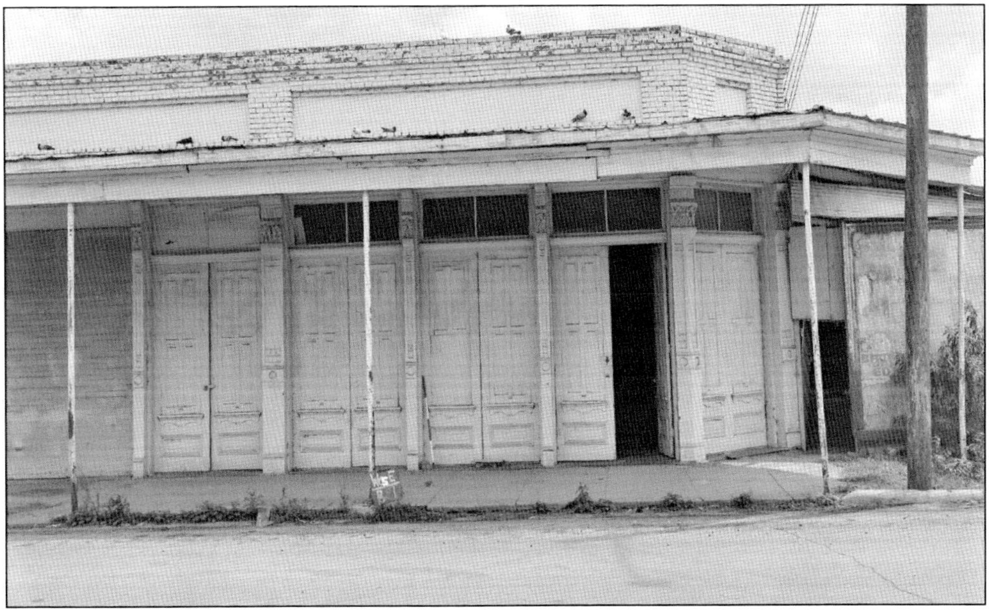

At First Street and the railroad tracks in the early 1980s, this building seemed valued more by pigeons than anyone else. It is tough to tell from today's vibrant downtown historic district, but Brenham's city center did reach a low point when commercial traffic there was sparse. Imaginative business leaders and politicians bought into the Main Street program and turned things around.

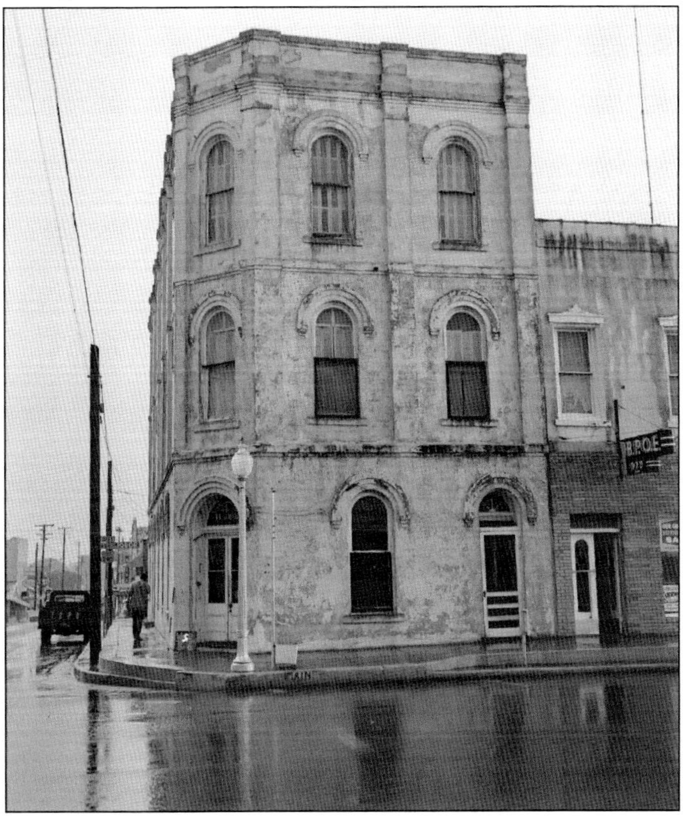

The Bassett and Bassett Bank at the corner of Market and Main Streets is beautifully rehabilitated today. It was Brenham's first bank, chartered at the close of the Civil War. A decade earlier, the Bassett brothers had served Brenham as lawyers and agents of the *Texas Ranger* newspaper out of Washington. The door immediately to the right of the Bassetts' building led upstairs to the Elks club lodge.

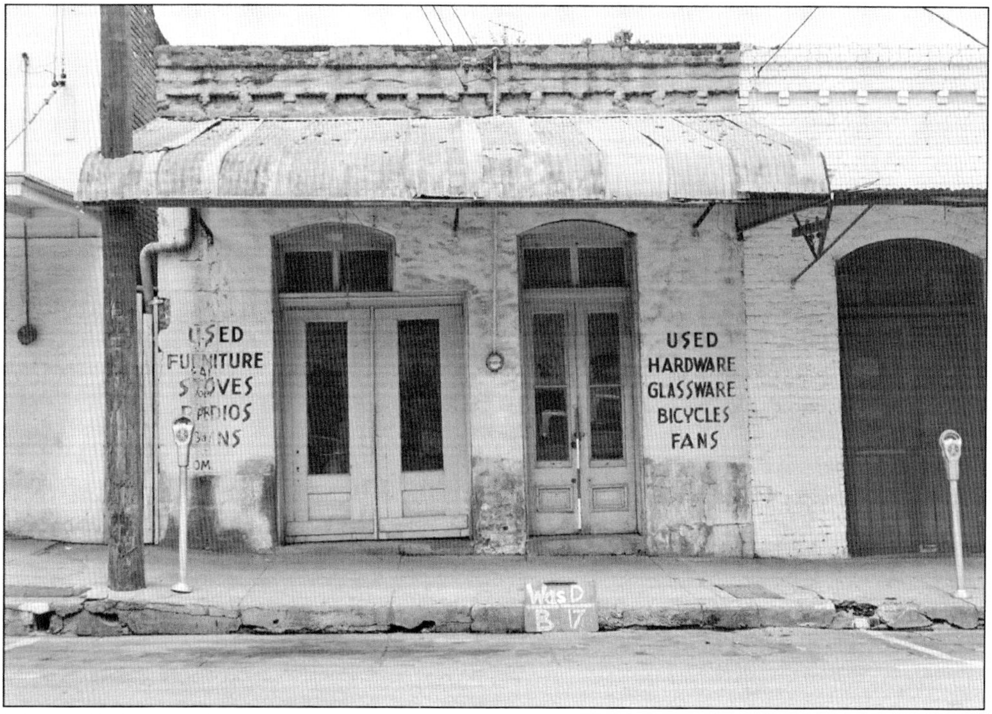

The small shop on Baylor Street near Commerce Street sold a variety of used goods, with several examples painted outside as advertisement in the 1970s. Earlier in the 20th century, it operated as a hay and feed business and a clothing store, but it was a casualty of the period of neglect to befall downtown. Today, only a small section of front wall survives, with advertising intact.

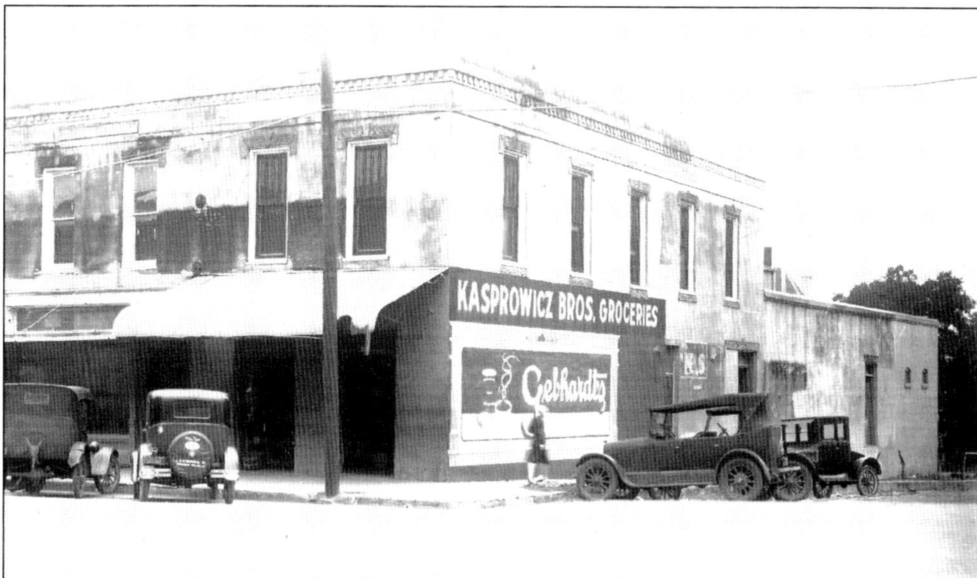

In Brenham in the 1920s and 1930s, the name Kasprowicz might appear in advertisements or the baseball box score. Max Kasprowicz starred at Brenham High and Texas A&M, and then with a semiprofessional team, the Sun Oilers. His father, John, a Polish immigrant, operated a grocery store on St. Charles Street.

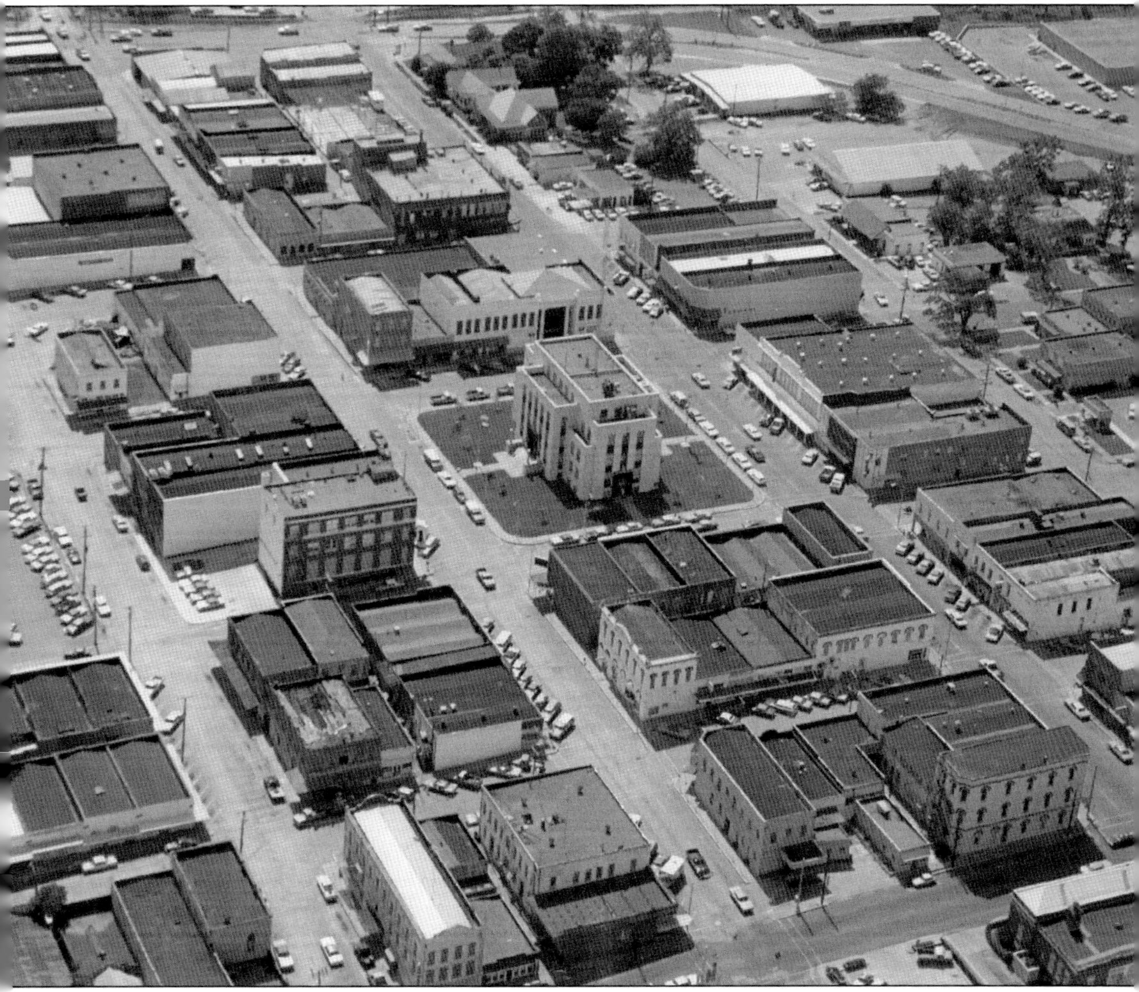

This 1950s aerial photograph of downtown Brenham offers a wealth of information. The courthouse is centered in the shot, and the post office occupies the extreme lower right corner. The overall footprint along the two main streets has changed relatively little in 70 years, although the city government's home along Vulcan Street in the upper right is quite different. The confection of a Romanesque city hall had been replaced with a modern municipal complex that also kept the fire station and library nearby. A few decades later, city hall moved down the street again into a larger complex, and the library went farther north. A few of the old downtown buildings had gained modern skins by the 1950s, but the aerial view of their roofs sometimes gives them away. One notable absence is the courthouse gazebo. It would eventually return, at least in replica form, for the country's bicentennial in 1976.

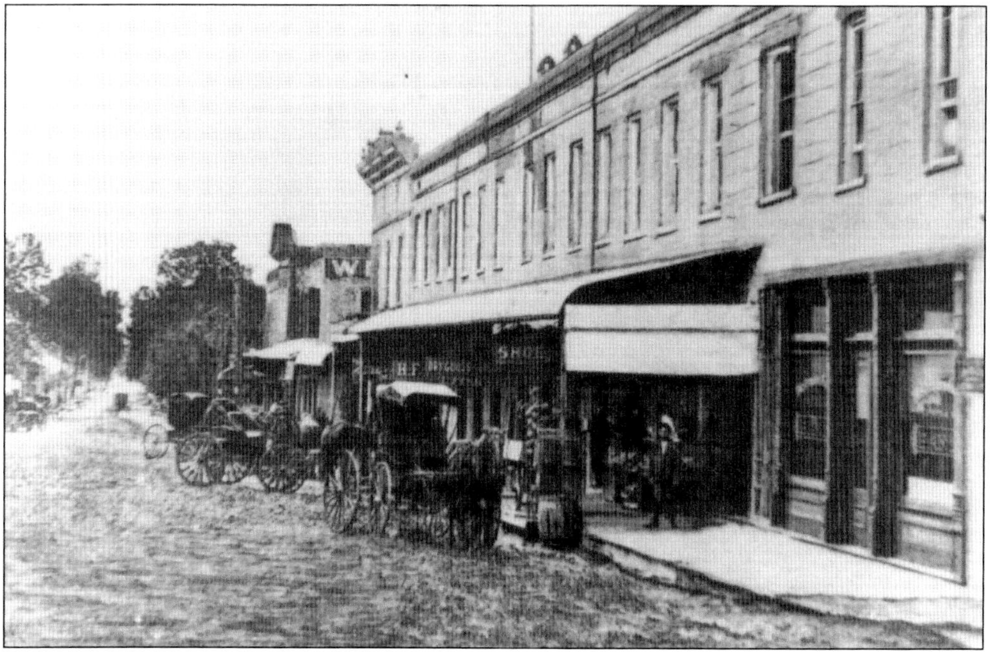

Brenham's Main Street, looking west in the late 1800s, shows the buggies of several customers outside H.F. Hohlt's first store. The dirt streets would turn to mud with the slightest rain. Muddy roads radiating out into the county could become a major hindrance to Brenham's commerce and activity when a gully-washer came. The entire county fair was once canceled due to impassable mud.

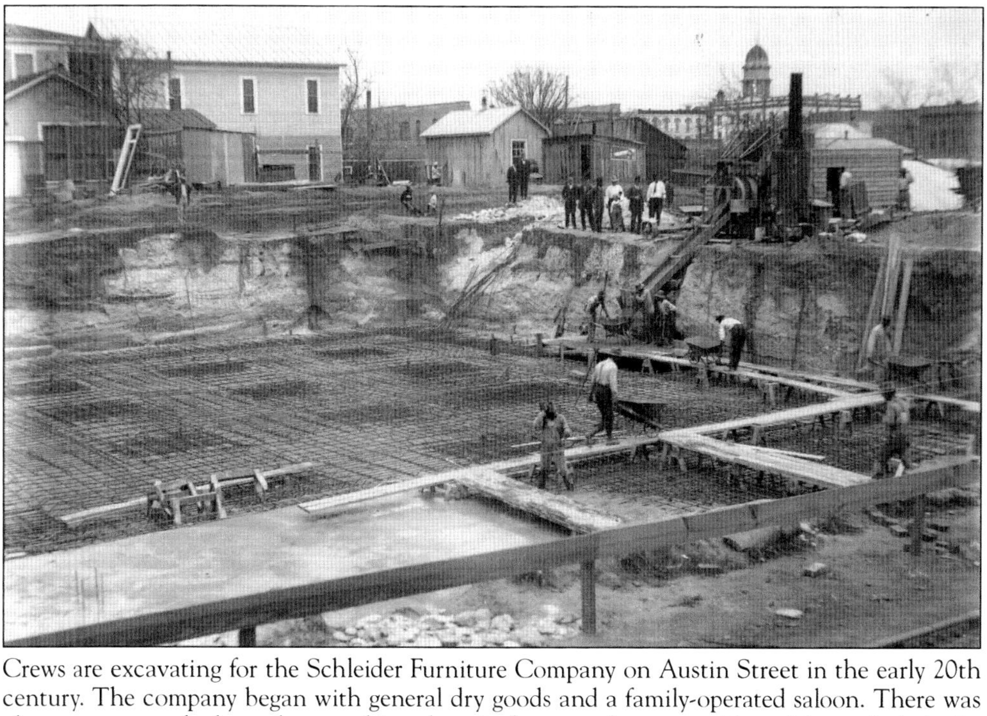

Crews are excavating for the Schleider Furniture Company on Austin Street in the early 20th century. The company began with general dry goods and a family-operated saloon. There was also a wagon yard where those making the trip from rural communities might park their rig. The basement being excavated served as Brenham's official fallout shelter during the Cold War.

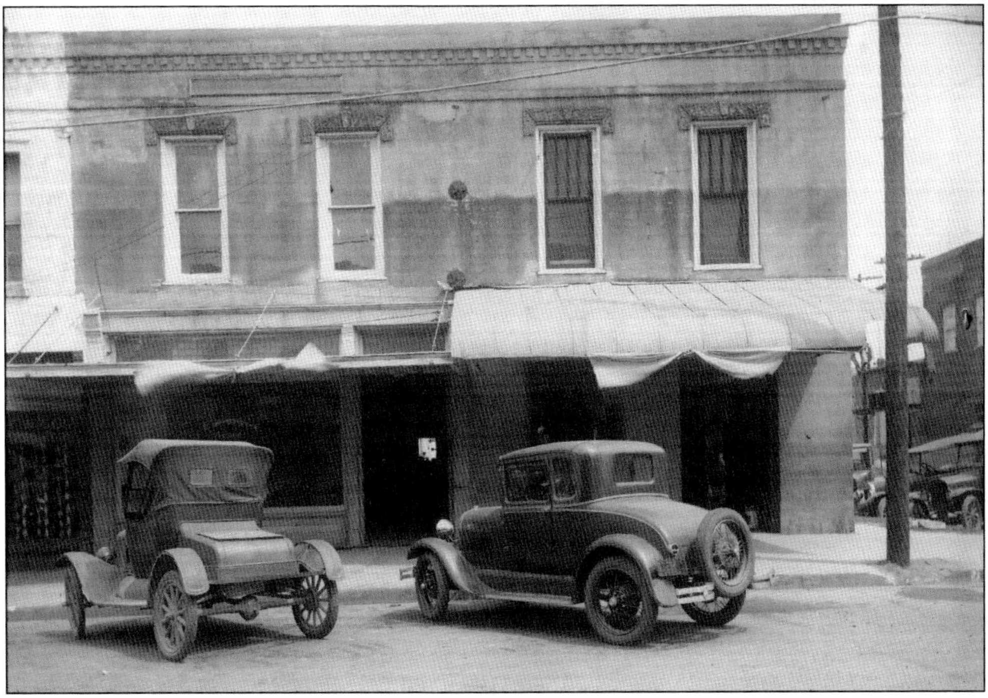

The Schramm Saddle Shop on Main Street was a mainstay during the days when leather goods were an essential part of horse-based transportation. Well-known doctor W.F. Hasskarl Sr. arrived in Washington County in 1910, and one of his early purchases was a saddle and new saddle bags from Schramm's that helped him make his country rounds.

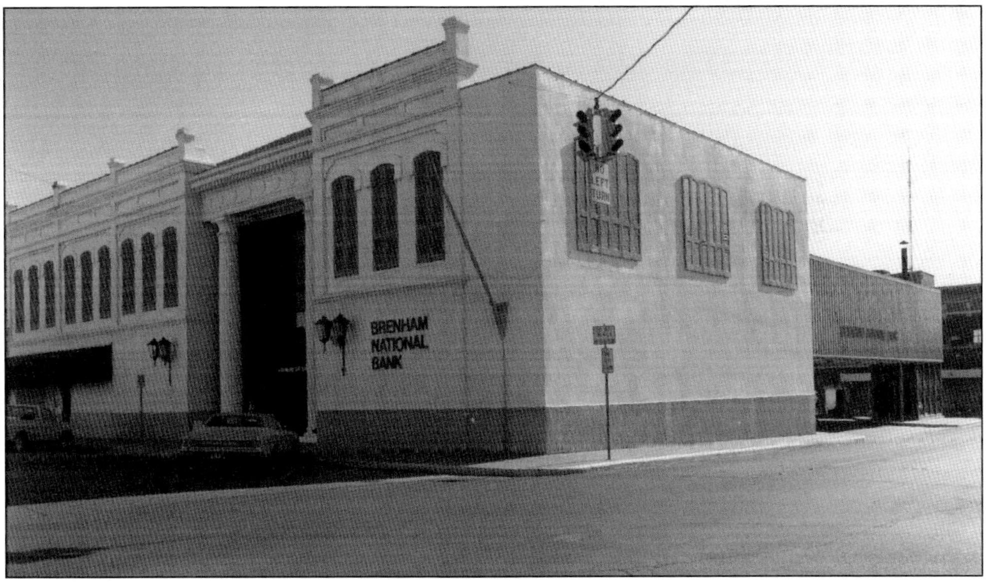

Brenham National Bank occupied the building at Main and Park Streets that is the Washington County Courthouse Annex today. The local name most closely associated with that institution is Tieman Dippel, and that name crosses multiple generations. The senior Dippel served as county sheriff for 20 years, retiring in 1960 to become bank president. He changed the name from Farmer's National Bank early in his tenure.

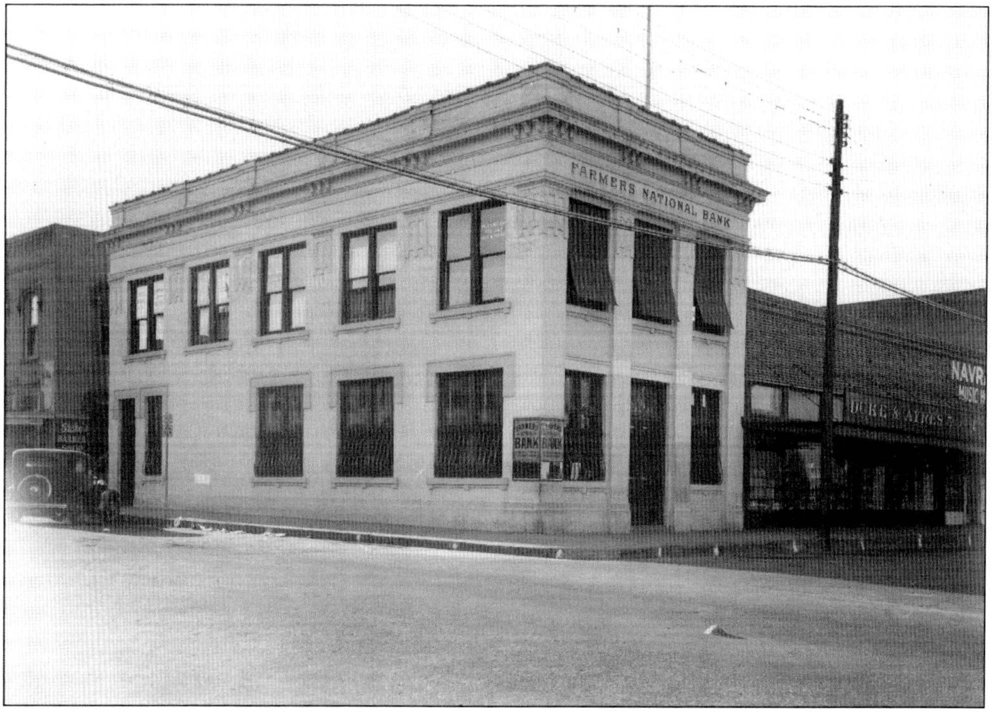

The Farmer's National Bank on Main Street across from the courthouse square opened in the late 1920s. Duke & Ayres next door was the type of variety store known as a five-and-dime, though the sign suggests it sold items up to a dollar. The ghost sign from Navratil's Music House remains visible today.

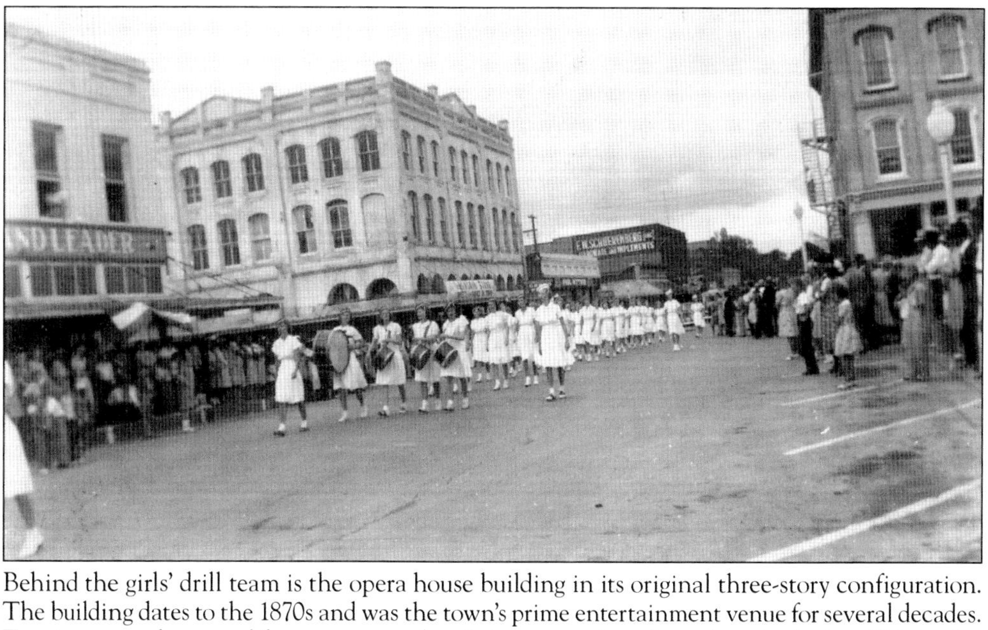

Behind the girls' drill team is the opera house building in its original three-story configuration. The building dates to the 1870s and was the town's prime entertainment venue for several decades. Touring stage shows and famous actors played the stage, often for only a single day. This is also where, in 1898, locals saw their first Edison moving pictures.

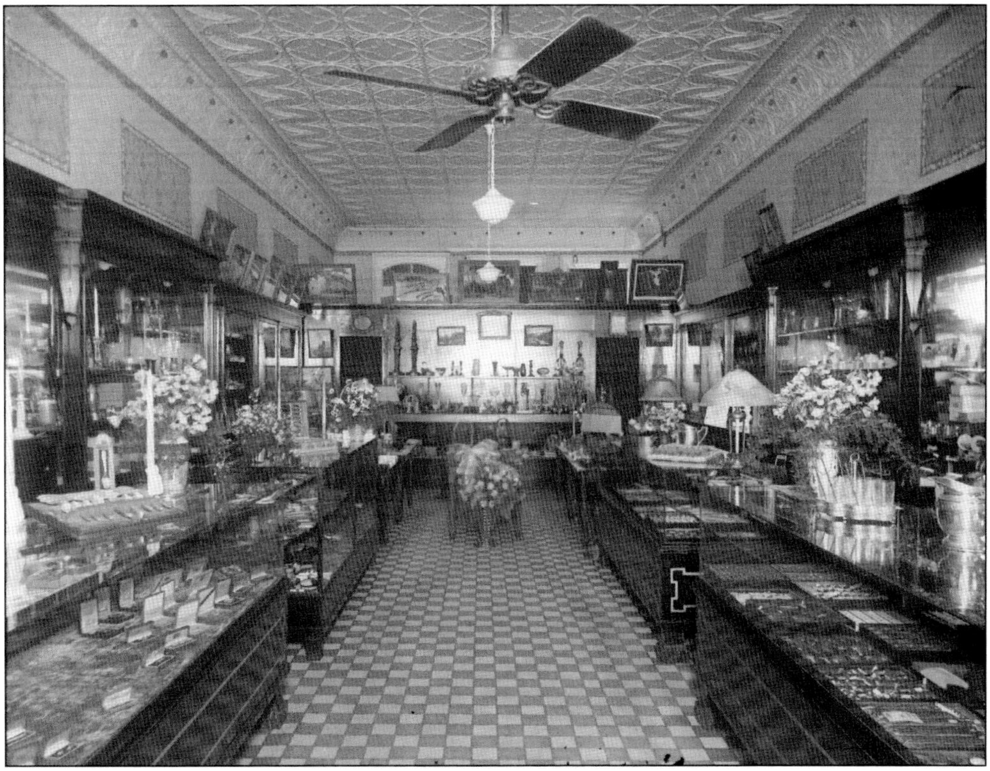

Arp's Jewelry at Alamo and Park Streets in the old Giddings and Giddings Bank Building was one of several jewelry stores in downtown Brenham. A mid-1930s ad for the store listed jeweled Gruen watches for Christmas gifts in the $30 to $40 range. The top of the line engagement diamond set on a 14k gold ring ran as high as $100.

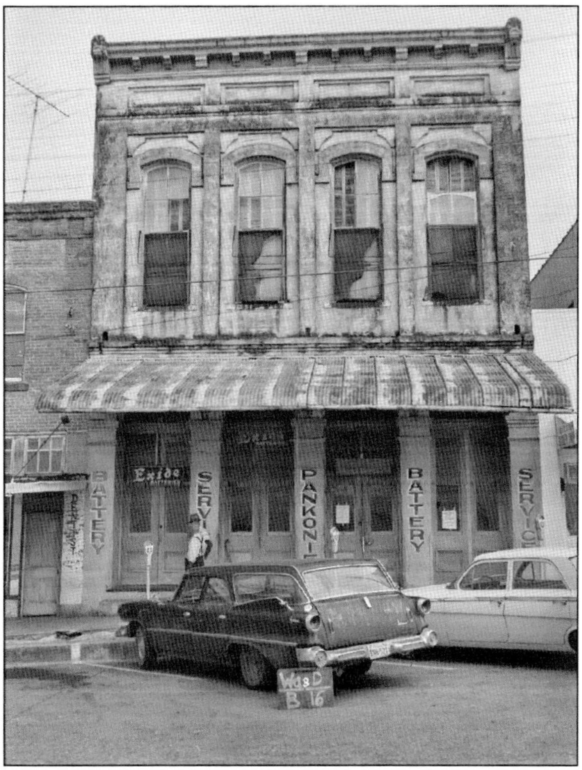

The block of Douglas Street south of Alamo Street housed a car battery service by the 1970s. Previously, it had been home to a succession of lively saloons that dated back well into the 1800s. With the building having fallen into serious disrepair, the decision was made to demolish it. Today, Toubin Park occupies this space.

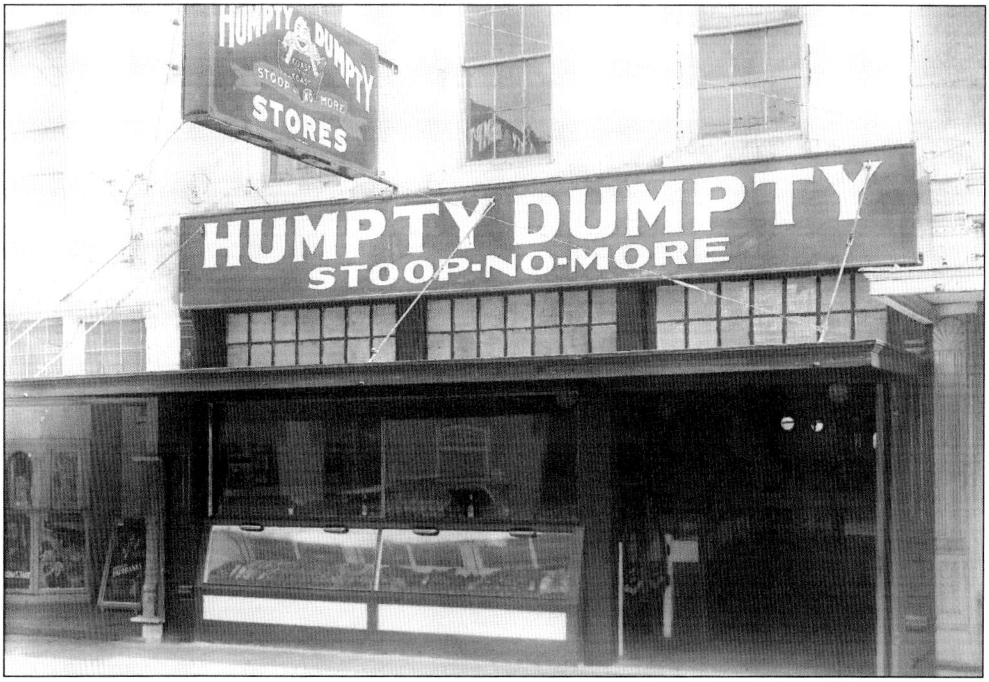

The Humpty Dumpty grocery on Main Street next door to the Rex movie theater began operations as a Piggly Wiggly franchise. The owner, World War I veteran and decorated hero Eugene Eversberg, made the switch in the 1920s, about the time of this photograph. He became the first grocer in Brenham to equip his store with new Frigidaire dry refrigeration in the freezer and dairy case.

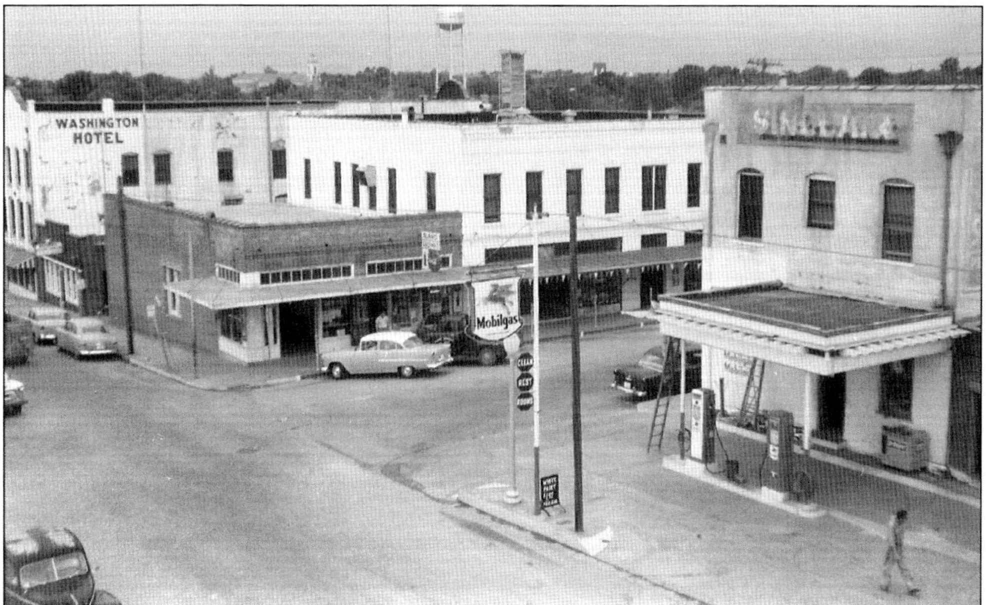

Looking southwest from the post office roof, postmaster Wilson Munz captured the gas station across the street at Market and Alamo Streets. It had previously been a Sinclair and before that a Gulf dealer. At the far left was the Washington Hotel, which had served in that capacity since 1876. The building included a small café and 33 guest rooms, some with private baths.

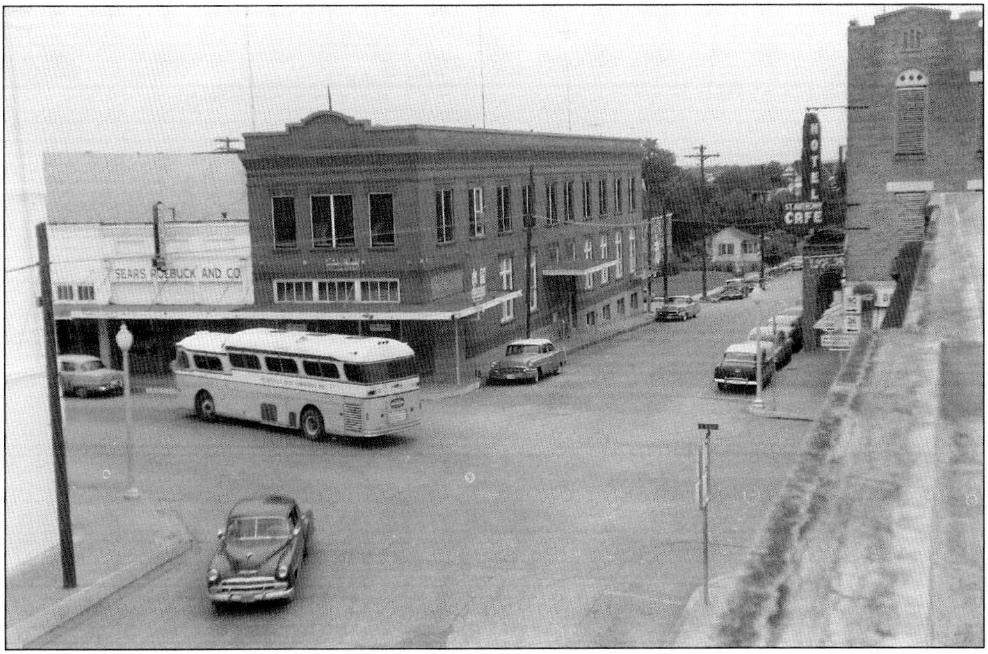

A Kerrville Bus Company liner turns west onto Main Street in the 1950s in front of the Banner-Press Building. Today, radio station KWHI resides there, keeping the news and communication connection. That station, Brenham's first, was started by Tom Whitehead Sr. and began broadcasting in May 1947 at 1,000 watts. Early shows were offered in English, German, Polish, and Czech.

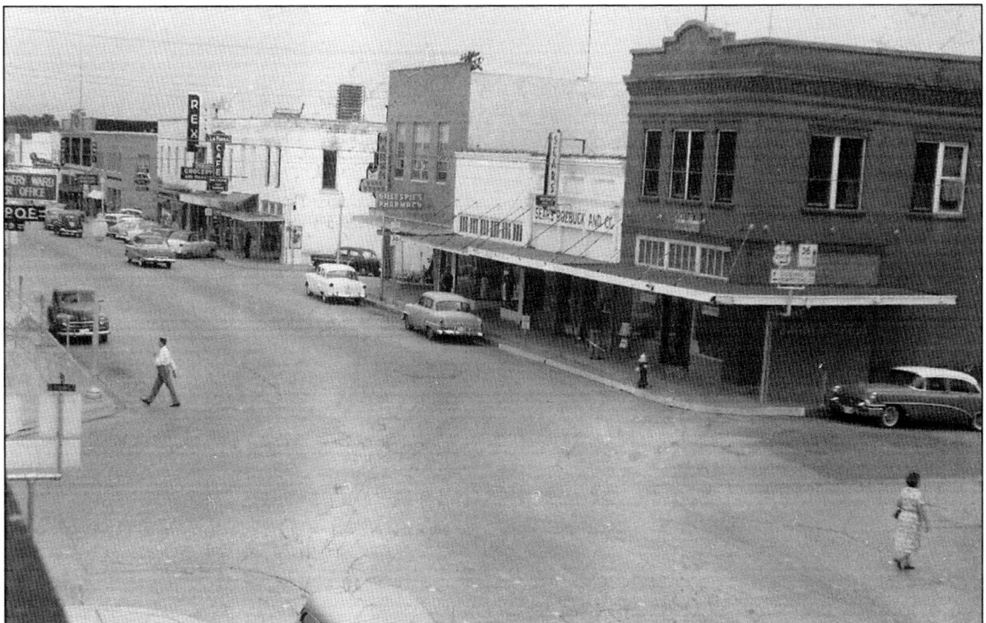

Postmaster Munz caught another mid-1950s look down Main Street west from atop the post office. It shows the local department store owned by the Marsh family and its national competitors Sears Roebuck and Montgomery Ward. One block farther west is the Rex movie theater, where many a local kid saw their favorite Western heroes.

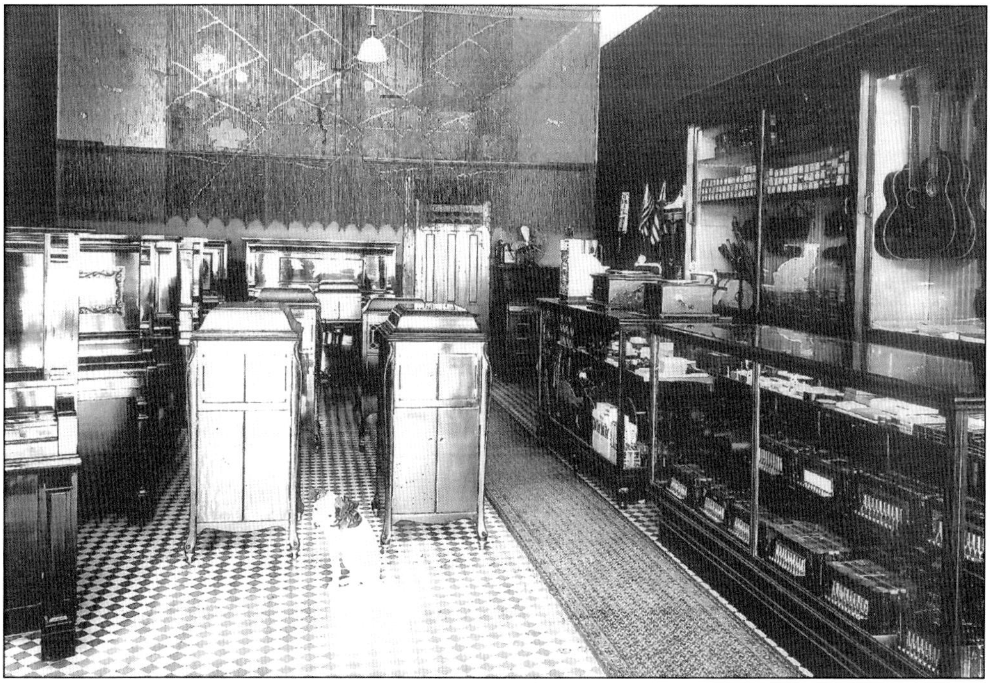

Navratil's Music House on South Baylor Street offered musical instruments and Victrolas to the discerning customers of Washington County. There were music lessons to be had, and the latest sheet music was available. The Victor Music Company's mascot, Nipper the dog, was a popular feature inside the Navratil showroom.

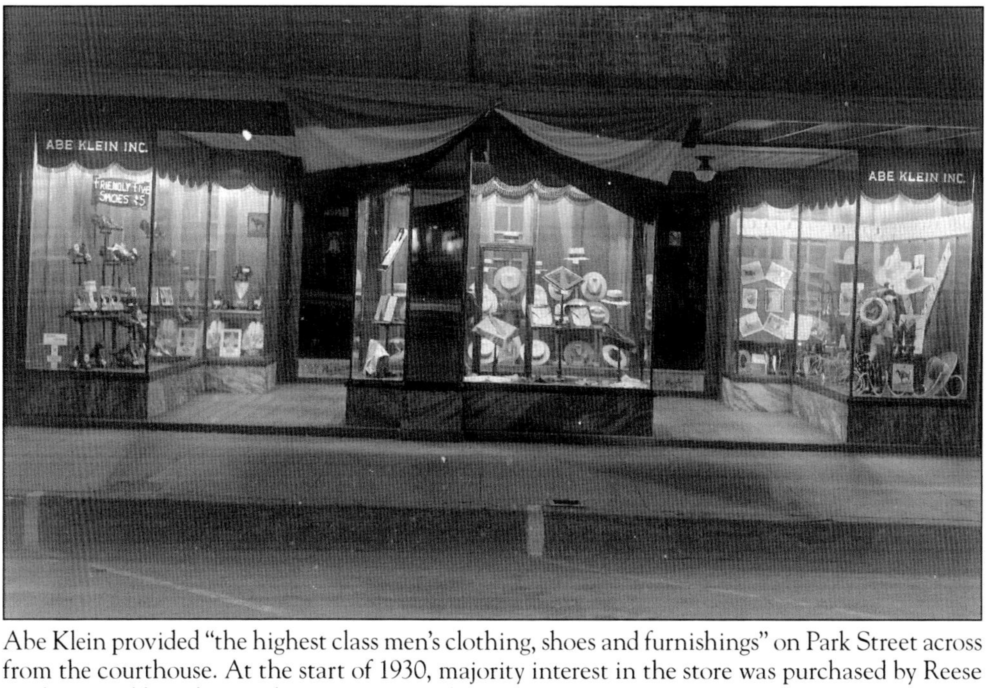

Abe Klein provided "the highest class men's clothing, shoes and furnishings" on Park Street across from the courthouse. At the start of 1930, majority interest in the store was purchased by Reese Lockett, Buddy Fisher, and Henry Ruetz, who vowed to continue serving customers. Klein and his wife, a local bridge champion, moved to Dallas.

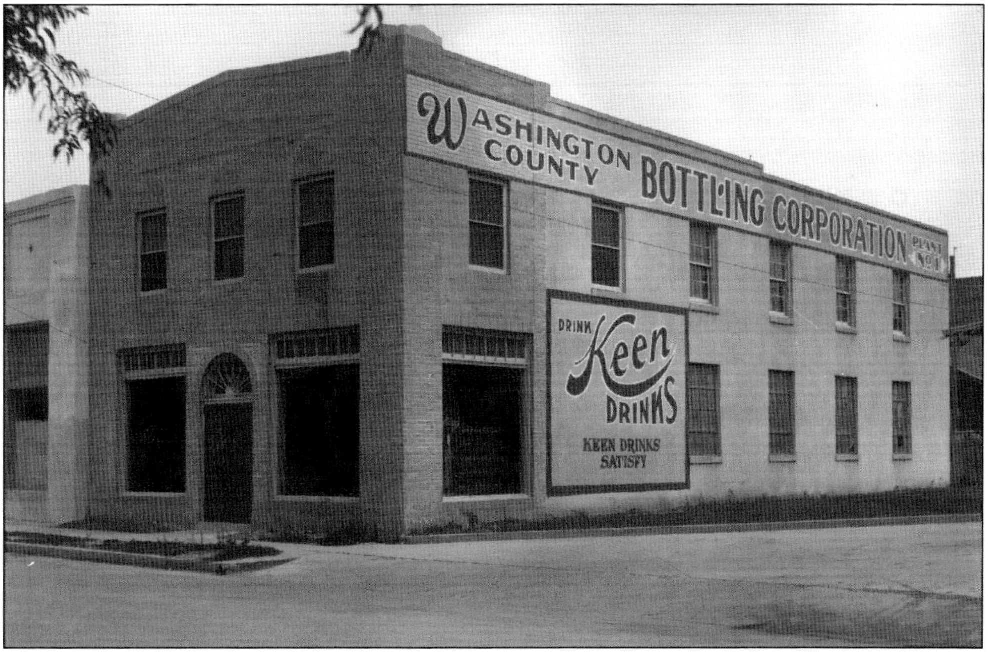

The Washington County Bottling Corporation, at 307 West Main and Austin Streets, advertised Keen brand soft drinks. It was also the local bottler for Dr. Pepper. In the 1930s, it promoted that beverage as more nutritional than many foods, adding that it "eliminates most stomach gas" and deters germs that cause typhoid fever and diphtheria.

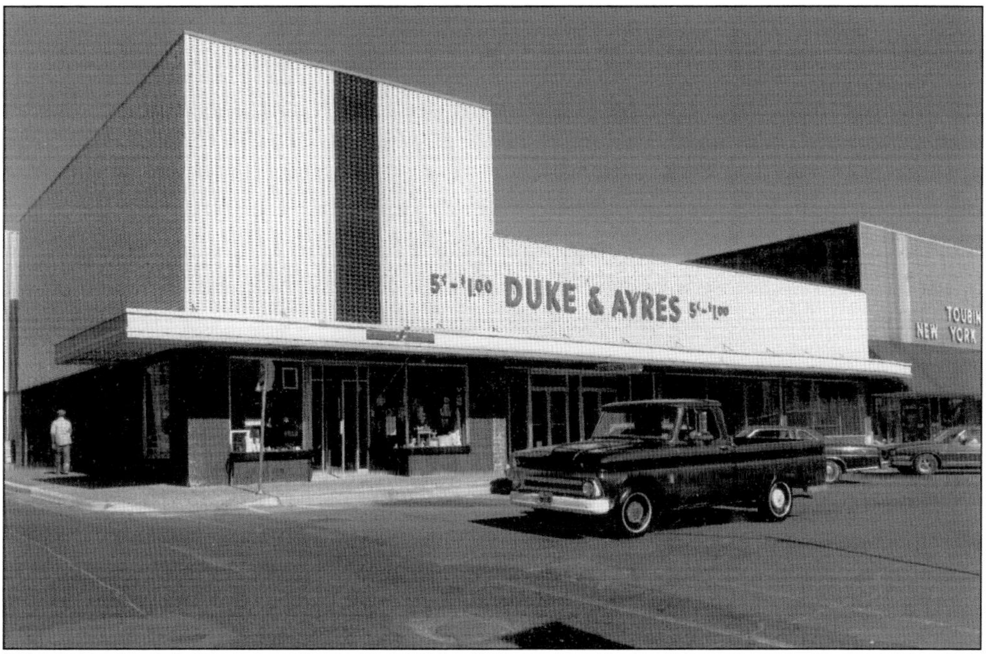

Duke & Ayres five-and-dime and Toubin's New York Store both sported mid-century cladding in the name of modernization. The Toubin family acquired their business in the early 1920s and expanded it a decade later. Along with families such as Marsh and Cohen, they were part of a rich tradition of Jewish store owners in downtown Brenham.

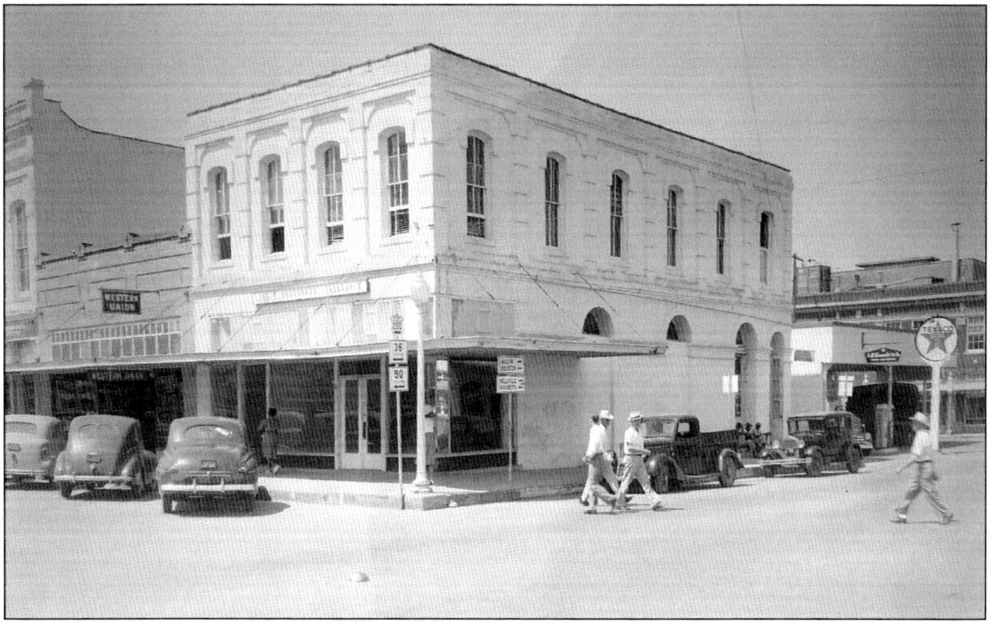

This 1940s photograph shows the southwest corner of Main and Park Streets. The decorative urns atop the Simon Theatre are just visible in the background. Western Union had a long existence in its space, serving as a connection between Brenham and the wider world. The Farmer's National Bank moved into the former drugstore space on the corner, later changing the name to Brenham National Bank.

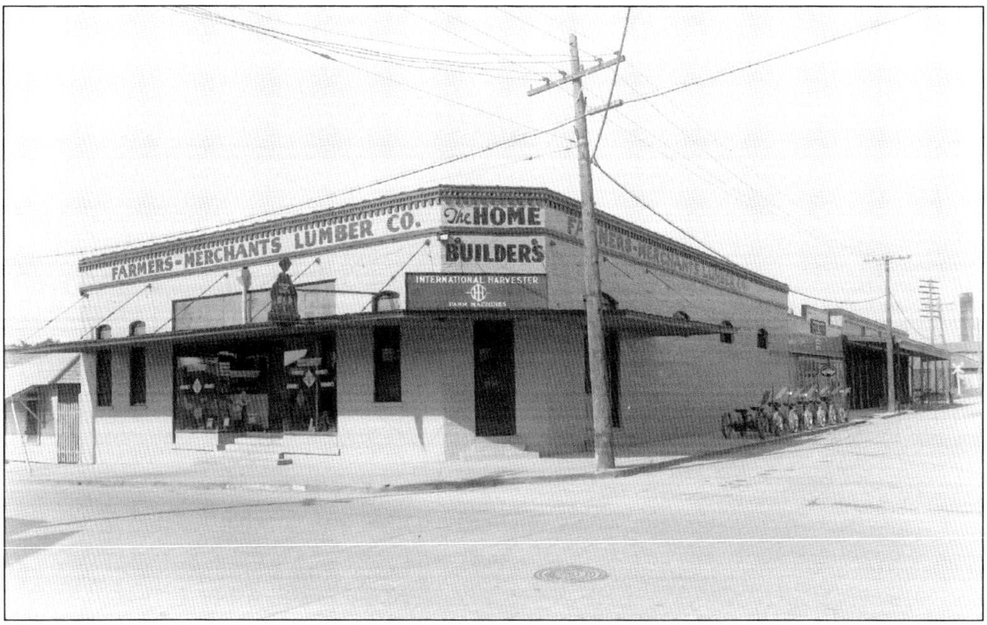

The Farmers and Merchants Lumber Company was one of several large lumber operations near the Houston & Texas Central tracks that border the south side of downtown Brenham. When this 1920s photograph was taken, the company was also a dealer of International Harvester farm machines and Sherwin-Williams paint. Horse-drawn mowers are lined up down the sidewalk. (Briscoe Center for American History, University of Texas at Austin.)

It is tough to fathom a tire store on courthouse square nowadays, but when Main and Alamo Streets were the principal highways, it made sense. The uniformed employees of this Goodyear business stand ready to install new tires right on Alamo Street. Upstairs of retail businesses such as these were many of Brenham's doctors, lawyers, and dentists.

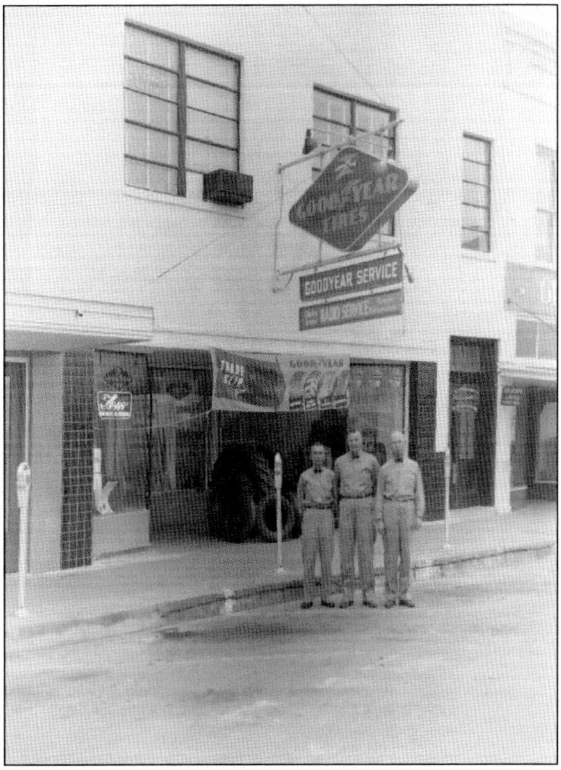

Brenham boosters, complete with brass band, gather in front of city hall on Vulcan Street. Mayor James A. Wilkins led the push for the new municipal building. The Richardsonian Romanesque structure was completed in April 1903, almost exactly one year after the bond ordinance to build it was passed. Its loss is still lamented by many long-tenured Brenhamites.

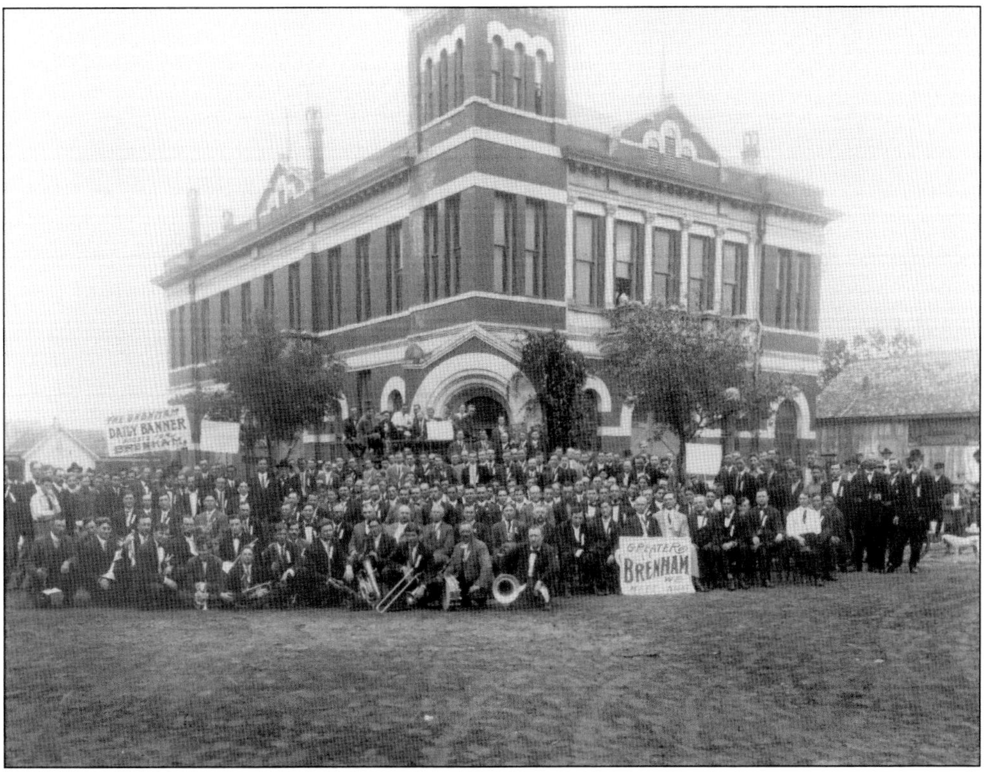

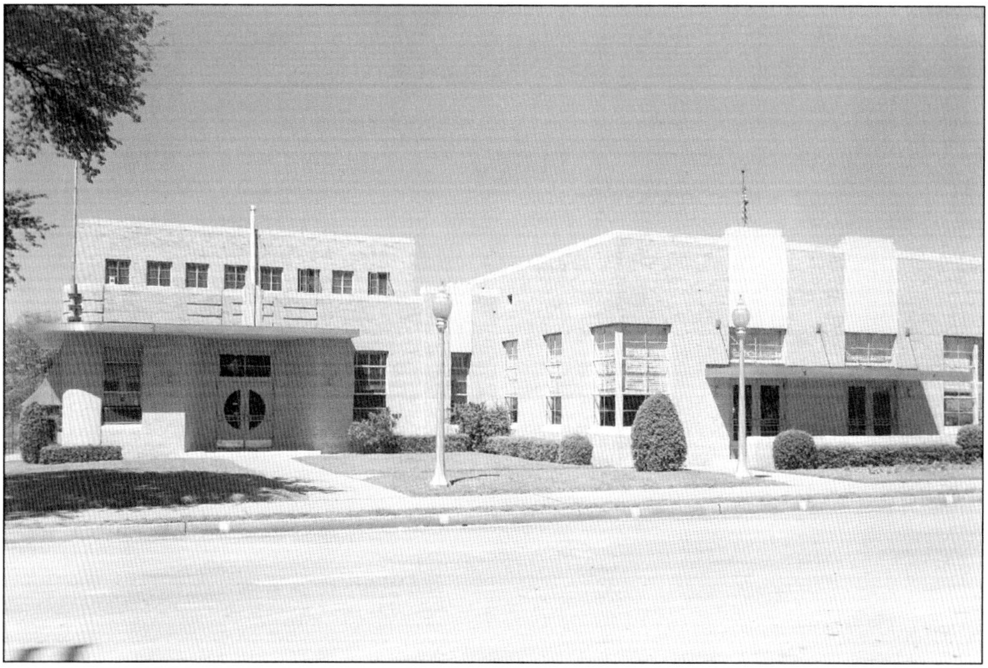

The Romanesque city hall did not last long as the seat of Brenham's government. Around 1938, an Art Deco replacement was constructed nearby. It included not only offices, but also a public auditorium and the fire station. A new library had opened down the street just a few years prior.

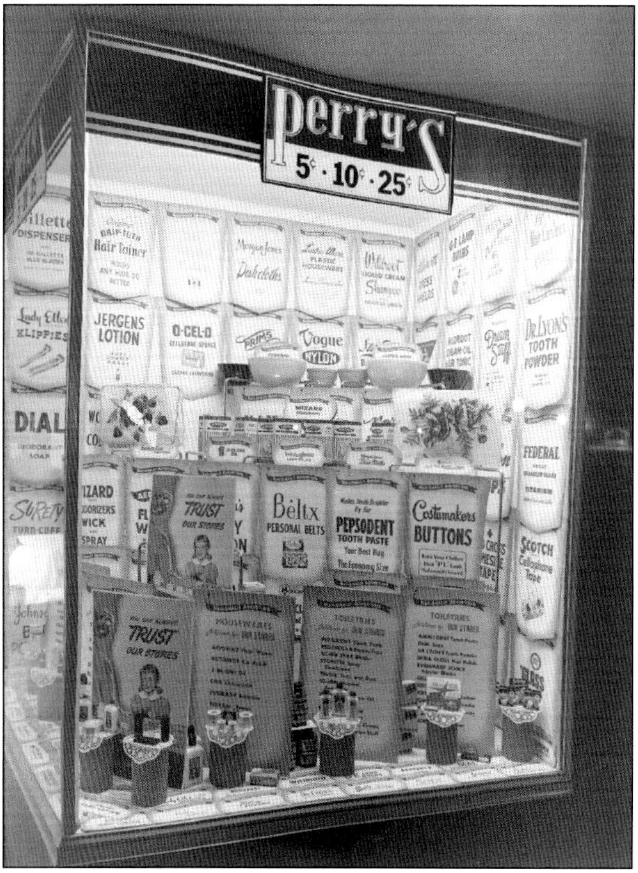

Perry's five-and-dime was a mid-century institution in downtown Brenham. The inexpensive merchandise was so popular during the Depression that the business opened a larger store on Alamo Street in 1932 and kept its previous location on the east side of the square open. The posted prices were a tad misleading, since they also offered bed sheets for 49¢ and dress shirts for 69¢.

Two

INSTITUTIONS AND ORGANIZATIONS

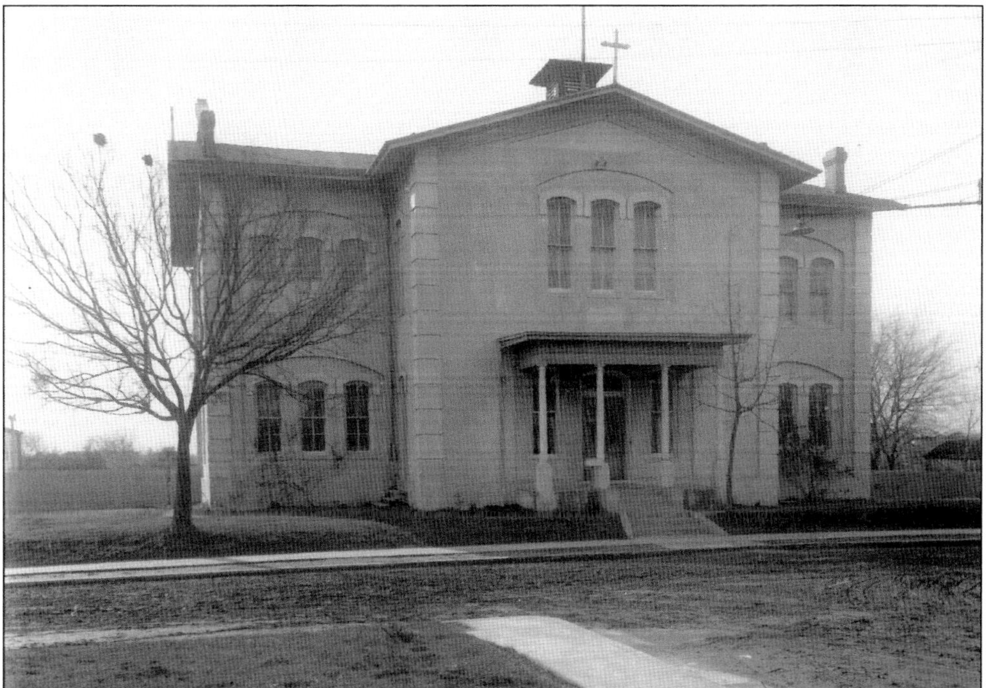

The wonderful old school building on East Alamo Street underwent a major renovation in 2021, preserving it for the future. It started life as the school for Brenham's white students in 1883, then was purchased by the Catholic church in 1909 to serve as a private school and convent.

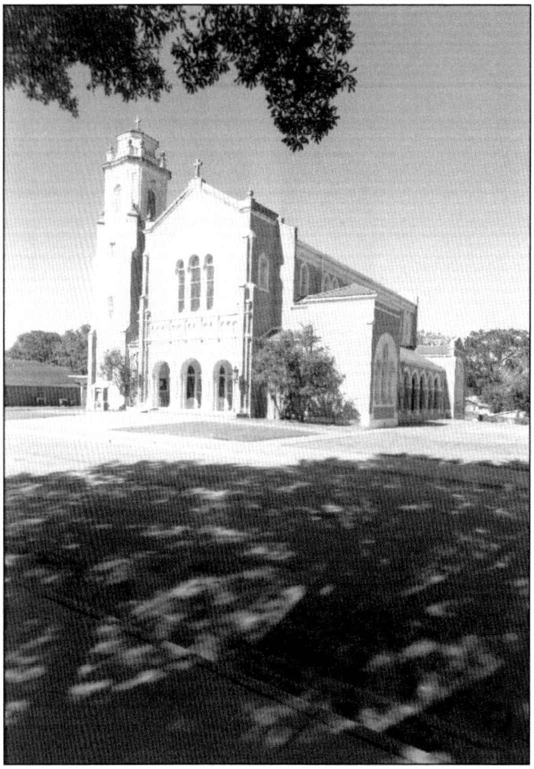

St. Mary's Catholic Church with its distinctive tower opened in 1936. The original church, at the same location, dated to 1870. The plot of land for local Roman Catholic worship was donated by B.H. and Jefferson Bassett, who were prominent Brenham bankers and financiers at the time.

St. John African Methodist Episcopal Church, whose congregation gathered in 1905 for this photograph, was formed in the Camptown area in the years immediately following emancipation when there was a Union soldiers' camp that gave the area its name. Like its neighbor, Mount Rose Missionary Baptist Church, St. John's first worshippers were newly freed slaves. Some early services were held in the federal dining hall at the camp. (St. John Church.)

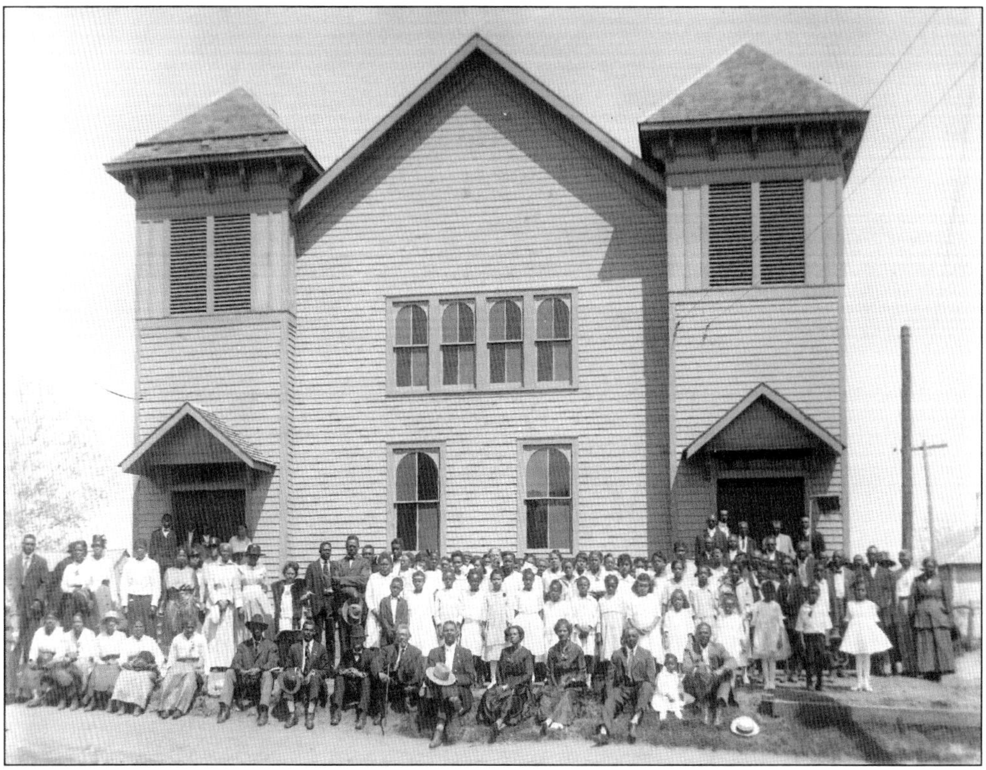

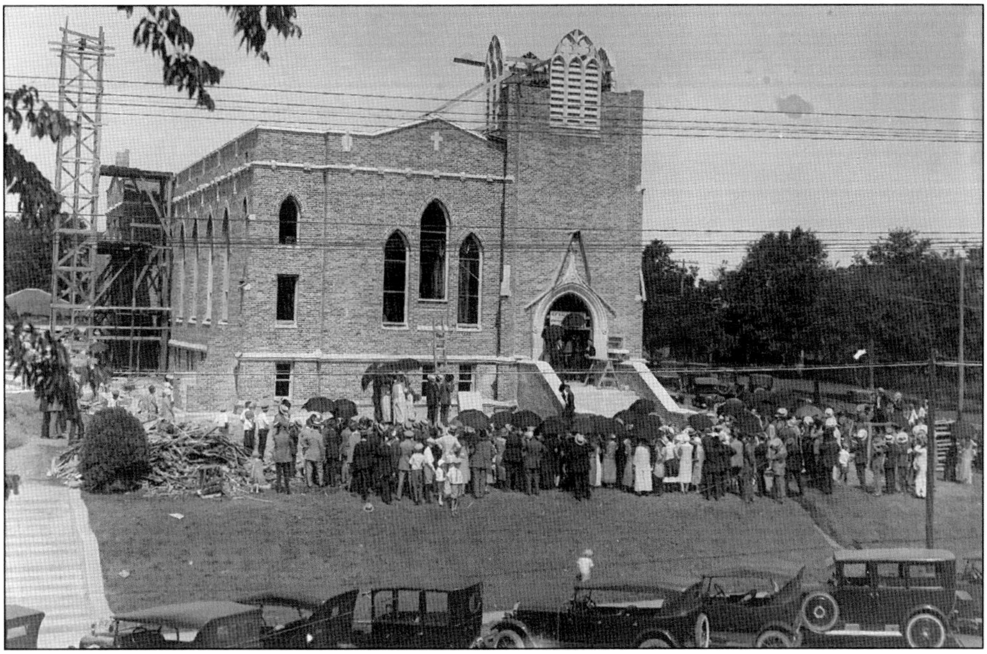

St. Paul's Lutheran Church, Brenham's largest congregation for decades, hired Bellville-born, Houston-based architect Alfred Finn to design a new building in 1925. The sanctuary was dedicated two days after Christmas on the last Sunday of the year, with Rev. Arthur Hartmann presiding over the celebration.

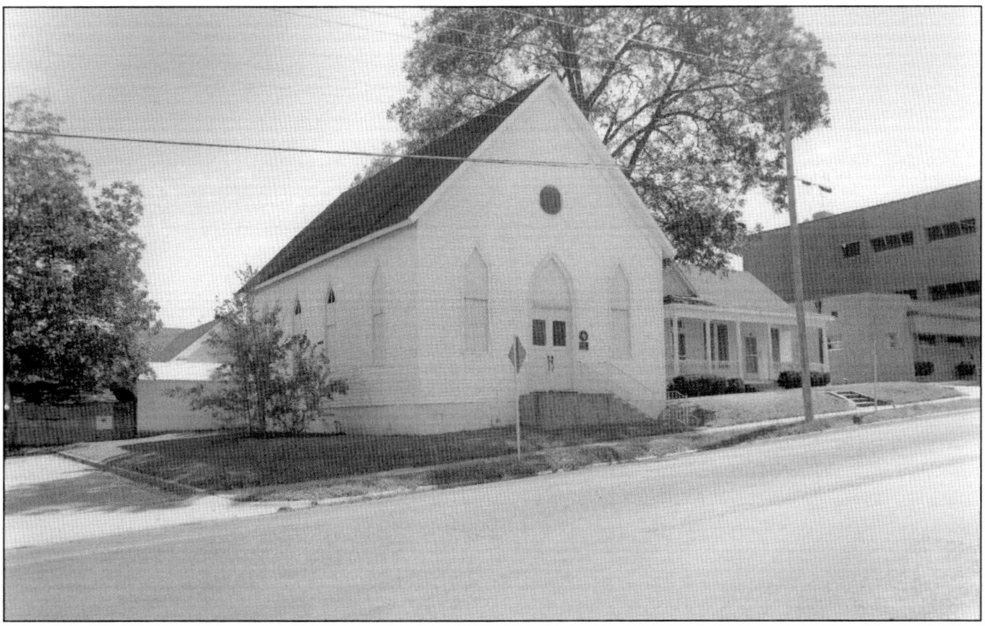

Synagogue B'nai Abraham officially formed in Brenham in 1885, the first time there were enough Jewish men over age 13 to comprise the required Orthodox quorum. Jewish families had lived in Brenham since prior to the Civil War. A building for worship was opened on North Park Street in 1892, but after a fire, a new one replaced it a year later. (Toubin family.)

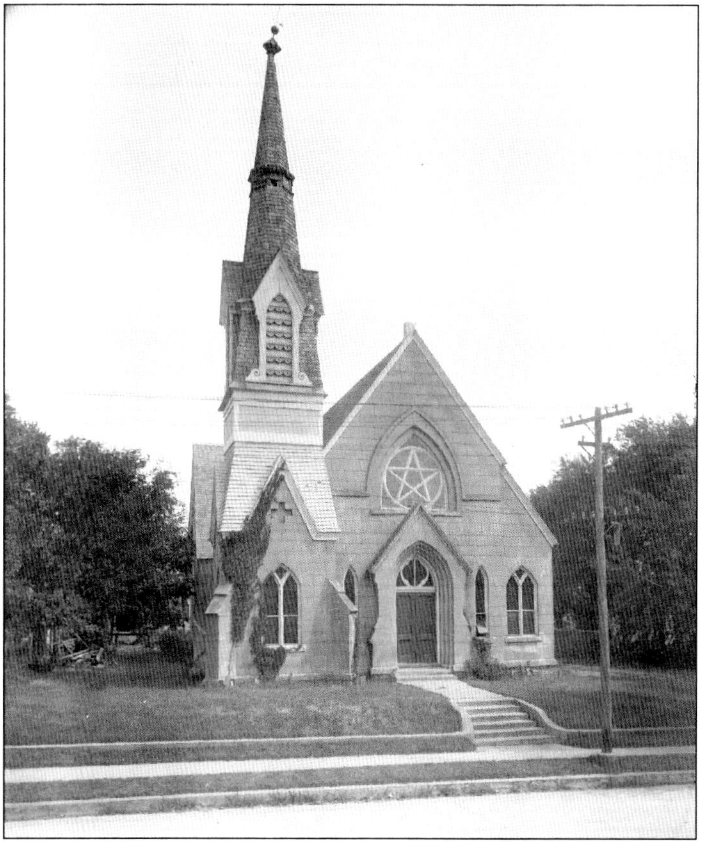

The Brenham Presbyterian Church near the Blinn College campus was erected in 1879, only two years after the congregation's founding. For a few years in the early 1900s, regular services were suspended for lack of members, but the church reorganized in 1919 and resumed operations. Repairs and additions to the church took place in the 1950s.

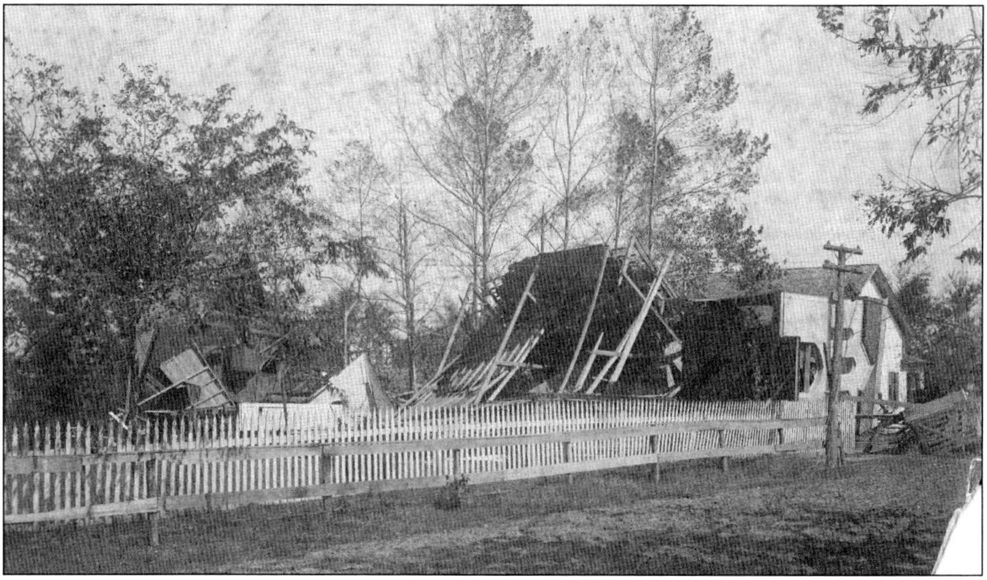

Brenham's Lutheran church on Clinton Street was blown over by high winds from the Great Hurricane of September 8–9, 1900. The church was not the only total wreck following the storm. The public school lost a roof, three church steeples came down, and total damage in the city exceeded $100,000.

The Evangelical Lutheran Church had two buildings on Clinton Street. The first was less than a decade old when it was destroyed during the 1900 storm, but the congregation replaced it. In 1925, a larger parcel of ground was procured on South Austin Street. By the end of World War II, it was the largest congregation in Brenham.

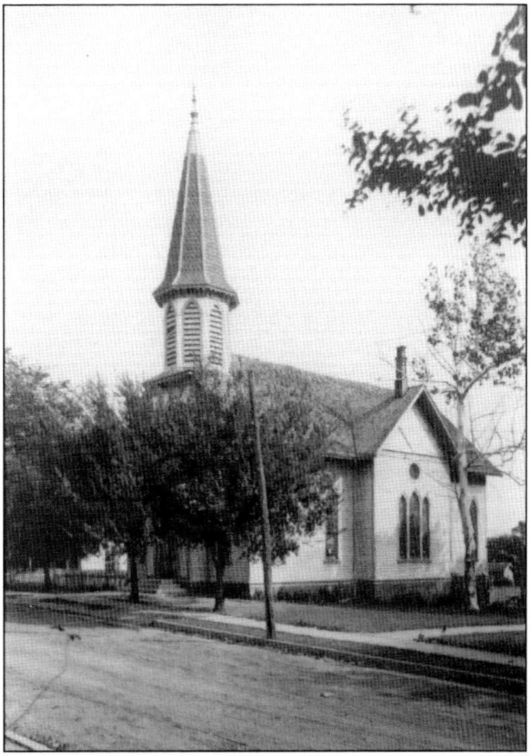

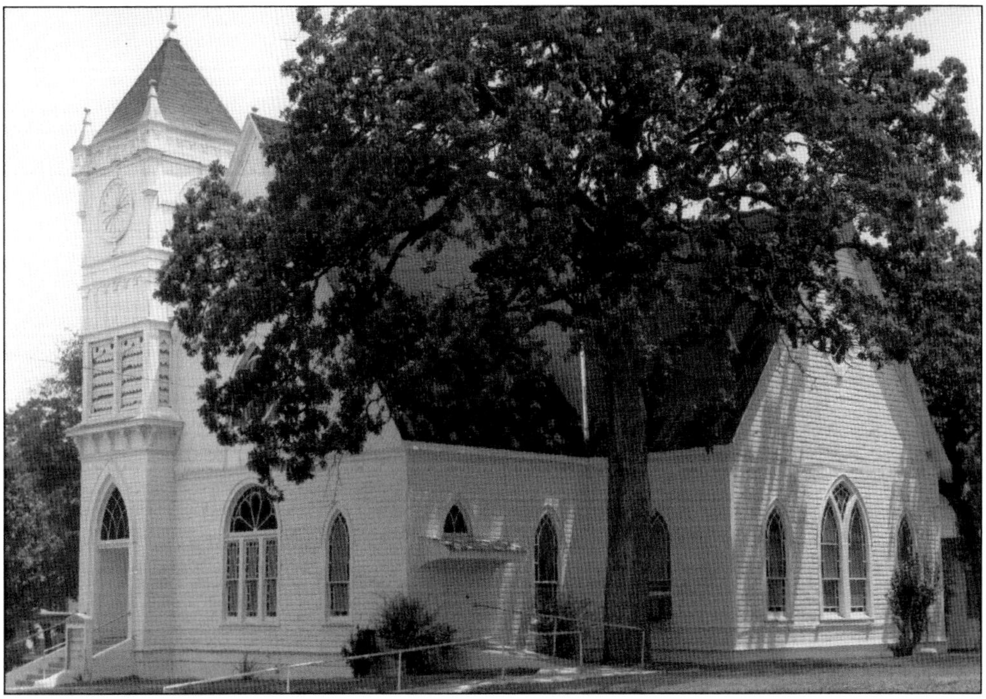

First Christian Church on Cottonwood Street traces its history to the immediate aftermath of the Civil War when Rev. A.J. Bush preached to followers in their homes. An earlier church building burned, but the present sanctuary was dedicated to replace it in January 1899.

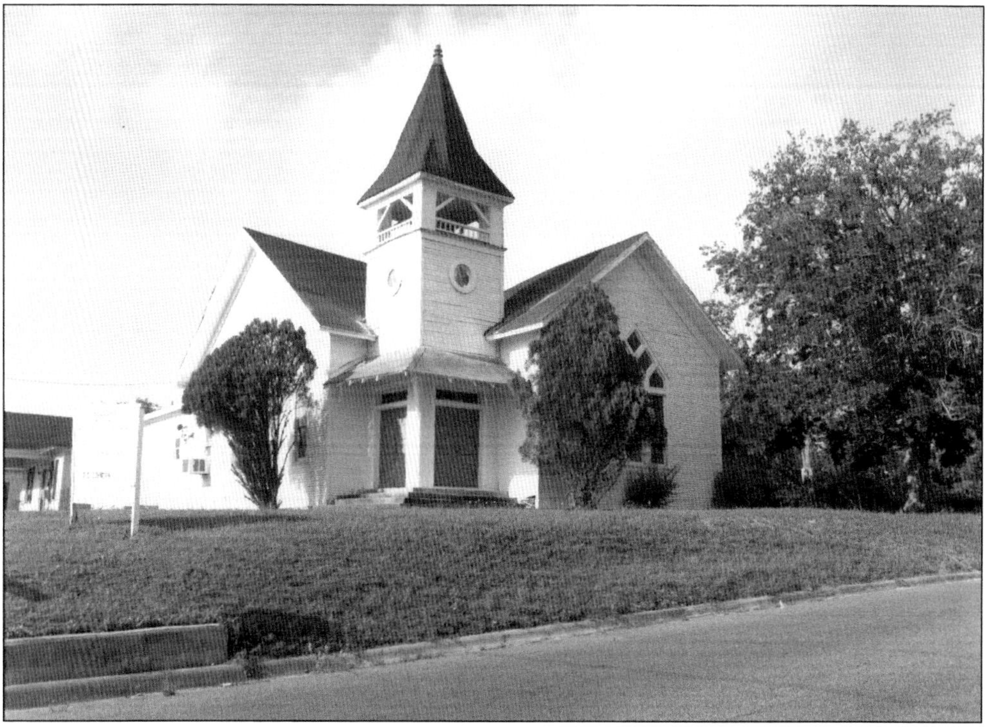

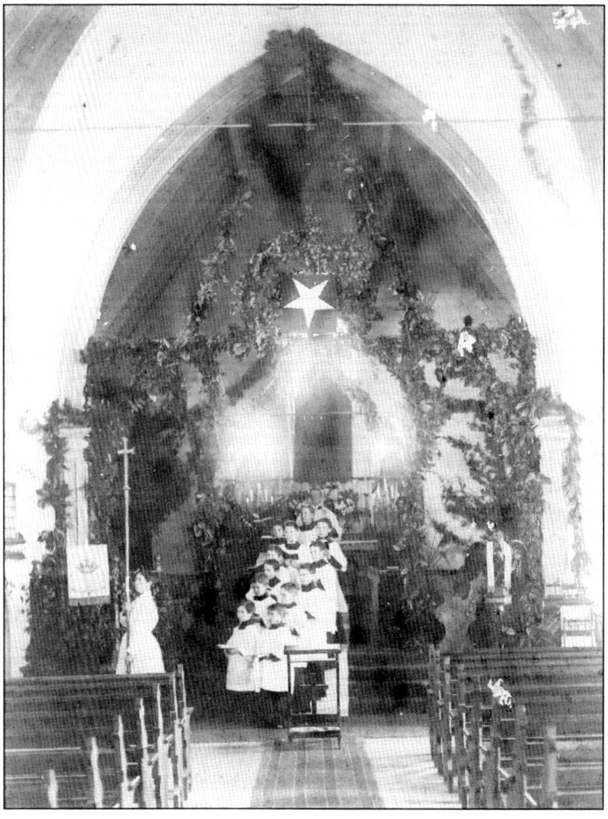

Mount Zion Methodist Episcopal Church was founded on the west side of Brenham in the Freedom Colony of Watrousville in 1877 with services held in a brush arbor. The emancipated slaves who comprised the congregation purchased land and constructed a building the following year. In the 1920s, after a damaging storm, this structure rose on the same spot.

The boys' choir at St. Peter's Episcopal Church, a building which sat for years at the corner of Vulcan and Baylor Streets, performs at Christmas 1896. Fred Seabright Leigh was the priest, and Revenal Luhn was the crucifer. Howard and Emmitt Gardner and another Luhn boy are among the singers.

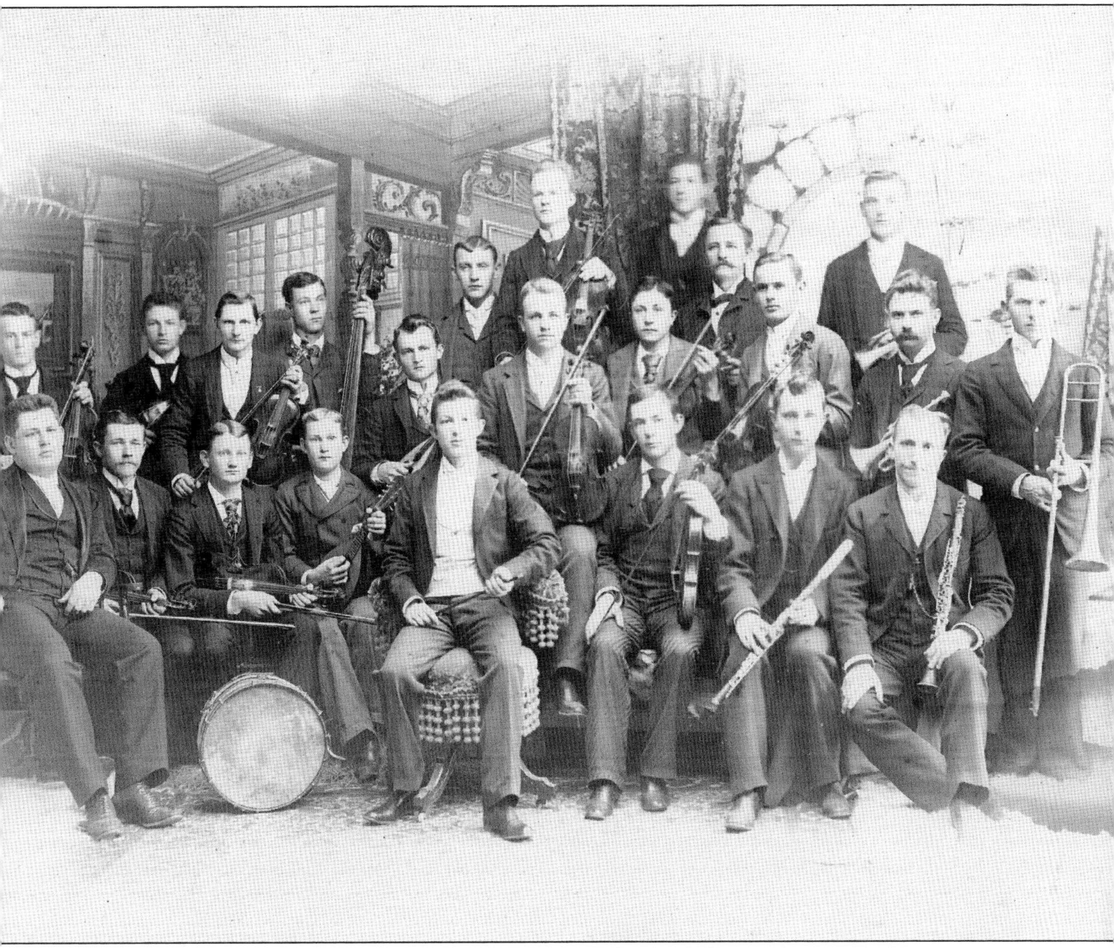

Brenham's Young Men's Orchestra assembled in Holland's Photography Studio to pose for a portrait about 1894. They formed a fine arts complement to four local brass bands, two white and two African American. The orchestra practiced often at Vorwaert's Hall late that year and the next, and their work paid off. The ensemble played dances and concerts at a variety of locations around town, including the Grand Opera House, for barely over a year or so, but their reviews were solid. One local writer suggested that the gentlemen might "astonish the professionals." Several of their engagements throughout 1895 were concerts held jointly with the Ladies' Glee Club, and their accompaniment of European-trained soprano Marguerite Fischer's vocals brought consistently deafening applause. Such evidence suggests a desire to impress the young women's group may have played a significant role in the formation of the men's organization.

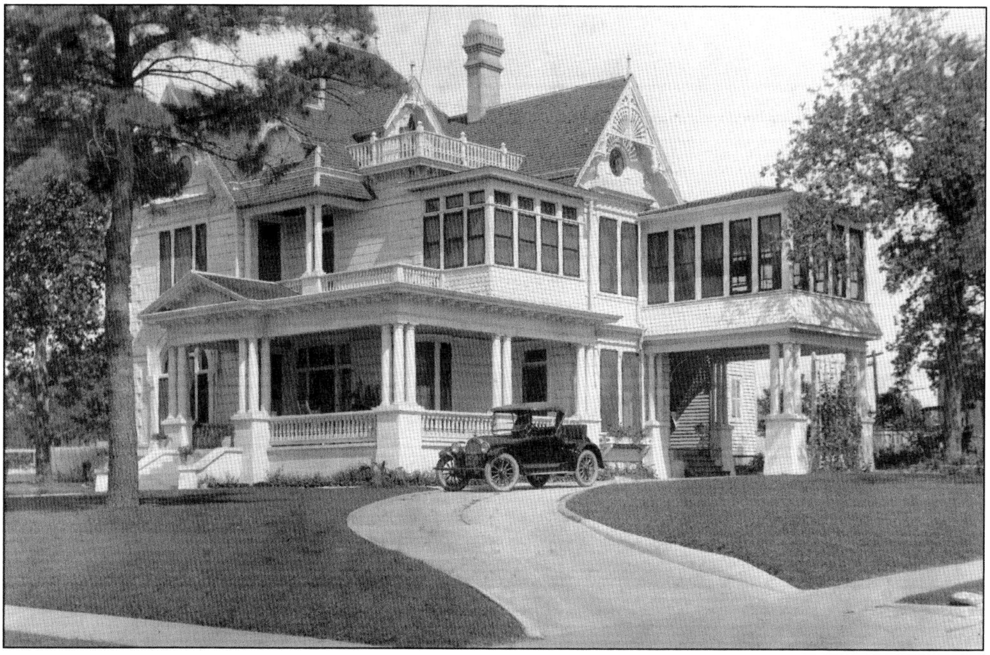

The grand home of the Frank W. Wood family on Academy Street is still standing. Wood, who owned a lumber company bearing his name, also developed two Brenham neighborhoods around the start of the 20th century. Woodlawn Heights and the Frank Wood No. 2 developments were both northeast of downtown.

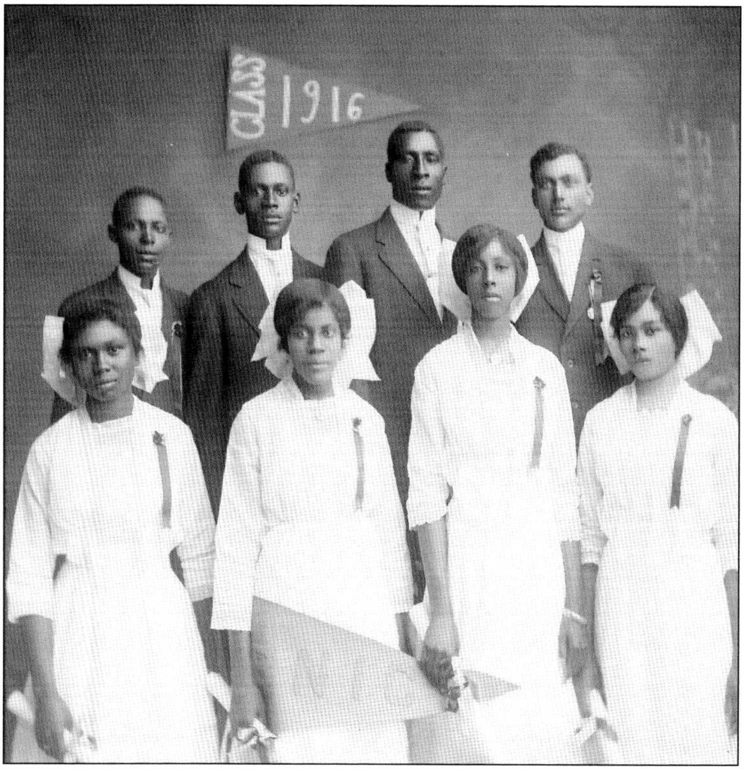

The Brenham Normal and Industrial College was founded north of town in the first decade of the 20th century to give African Americans an education that would "fit him for the arduous duties of life." A scholarship program extended to all Texas counties, allowing county judges to recommend candidates who could get an education for $50 a year or less.

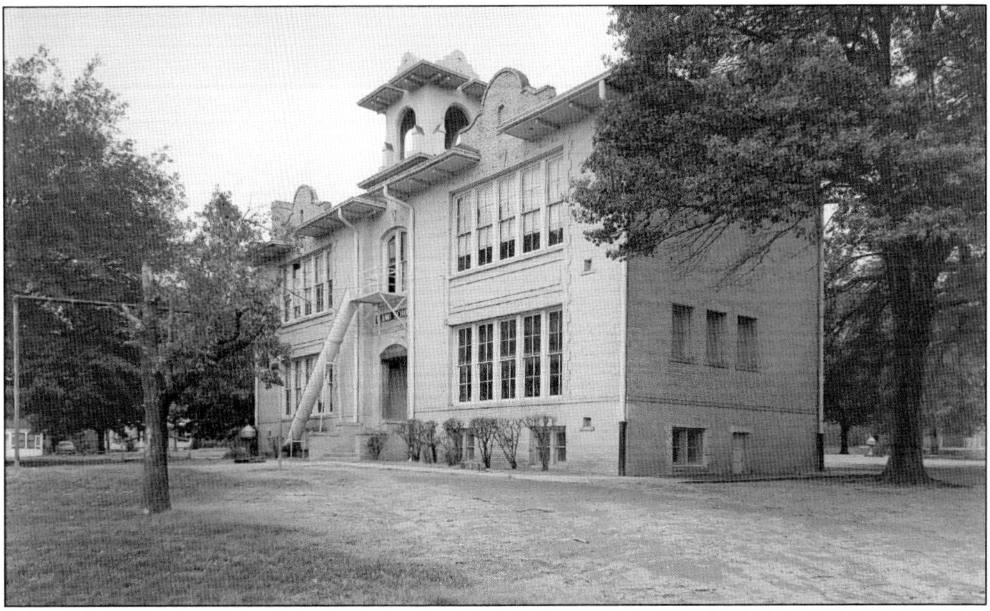

Alamo School was on Germania Street, on the lot now occupied by the Catholic church's community center. The cafeteria sat in the half-basement while first and second graders had the ground floor, and third and fourth graders the top floor. Most of them dreamed of using the fire escape slide for play.

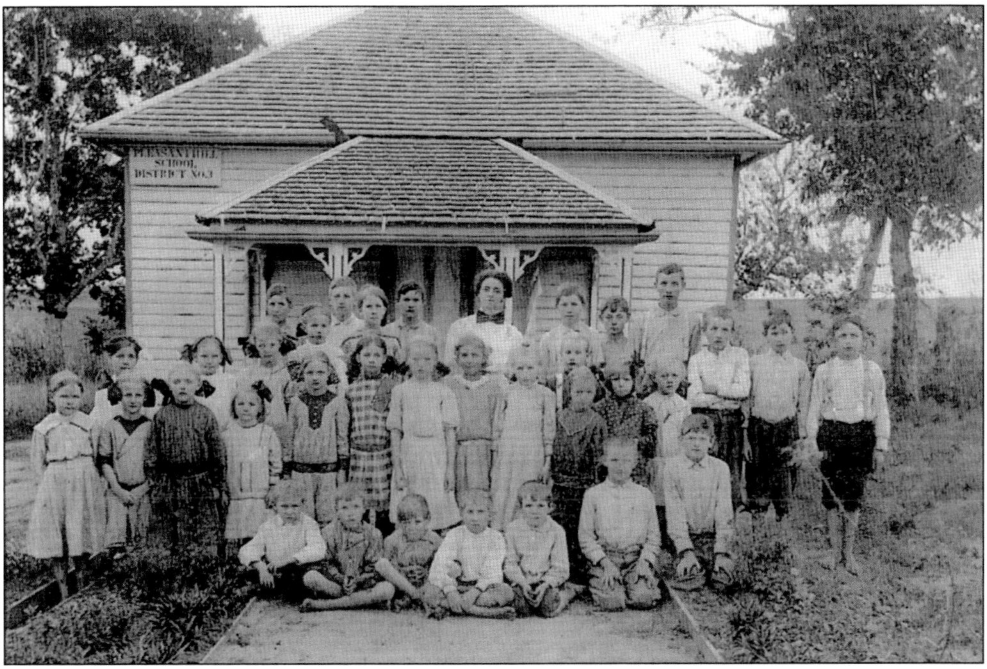

Students at the original Pleasant Hill School in 1912 exclusively bore German surnames. Their teacher, Otillie Klaener Bockhorn, stands in the back row with the older boys, many of whom did not wear shoes to school in warm weather. The town, in extreme southern Washington County, had already begun to decline in population, losing its post office, but the school and two churches hung on.

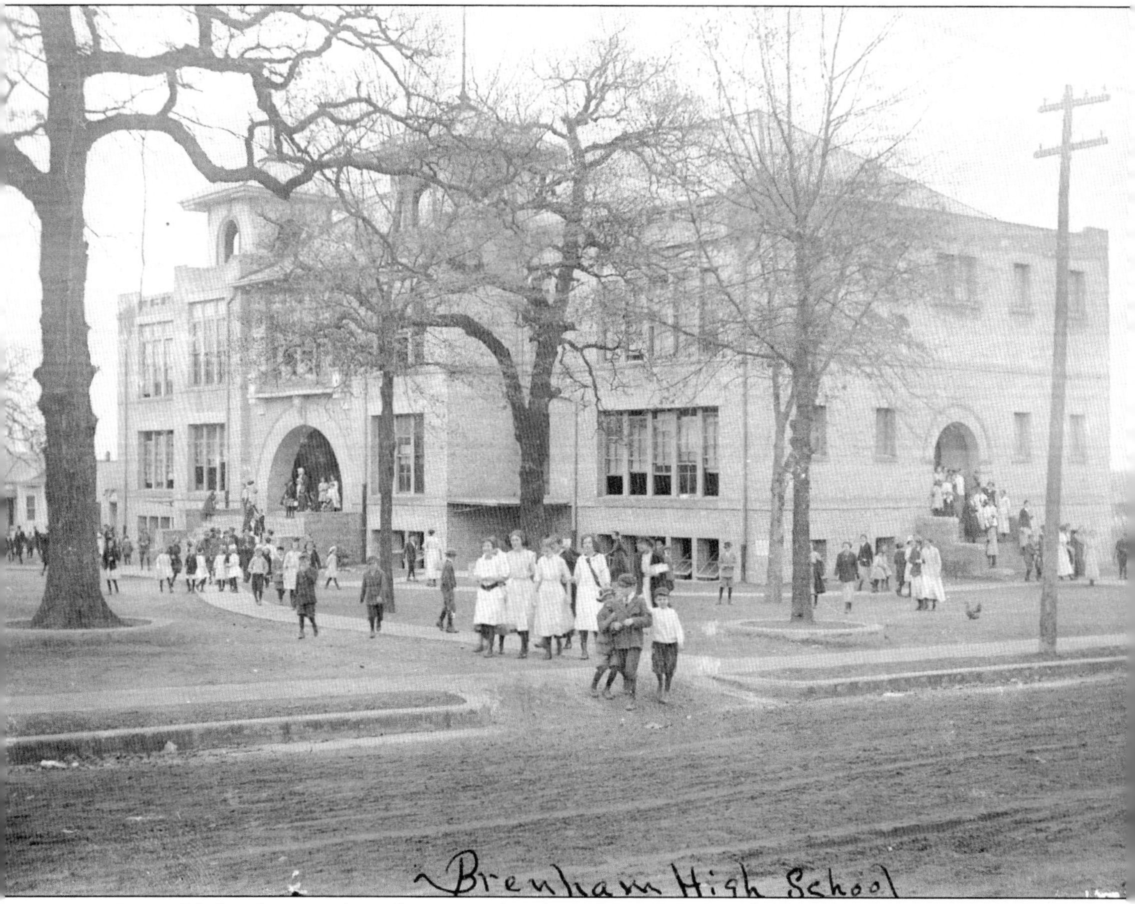

Central School opened on the west side of Market Street not far north of Vulcan Street for the fall semester of 1908 to accommodate high school students who were crowding the existing building. The city undertook an ambitious public subscription program to raise much of the $50,000 needed for its construction. Preparations for the new building continued all summer with excited reports of new sewers being installed and new furniture put in place prior to the first day of classes on September 7. The oversized arch at the main entrance to Central School quickly became a favorite photograph spot in Brenham for groups of all sorts. When a new high school opened in the late 1920s, Central School became an elementary building. It was sold and removed in the fall of 1956. Chase Bank occupies the property today.

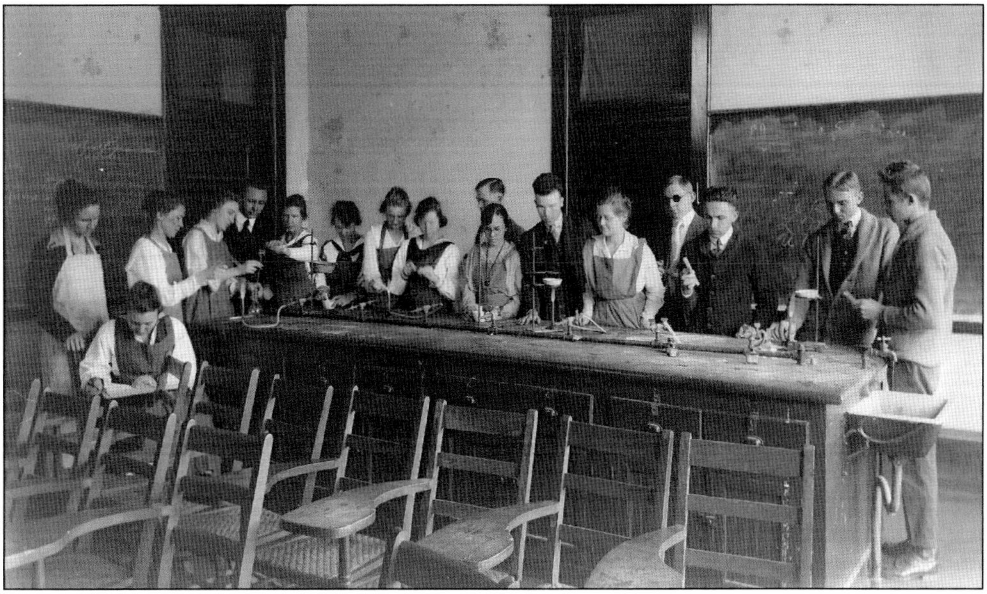

High school classes, held in the Central School on Market Street, offered a chemistry lab around the time of World War I. Students formed the Edison Science Club in 1917 with Coral Clark, the high school science and mathematics teacher, as the faculty sponsor. The club had seven inaugural members who gathered weekly for educational experiments.

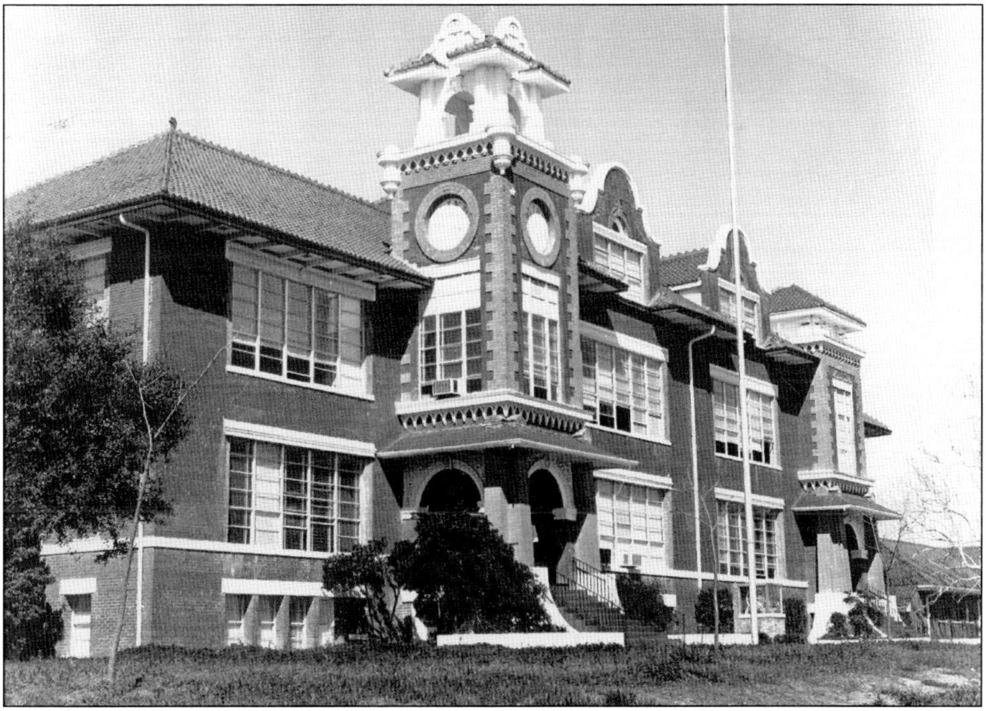

Old Main at Blinn College opened in 1906 and was the design of architects C.H. Page and Brother of Austin. Charles Henry Page's father brought his family to that city in the mid-1880s so that he could work on the Texas State Capitol Building. Charles H. and brother Louis C. Page designed seven Texas county courthouses.

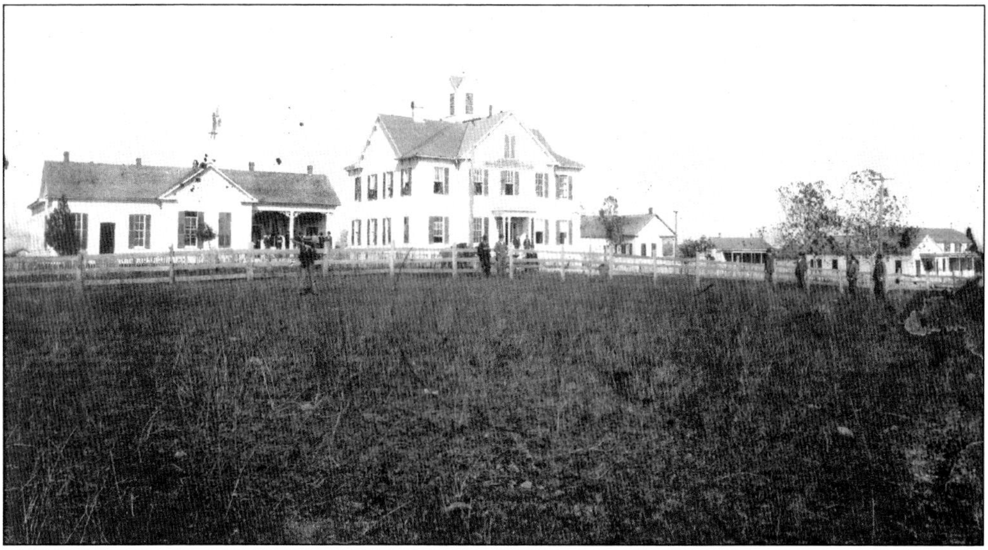

The German Methodist Church, which had been organized by Rev. Carl Urbantke a decade earlier, founded a college on the west side of Brenham in 1883. The name was changed a few years later to honor Rev. Christian Blinn of New York, who was a financial benefactor of the effort. The original wood frame buildings remained intact until at least the late 1920s.

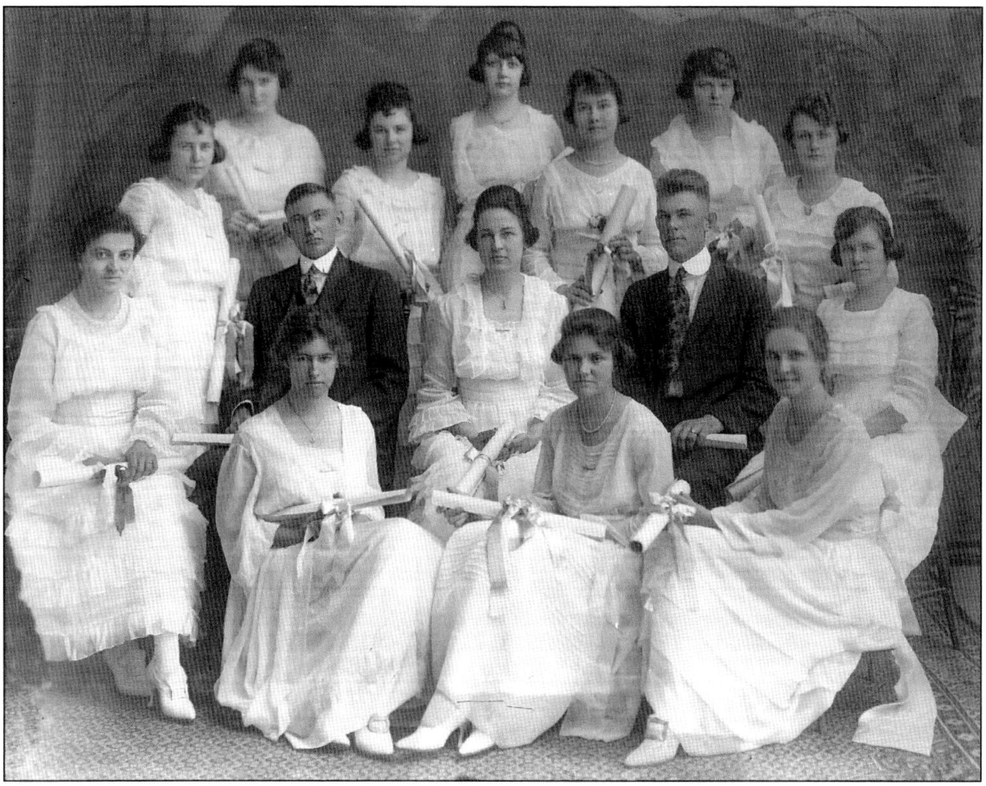

The two men in the 1919 graduating class at Blinn College may have liked their odds of finding an eligible young woman. For its first five years, the school was solely for men seeking to enter the ranks of Methodist clergy, but it was made coeducational in 1888. (Blinn College Library.)

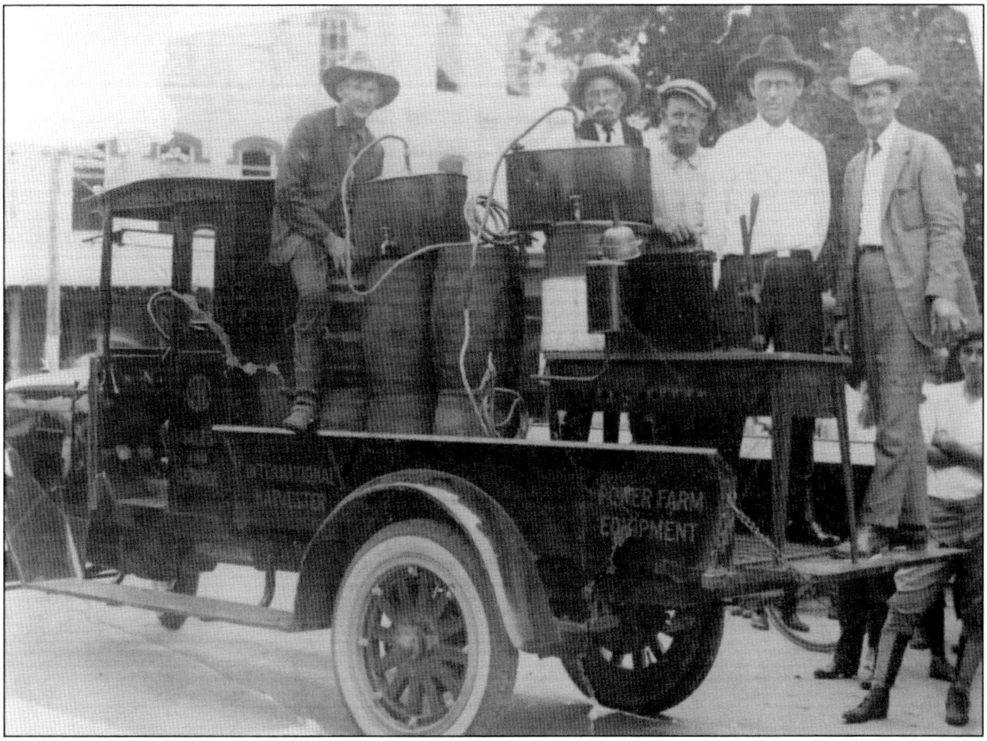

Controversial Washington County sheriff Burney Parker shows off confiscated stills in downtown Brenham in 1924, his 10th year as sheriff. In July of that year, Sheriff Parker openly resigned his membership in the Ku Klux Klan after making a motion to disband the local chapter. It was front page news in the *Banner-Press*. Parker soundly lost reelection.

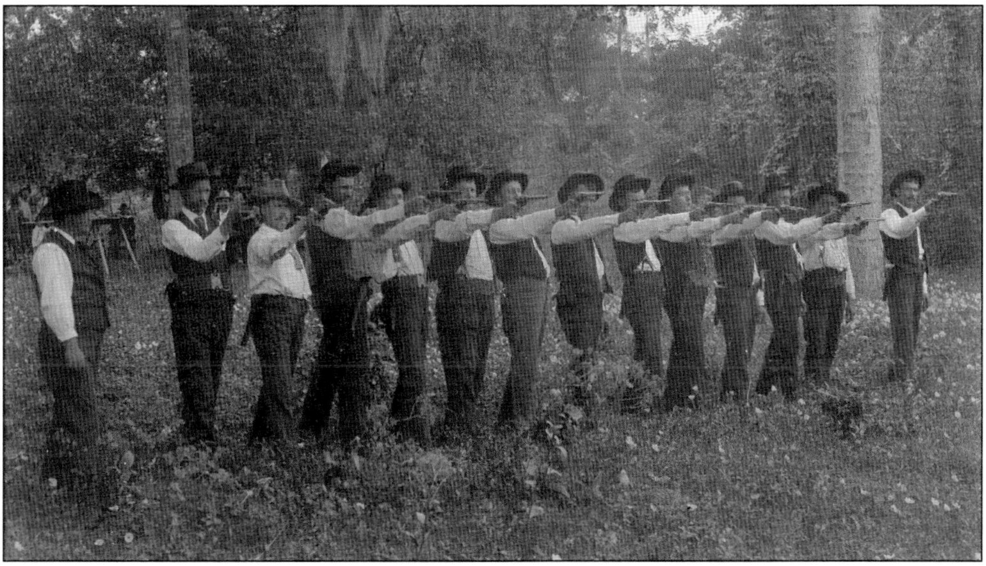

The local Schutzenverein, or Shooting Club, poses for a photograph with pistols on display. It was founded in 1877 with Capt. R. Schmerbeck in command. Membership was exclusive to German-born men. There was a robust social element and frequent events such as the combined German Day and Columbus Day celebrations of the late 19th century.

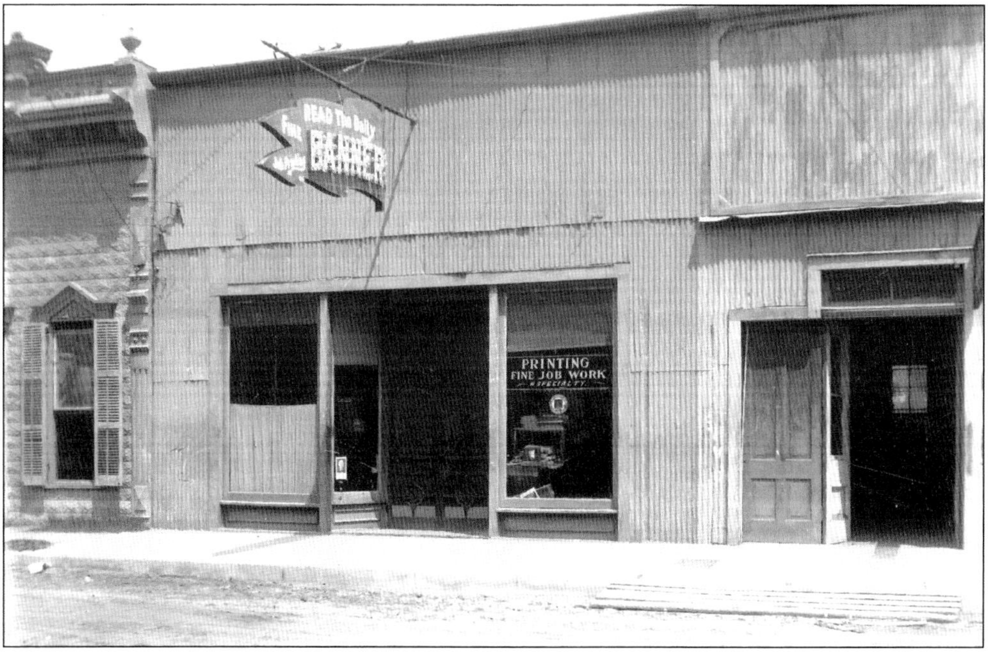

The *Brenham Daily Banner* newspaper did not boast a particularly impressive edifice on Alamo Street. As the signage noted, the paper also took on outside printing jobs and promised fine results. On October 1, 1913, the owners of this paper, having bought out their rival newssheet, began publishing under the name *Brenham Banner-Press*.

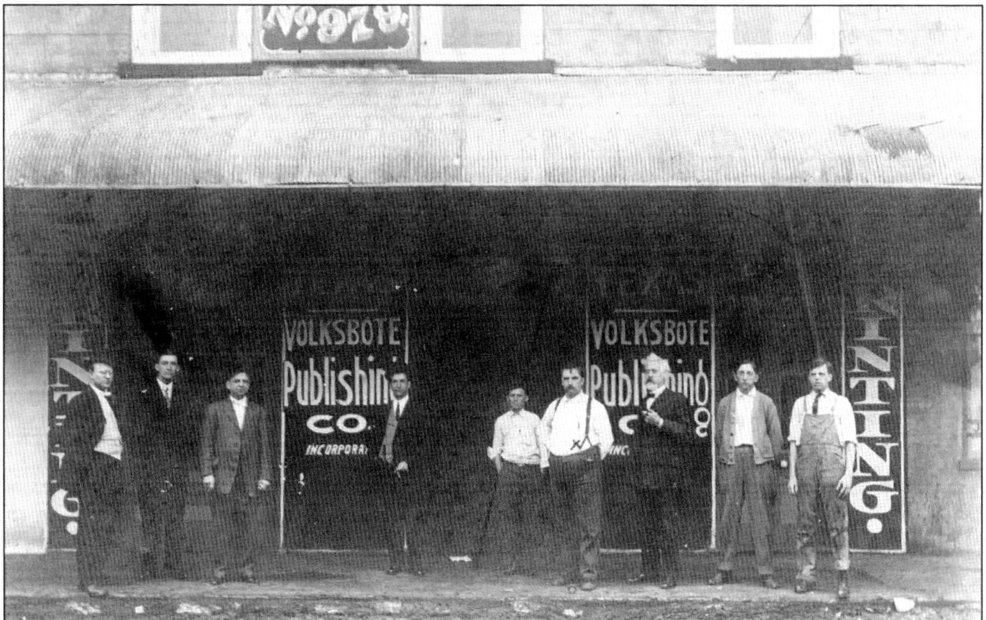

Volksbote Publishing was started by Henry Mueller in 1873. *Der Texas Volksbote* was printed in German and enjoyed a broad circulation both around Texas and in Germany. In 1919, reacting to virulent anti-German sentiment engendered by both World War I and the revitalized Klan, the name was changed to the *Brenham Weekly Messenger*, and the language switched to English.

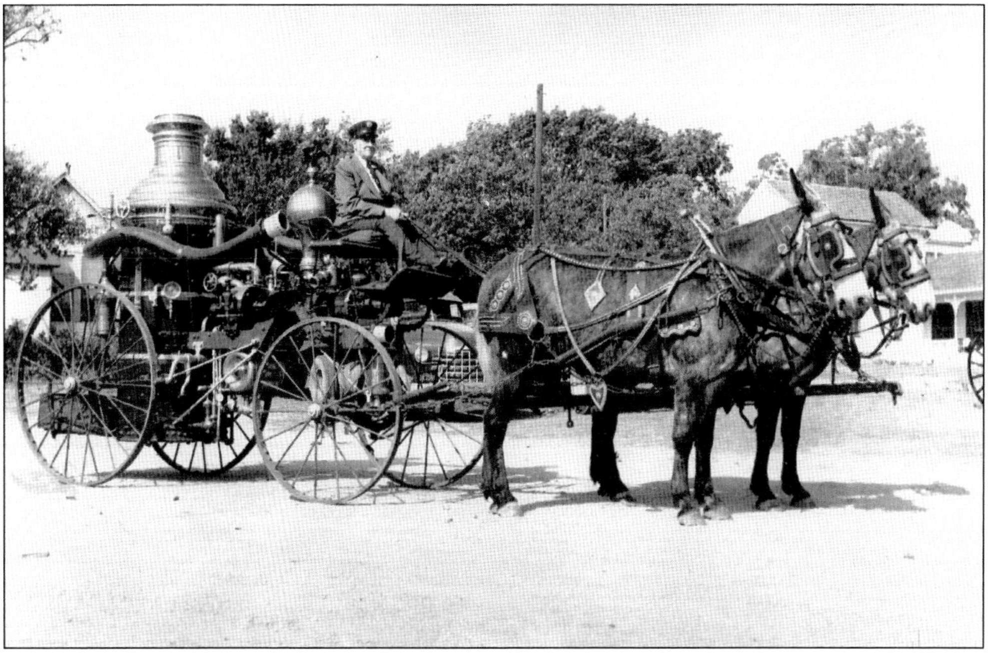

The Brenham Fire Department's prized Silsby steam pumper remained a mainstay at local festivities decades after it was taken out of service. It was purchased by Mechanics Engine Company No. 1. Though it was designed to be pulled by horses, it often responded to local fires under the power of the firemen themselves since horses were not always readily available.

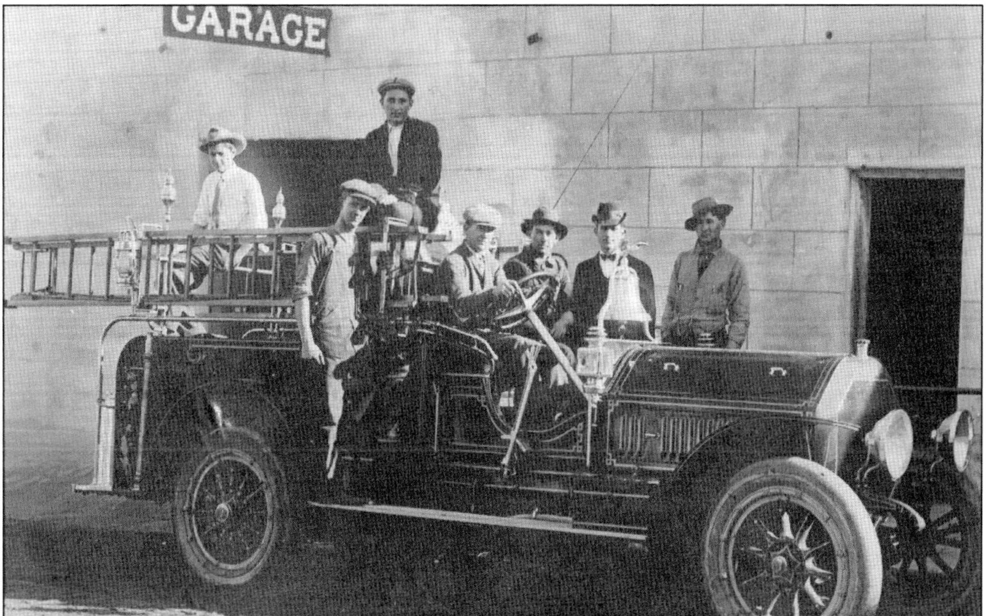

For the price of $5,000, Brenham Fire Department took delivery of this brand new 1911 Webb combination hose and chemical truck on July 3 of that year. Among the men photographed with the vehicle were Reese Lockett, E.P. Davis, and young E.W. Pflughaupt, the latter two of whom went on to serve the department as chief. (Brenham Fire Department.)

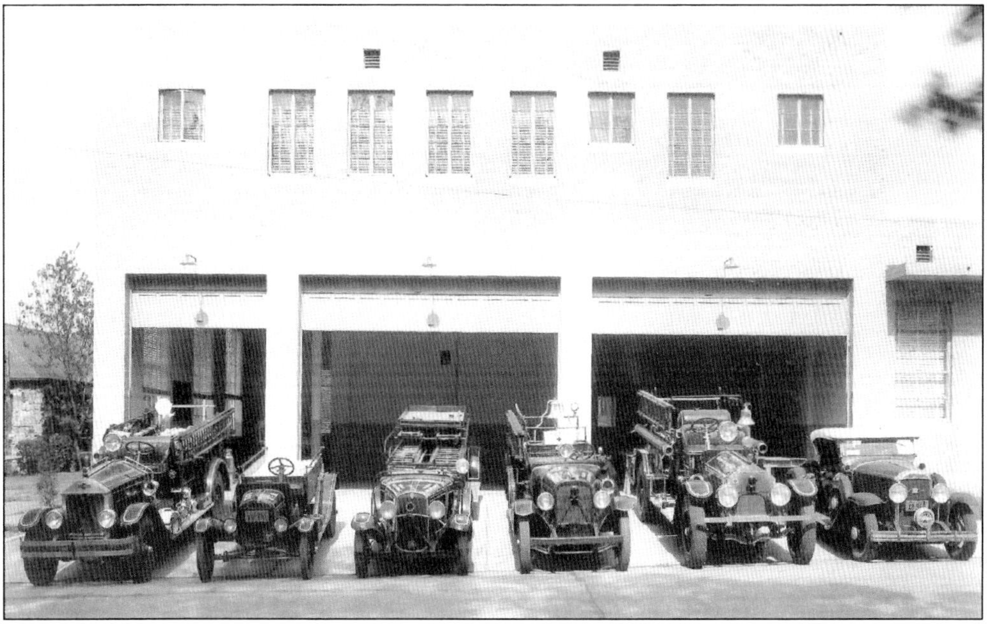

Trucks of the Brenham Fire Department stand ready at the station, which was on Park Street at Vulcan Street. Second from the right is *Samanthe*, a 1923 American LaFrance Type 38 that the City of Brenham bought new from the factory in Elmira, New York, in 1923. The department restored the engine to its original glory, and it is now housed at the local fire museum. (Gloria Nix.)

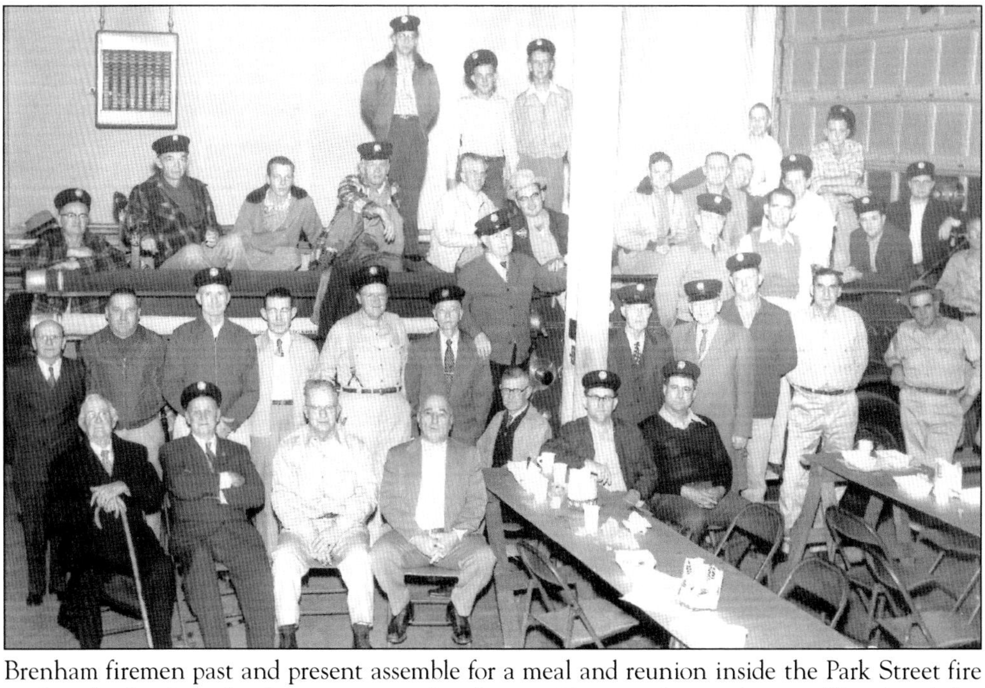

Brenham firemen past and present assemble for a meal and reunion inside the Park Street fire station. At the time, the department employed two paid responders, and most of Brenham's fire protection still came from volunteers who responded to bells and sirens. Some were as near as Carl Schlottmann's Phillips 66 Station across the street. A fire truck frequently started its response by circling the courthouse to pick up volunteers. (Gloria Nix.)

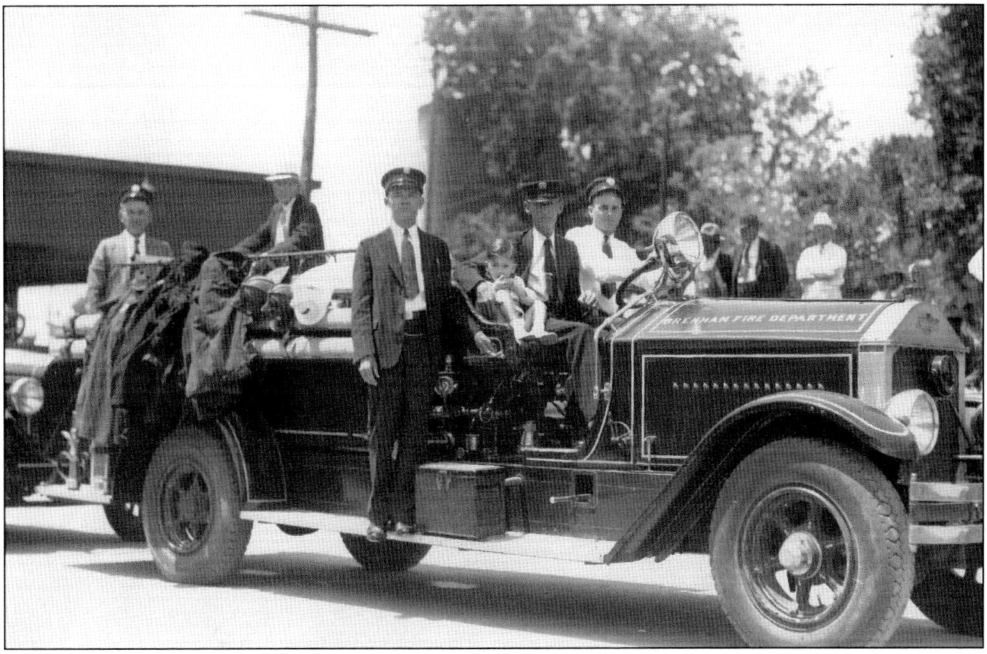

The Brenham Fire Department oversaw Maifest for over a century, and the parades always showcased the shiny engines. The fire department took over the event from the founding Volksfest Association in 1881, sponsoring that year's festival at the fairgrounds southeast of downtown. Those grounds were owned by another immigrant organization, the Germania Verein.

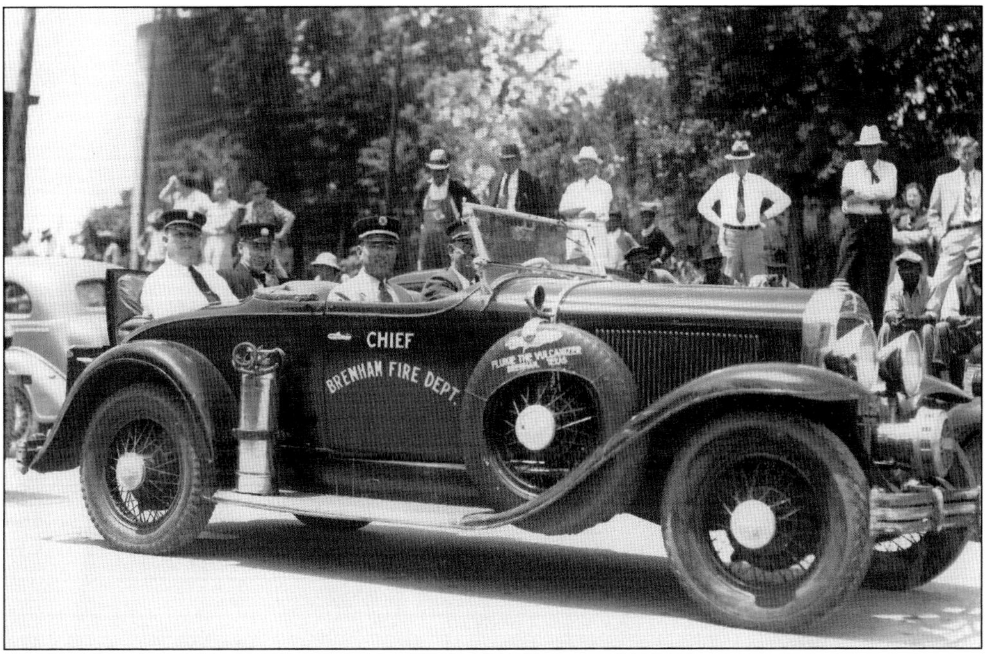

Brenham fire chief E.W. "Flukie" Pflughaupt rides in the Maifest parade along with assistant chiefs E.P. Davis up front and Grant Woods in the jump seat. Flukie served as the city's fire chief from 1937 until 1969. The spare tire cover on the car's fender advertises Flukie the Vulcanizer, a tire shop and service station at 401 East Alamo Street that was owned by the chief.

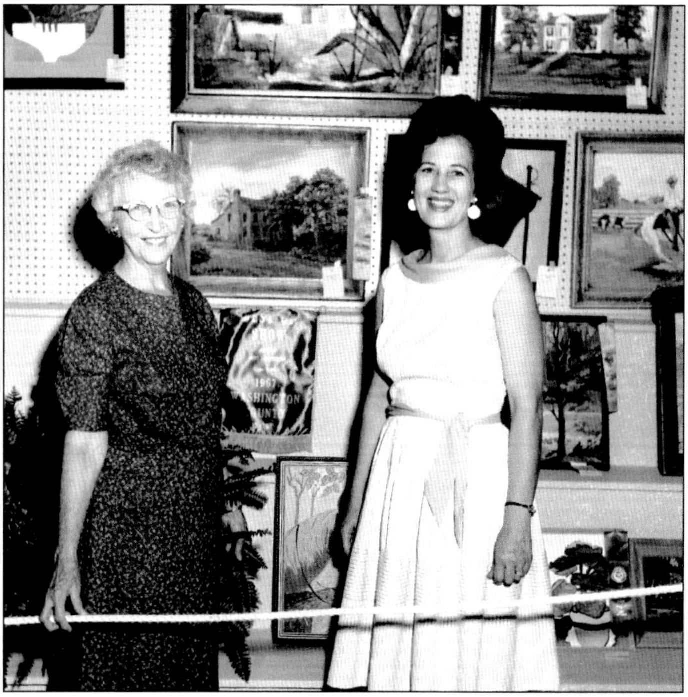

Local artists Golda Johnson and Lois Daniels display their work at the 1967 Washington County Fair. The art show remains popular with county fairgoers to this day. Johnson was instrumental in founding the Brenham Art Club along with Jeanne Hawley and Madeleine Schwecke in September 1956.

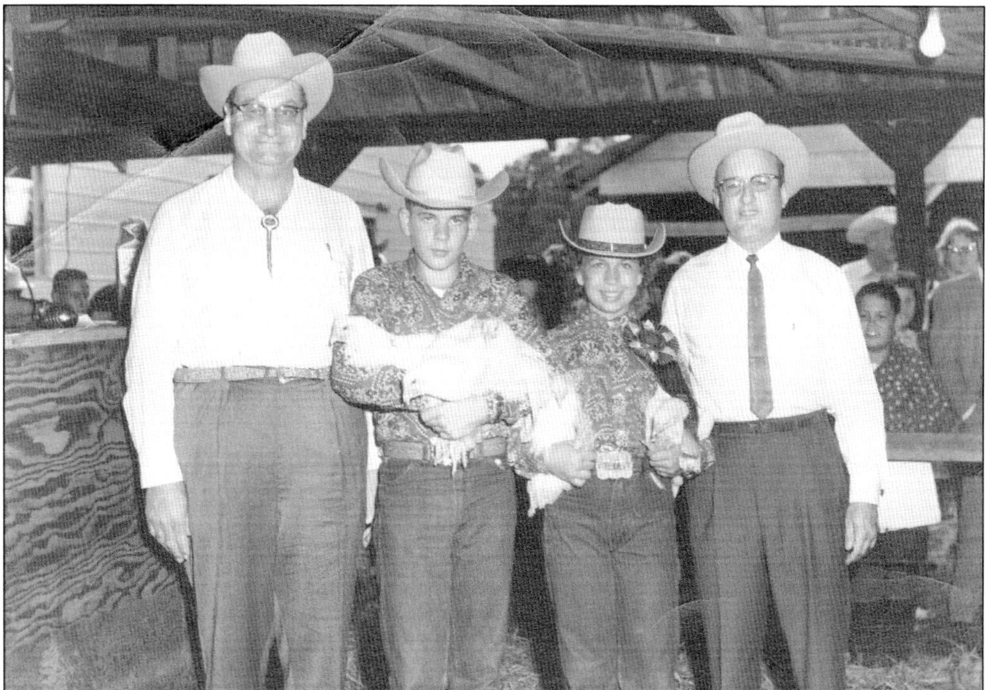

Brenham's Pearl Beer distributor Emanuel Lehrmann and Carl A. Schlottmann flank the poultry winners at the Washington County Fair. The fair was the first in Texas but had two prolonged gaps. In 1949, it moved from Fireman's Park to its own larger fairgrounds northeast of downtown. (Carl Schlottmann.)

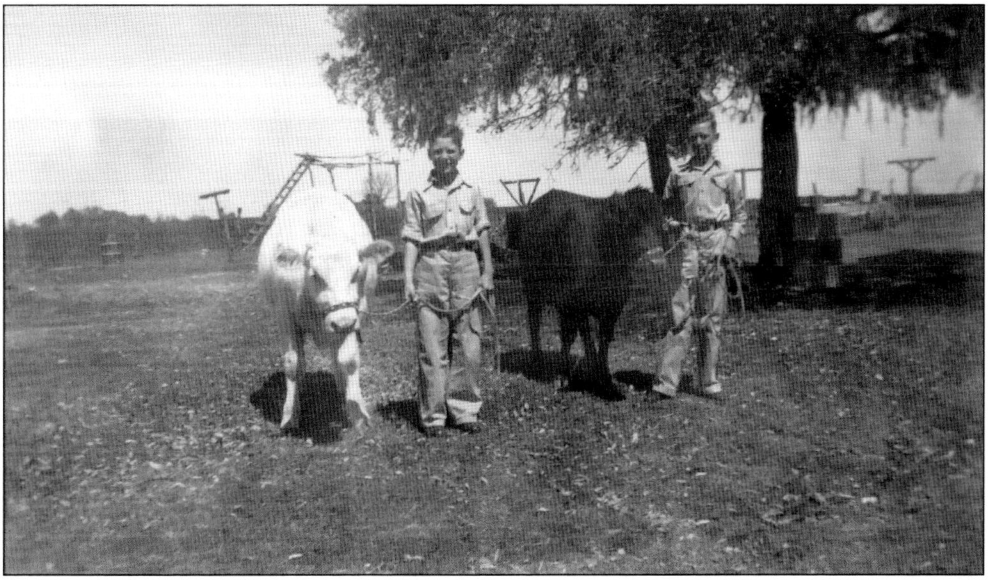

Eugene and Gilbert Janner raised cattle to show at the Washington County Fair, only to have the event canceled due to World War II. Local agriculture leaders rose to the occasion and created an opportunity for young local farmers to show their animals in 1943 despite the lack of a wider event. (Washington County Fair.)

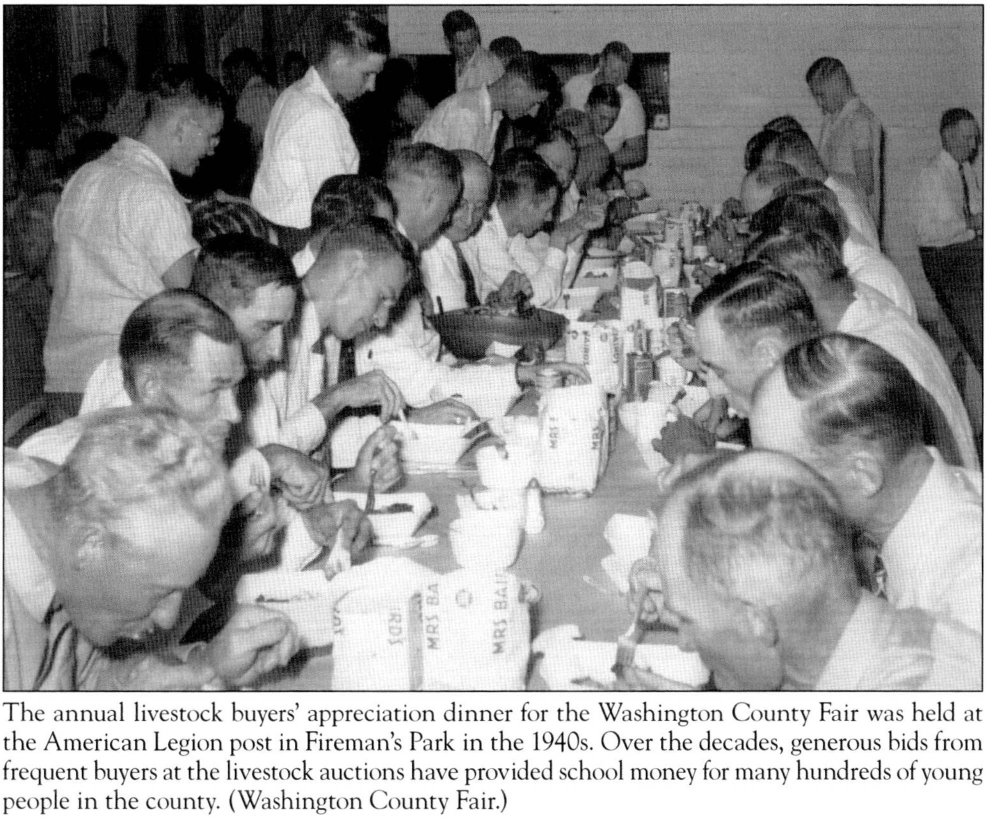

The annual livestock buyers' appreciation dinner for the Washington County Fair was held at the American Legion post in Fireman's Park in the 1940s. Over the decades, generous bids from frequent buyers at the livestock auctions have provided school money for many hundreds of young people in the county. (Washington County Fair.)

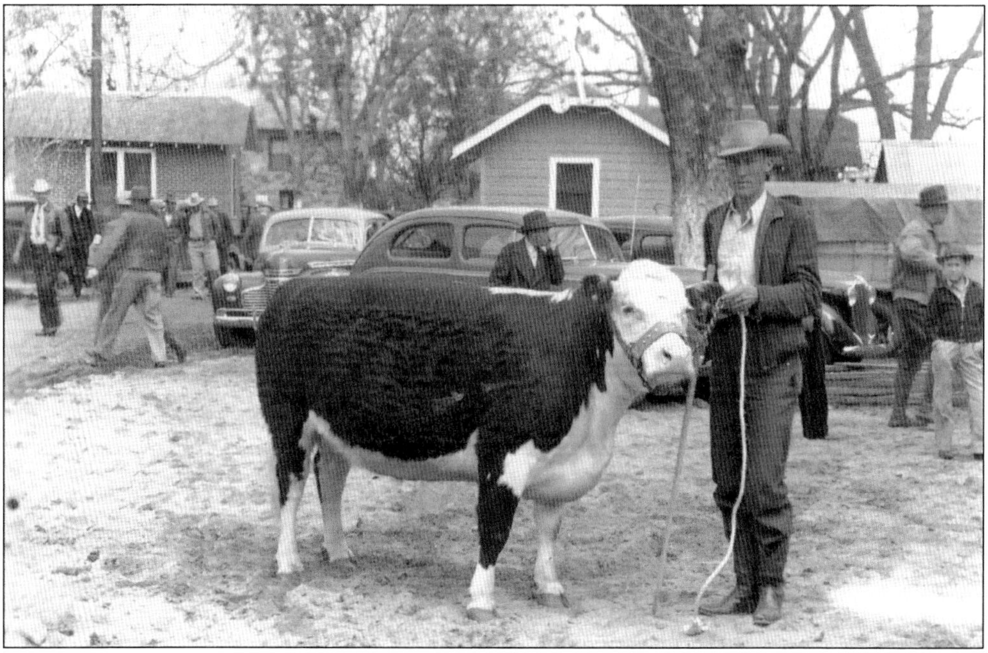

Holding the Washington County Fair and other livestock events in Fireman's Park meant bringing the animals into a residential neighborhood. When the fair resumed as an annual event in September 1929, an exposition hall was built at the park to accommodate cattle and other show animals. It served the community for two decades.

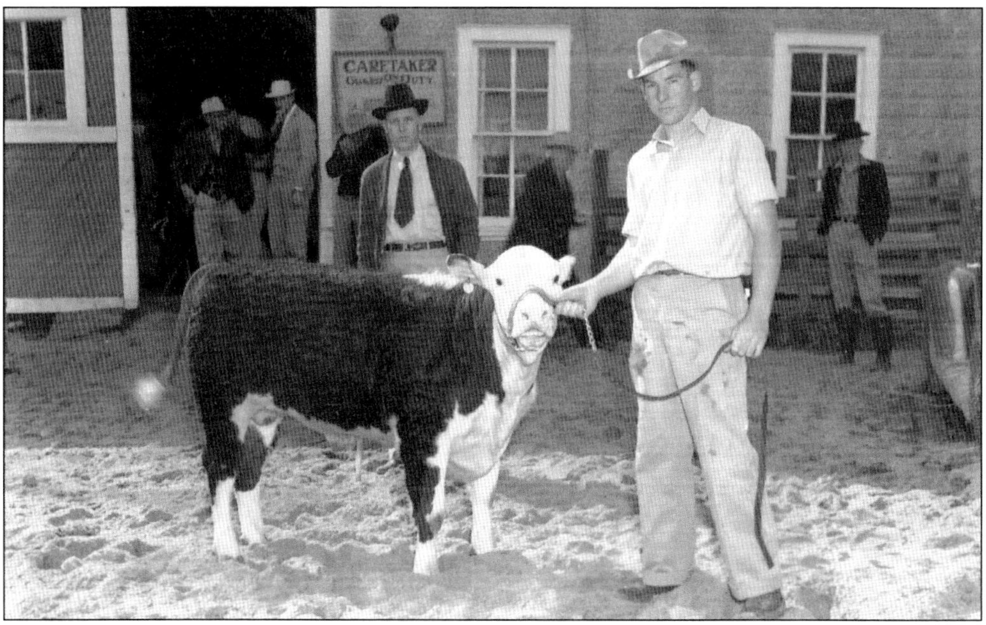

W. Arthur Schomburg poses in March 1941 with his entry for the feeder-breeder show. The event was the first of its kind and featured 50 calves from local 4-H and Future Farmers of America boys and girls plus 75 registered breeding cattle and 25 fat hogs. The two-day event included educational programs and an auction sale. Unfortunately, the attack on Pearl Harbor put an end to the promising idea.

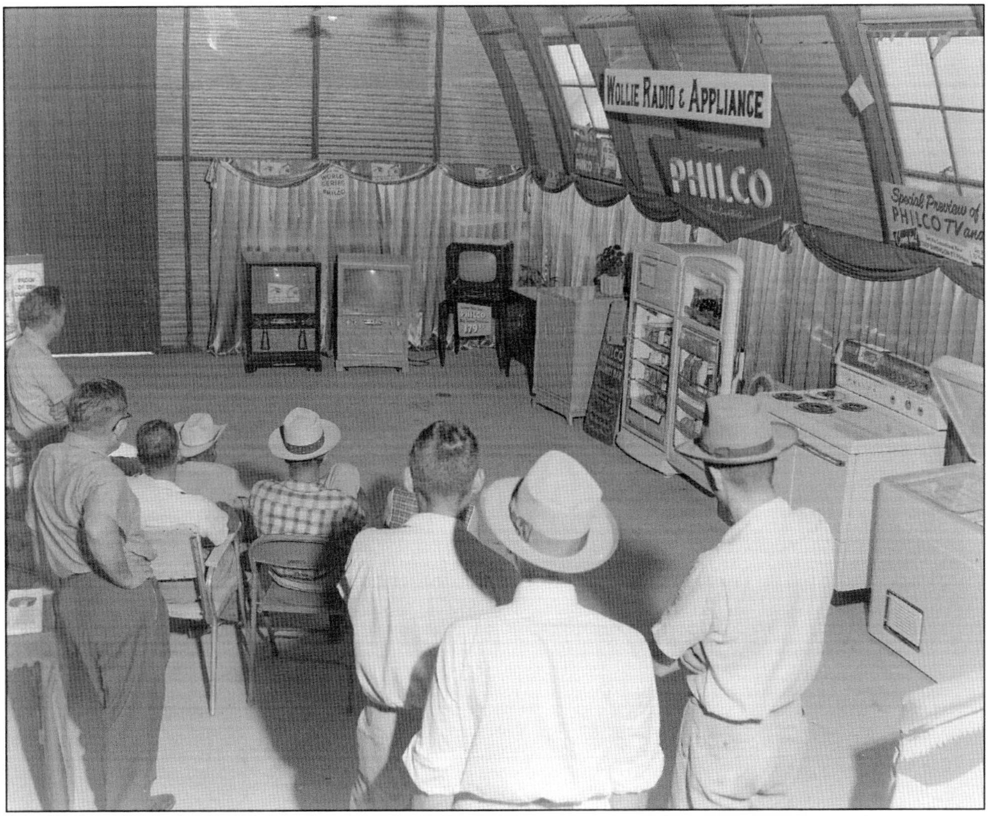

Wollie Radio and Appliance presented Philco televisions in its booth at the 1953 Washington County Fair. Among the viewers gathered were undoubtedly some who had never seen the contraption that was slowly becoming a new addition to some American homes. County residents who took the plunge for the new technology could sometimes get signals from the single station in Houston. (Washington County Fair.)

Though cattle, hogs, and poultry might garner more attention at the Washington County Fair, there is plenty more going on. The entomology winners in 1982 are a prime example. It is part of the fair's commitment to overall education that also includes competitions in art and photography. (Washington County Fair.)

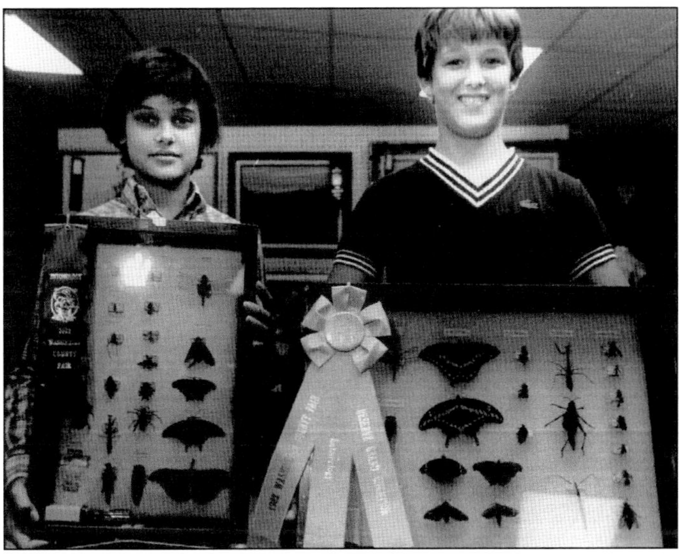

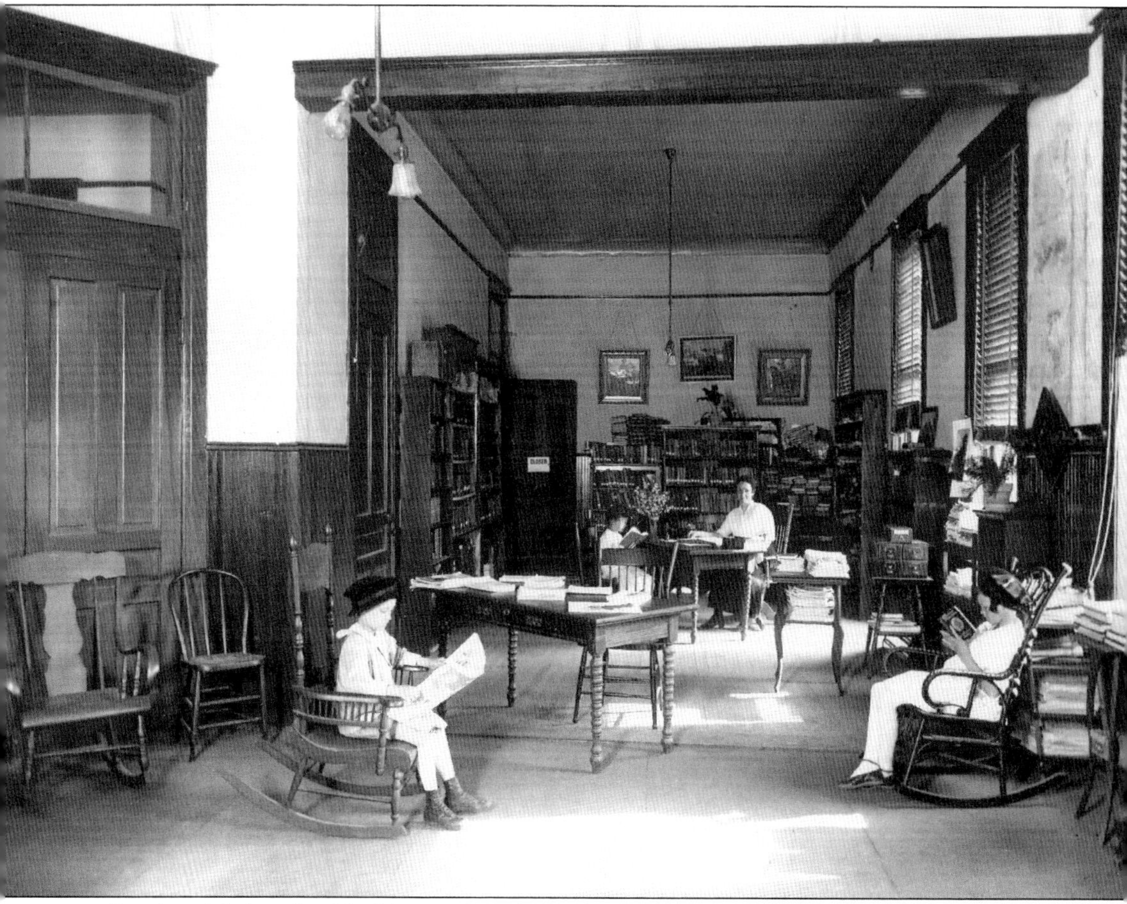

Brenham's beloved public library opened on February 19, 1901. Over a thousand invitations were issued to the opening reception in flower-bedecked rooms with a definite society air. The library's first home was in two rooms behind the Giddings & Giddings Bank Building. According to the *Brenham Daily Banner* from that day, the "light and airy" space was donated for the purpose by D.C. Giddings Sr. The library later moved to an upstairs space at city hall. It was founded by the "noble ladies of the Fortnightly Club," a group of literary local women who continued to manage the library into the 1970s, when paid staff under the direction of the city took over. At the time of its founding, there were over 40 public libraries in Texas, and all but the one in Galveston were due to the diligent and inspired work of women's groups such as the Fortnightly Club.

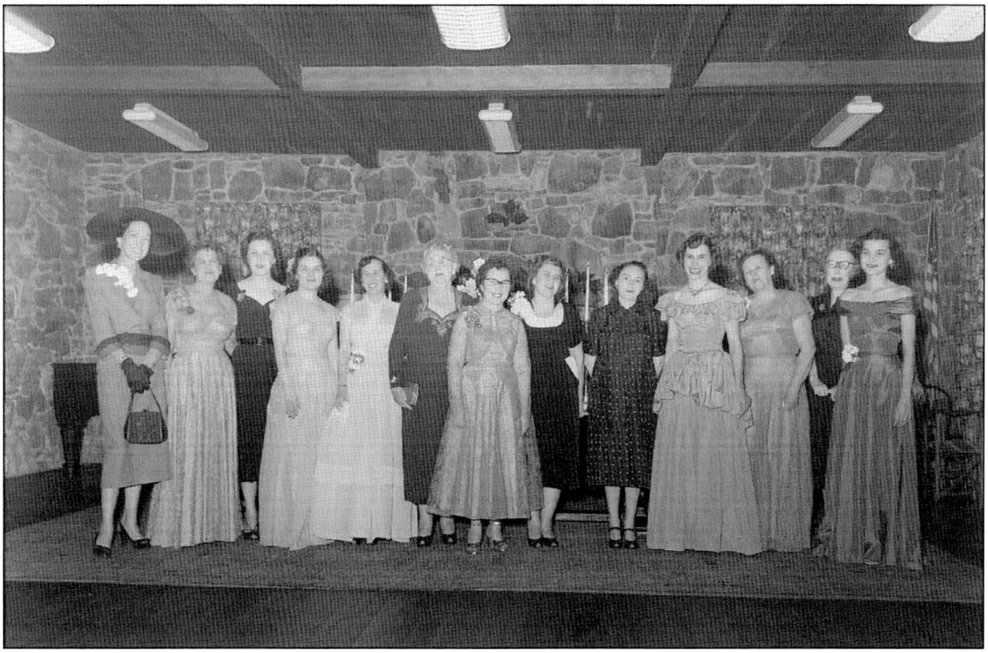

The Fortnightly Club poses during a formal tea in the early 1950s. The women's group was founded in 1895 and quickly set about work to establish a public library in Brenham, an institution they opened with books donated by the Brenham community. In their earliest years, they loaned their efforts to other civic improvements and fine arts. (Fortnightly Club.)

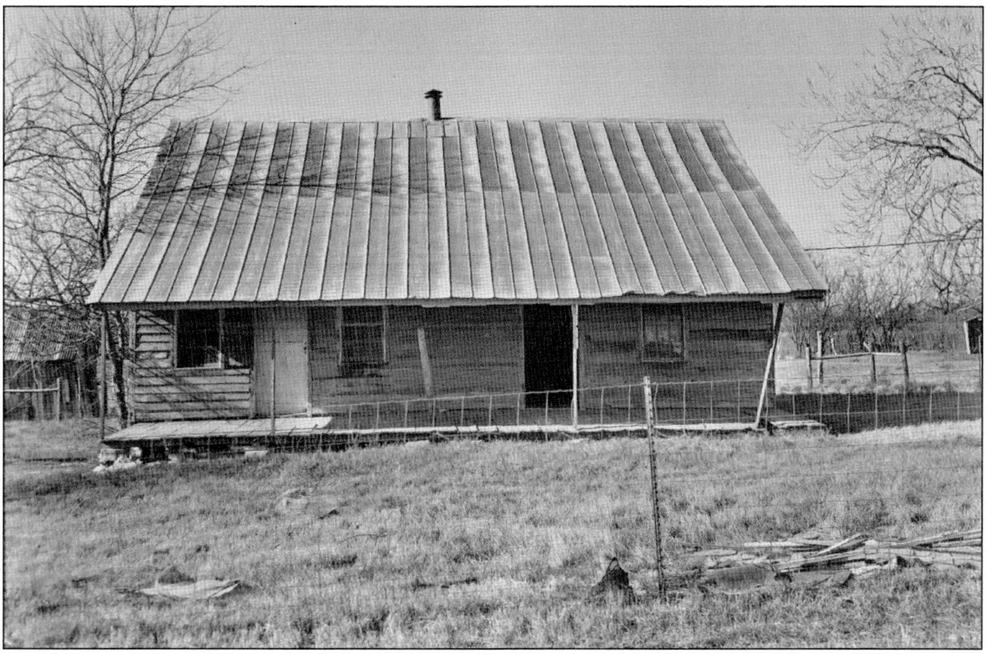

The home of John F. Coles stands about a mile north of the ruins of old Baylor University near Independence. Coles was one of the earliest of Austin's colonists, arriving on the Brazos River as early as 1822. Because of his promise to build a public meeting house, his homestead became a prominent gathering place, eventually growing into the town of Independence.

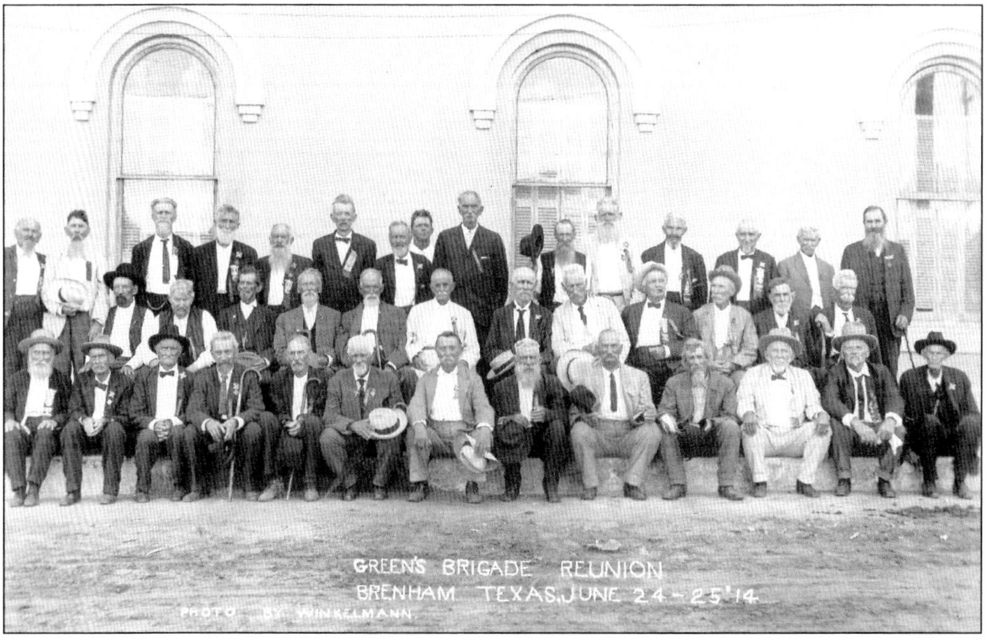

Survivors of Tom Green's Confederate Brigade held a reunion in Brenham in 1914. Tom Green was a veteran of the Texas Revolution, Indian raids, and the Mexican War before being elected colonel of a cavalry brigade that fought in New Mexico. The men who gathered in Brenham had served under Green in northern Louisiana, where their commander was killed in 1864.

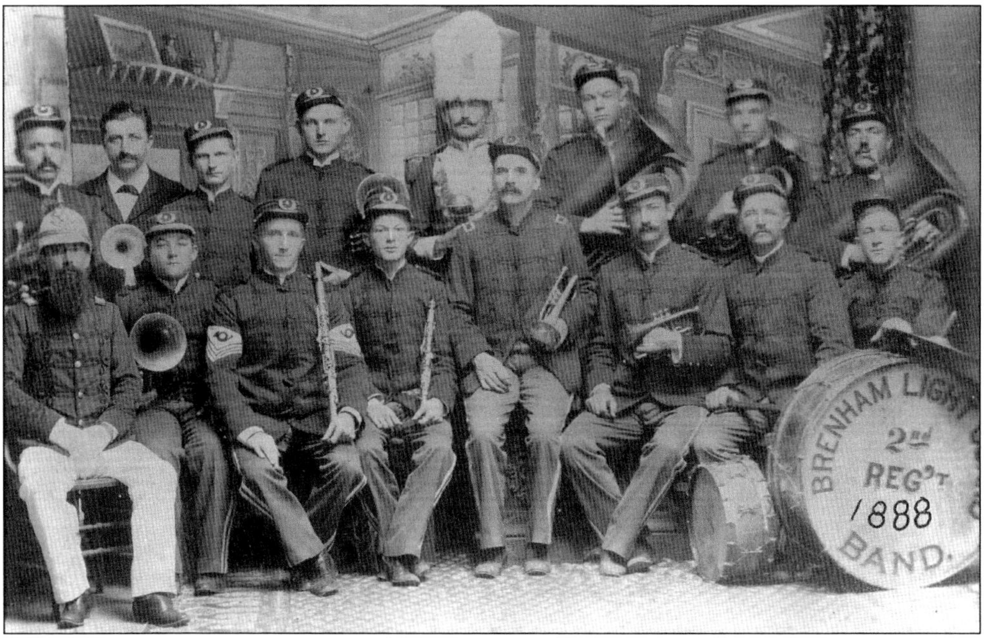

The Brenham Light Guard Band was a point of civic pride in the late 19th century, becoming the official band of the 2nd Texas Infantry. Leader G.H. Browning was succeeded by W.A. Jakel, and then F.J. Navratil. The band was called to active federal service in 1916 to serve American troops along the Mexican Border. Incorporated into another military unit, some members also saw service in France during World War I.

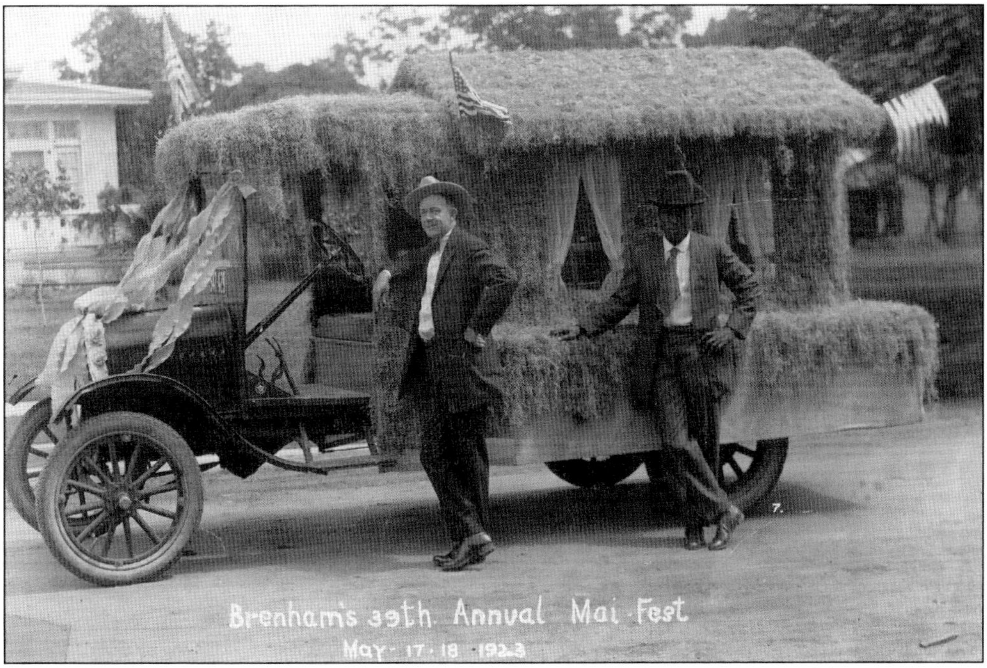

The Maifest celebration of 1923 fell in the midst of segregation and at the peak of the Klan's power in Washington County. That did not stop an integrated county agent's car from rolling in that year's parade. Agriculture extension services were operated out of Texas A&M and Prairie View A&M for white and black farmers respectively, though there was crossover in providing services.

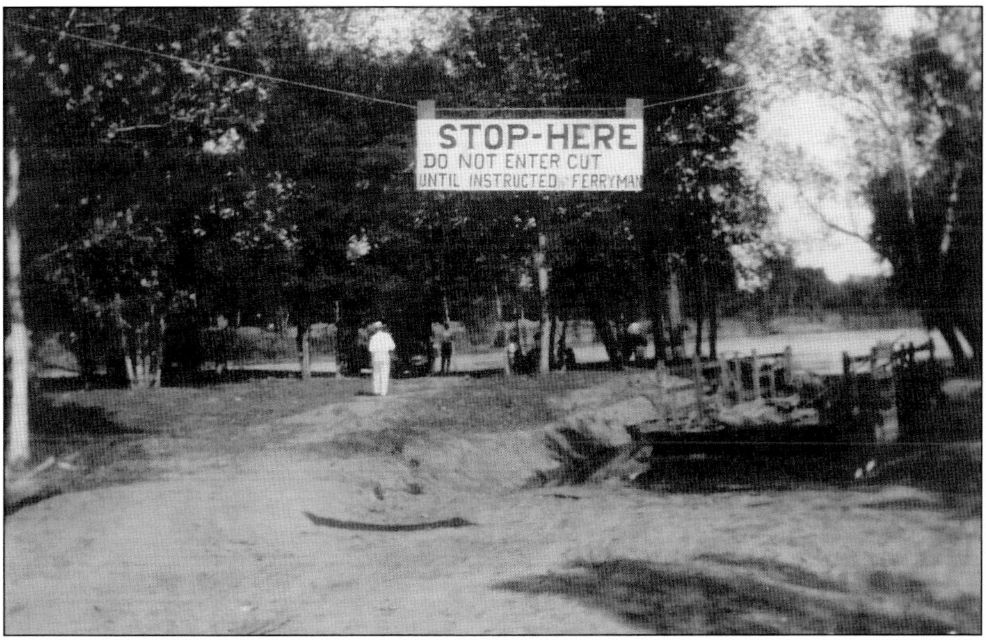

Though Washington County was on the verge of getting one of the state's earliest paved highways, crossing the Brazos River was still done by ferryboat in 1921. Many improvements to the slope and reliability of the approach had been made since early horse-drawn wagon drivers complained. The bridge on today's Highway 290 did not open until the end of the 1920s.

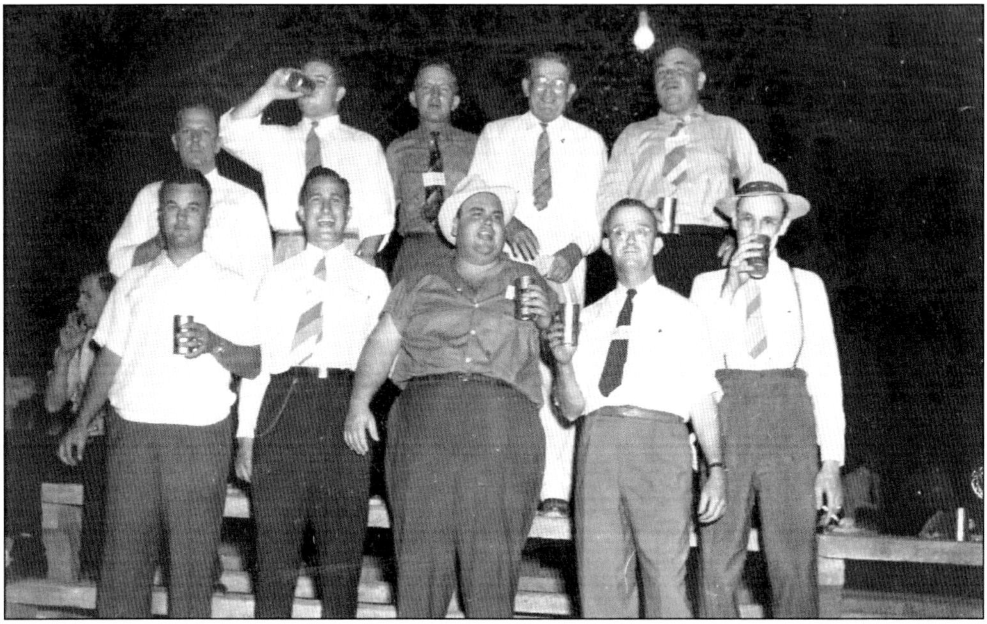

The Brenham Jaycees were a popular and active organization in 1941. It had been among the most vibrant business-promoting groups in town for nearly a decade, having fun and fellowship while moving younger people toward the senior chamber of commerce. Due to their youth, however, the group was forced to suspend operations only a few months after this photograph was taken because almost all of its members entered military service during World War II.

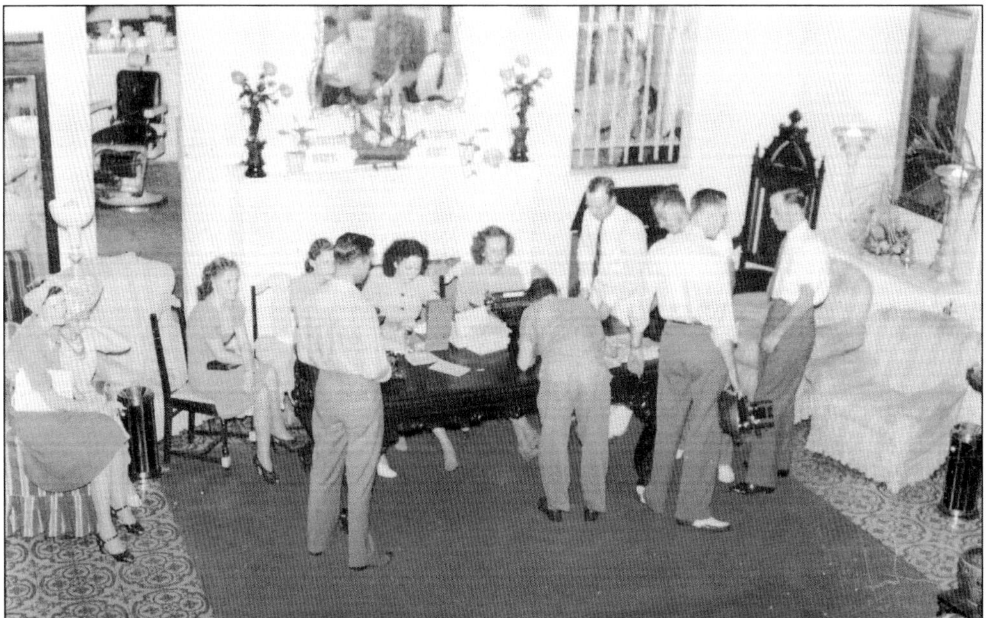

The district meeting of the Jaycees was held in Brenham in August 1940, headquartered at the St. Anthony Hotel. Behind the check-in table in the lobby is the barbershop. The local group got to trumpet several of its programs for the year, including raising money for a boys' dorm at Blinn, providing hot lunches in rural schools, and mounting a wildlife restoration program.

The Red Cross was vital during World War I, including in Brenham. Dr. Edmond Knolle was one of several medical professionals involved. Three Brenham doctors served in the US Medical Corps in France: Dr. P.D. Barnhill, Dr. Robert Hasskarl, and Dr. Hermann Hodde. Dr. Barnhill was killed there only three weeks before the end of the war.

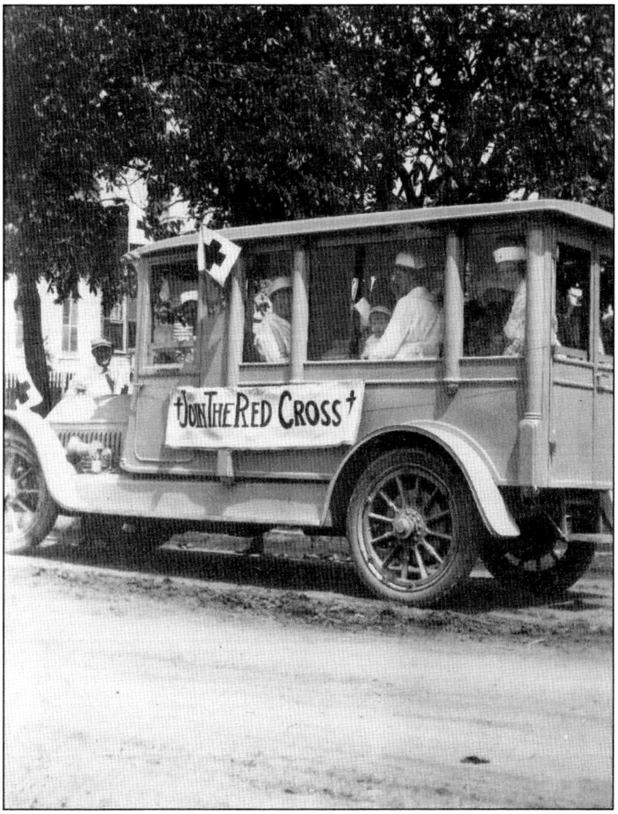

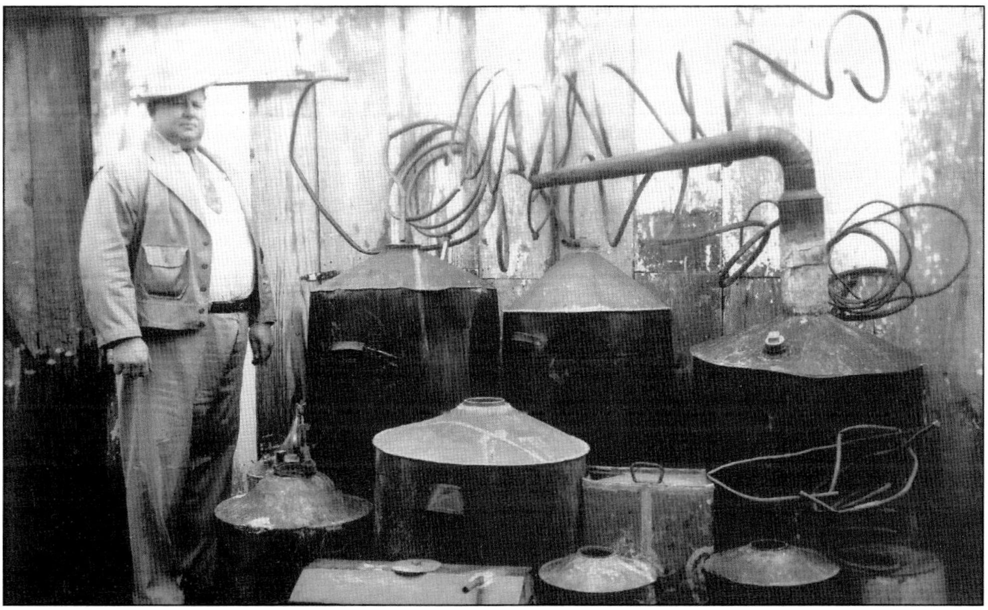

E.T. Zwernemann became a local liquor control agent at the end of Prohibition and stayed in that job for years afterward. Even though alcohol became legal again in the county, production of bootleg hooch persisted through well-hidden stills in rural areas. Enforcement, however, was generally accepted as being uneven.

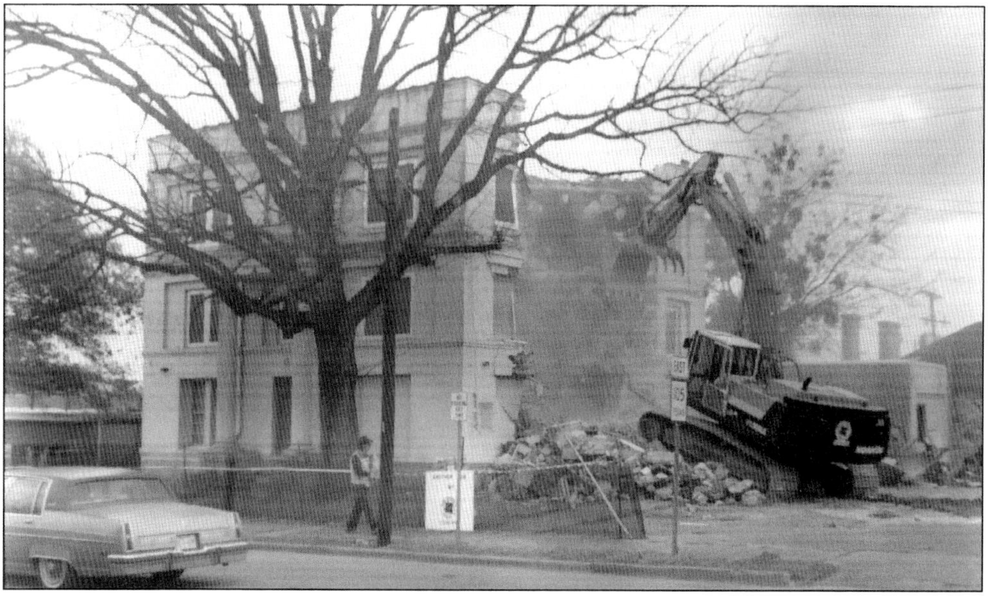

Washington County's jail has had several homes since the days of the Republic when a temporary wooden building held the county lawbreakers. This jail sat on East Alamo Street adjacent to the rock-faced cannery building. It was built in the first decade of the 20th century and replaced a smaller calaboose on the same spot.

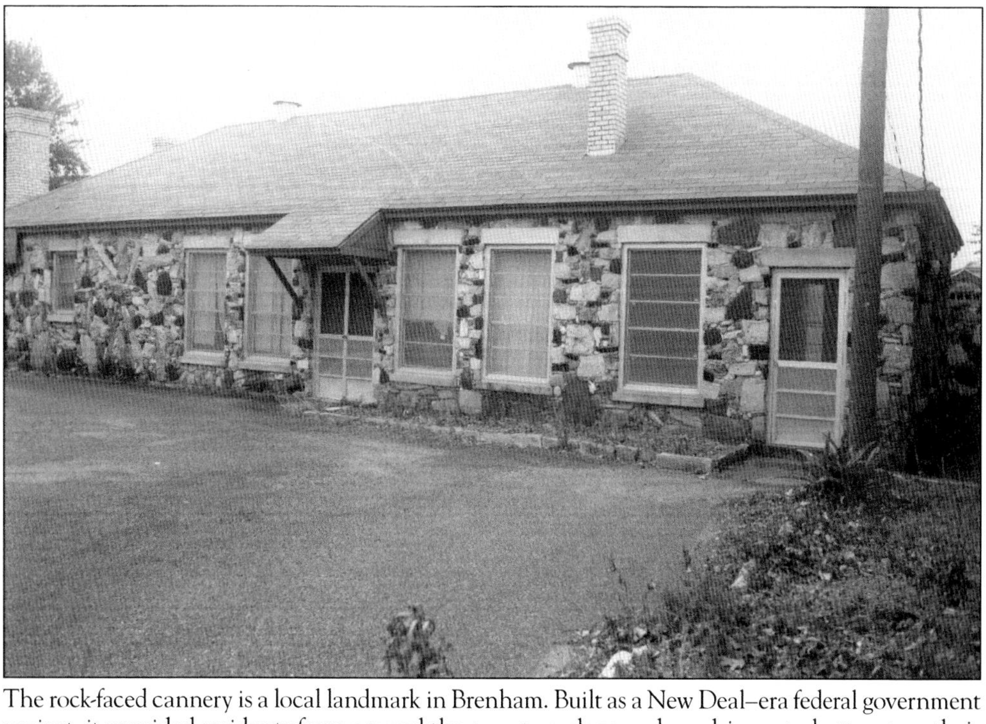

The rock-faced cannery is a local landmark in Brenham. Built as a New Deal–era federal government project, it provided residents from around the county a place and machinery to better store their farm produce for year-round use. Some of the canned food was also distributed to those in need. The cannery building and name both live on with the charity work of the Faith Mission.

Three

Events

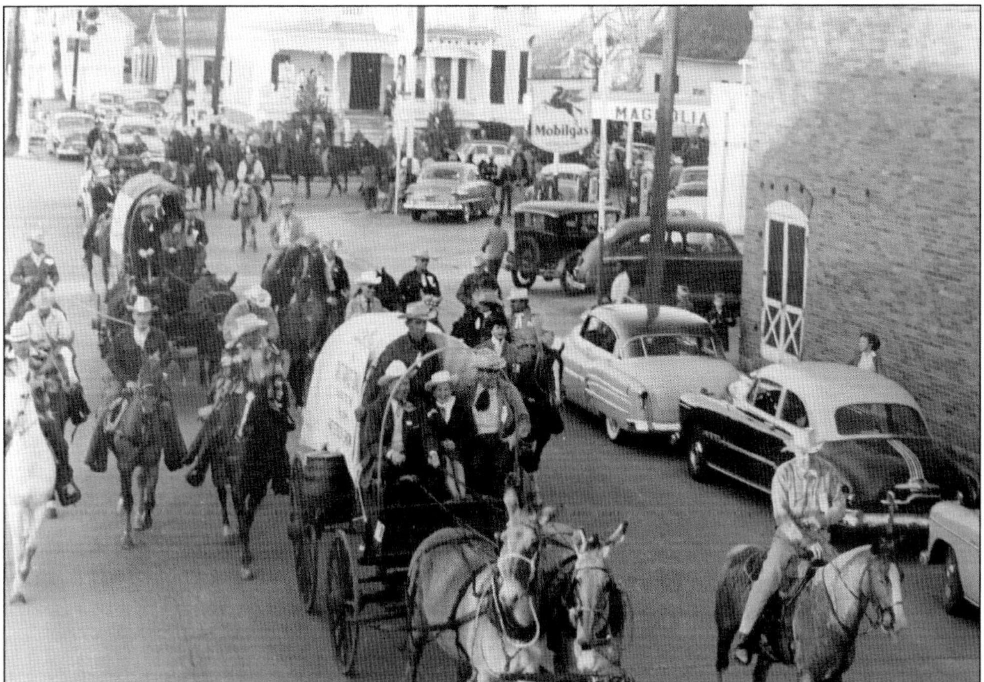

Salt Grass Trail riders make their way from Main Street onto South Austin Street, passing through an area unaccustomed at the time to seeing such a large number of riders on horseback. Singing cowboy star Gene Autry drove the wagon, and KPRC radio announcer Pat Flaherty, who had been one of the four inaugural trail riders, also occupied a front wagon seat. (Gloria Nix.)

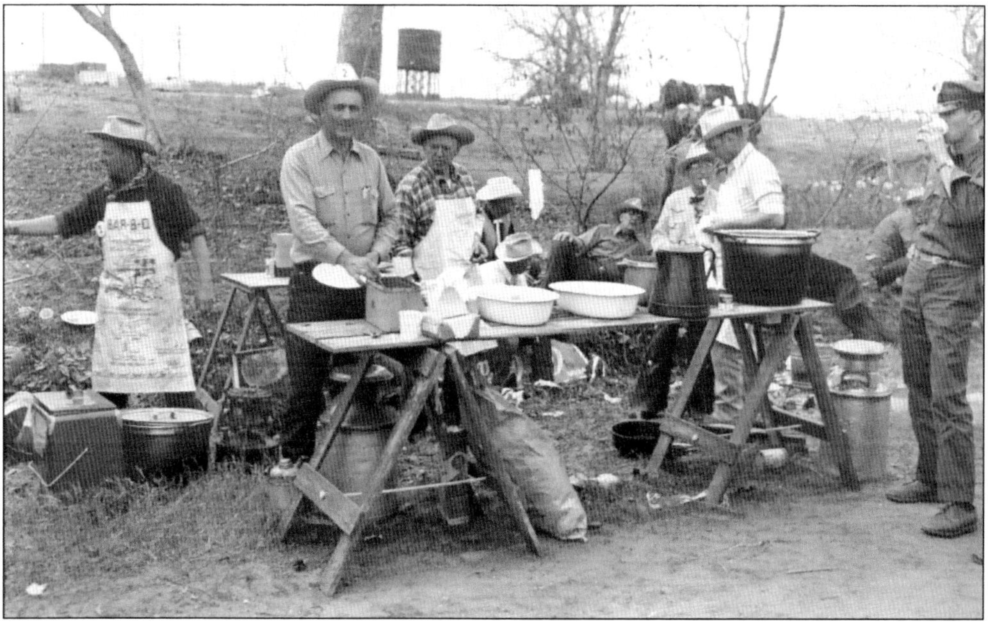

The first Salt Grass Trail started in 1952 with only four riders fulfilling a bar bet between Brenham's mayor Reese Lockett and his friend LH7 Ranch owner Emil Marks. Over drinks at Houston's Shamrock Hotel, the challenge of riding to Houston from Lockett's home in Brenham was crafted. A couple of years later, the number of riders had grown, but meal stations along the way remained primitive. (Gloria Nix.)

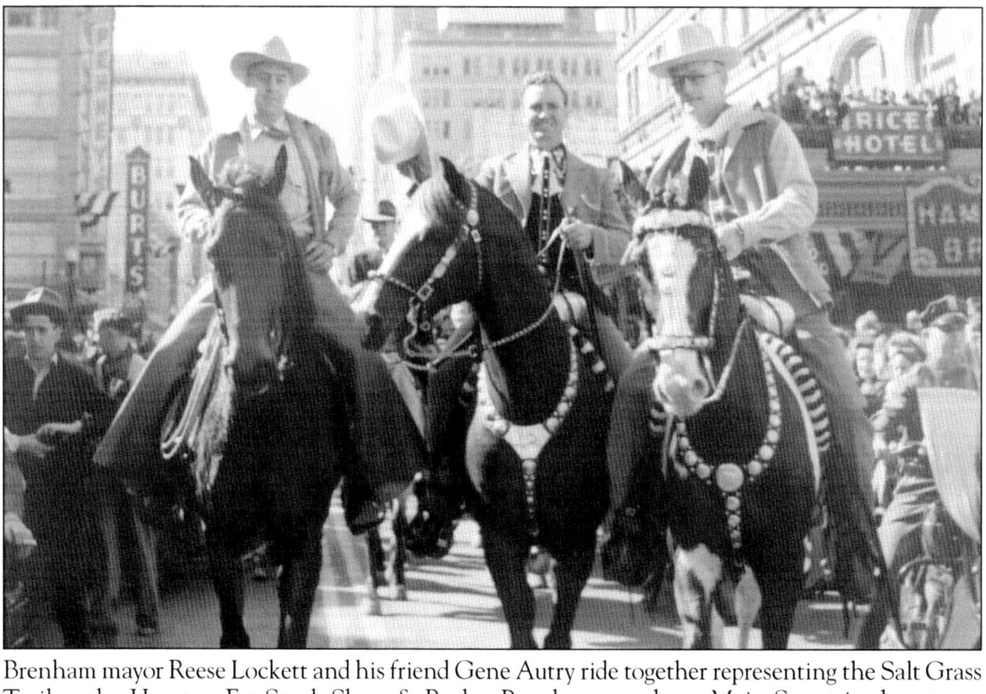

Brenham mayor Reese Lockett and his friend Gene Autry ride together representing the Salt Grass Trail as the Houston Fat Stock Show & Rodeo Parade passes down Main Street in downtown Houston. Lockett was a founder of the Houston show's trail ride tradition and remained involved in the giant event in Houston for many years. (Gloria Nix.)

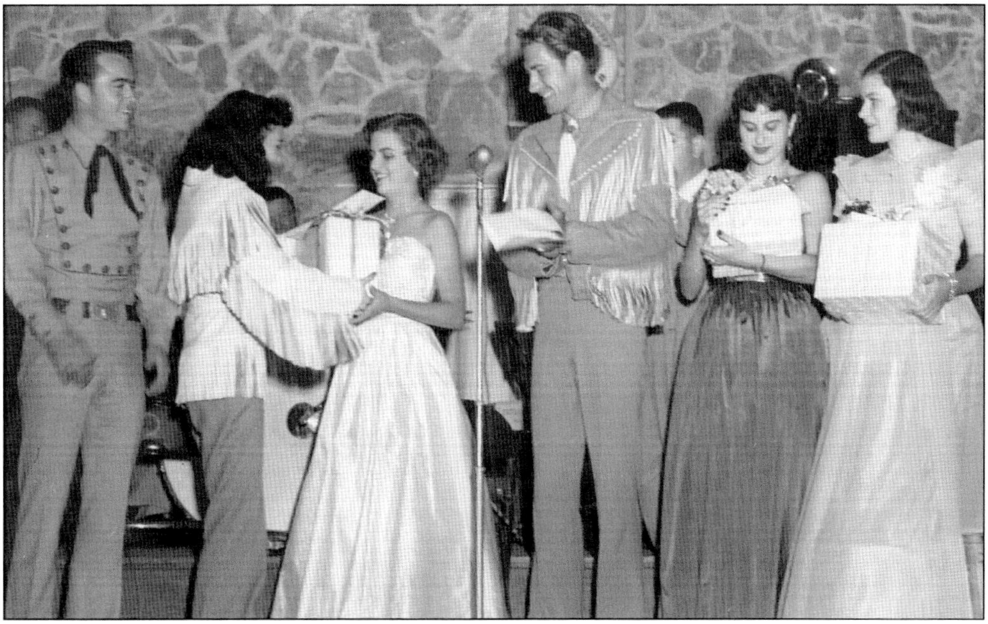

Gloria Nix accepts a gift during the Salt Grass Trail Dance in 1953. To raise money for the March of Dimes, queen candidates sold tickets to the dance, with the highest fundraiser becoming the top royalty. The charity began with Pres. Franklin Roosevelt's efforts to combat polio around the world, and the March of Dimes quickly became one of the top beneficiaries of America's charitable giving. (Gloria Nix.)

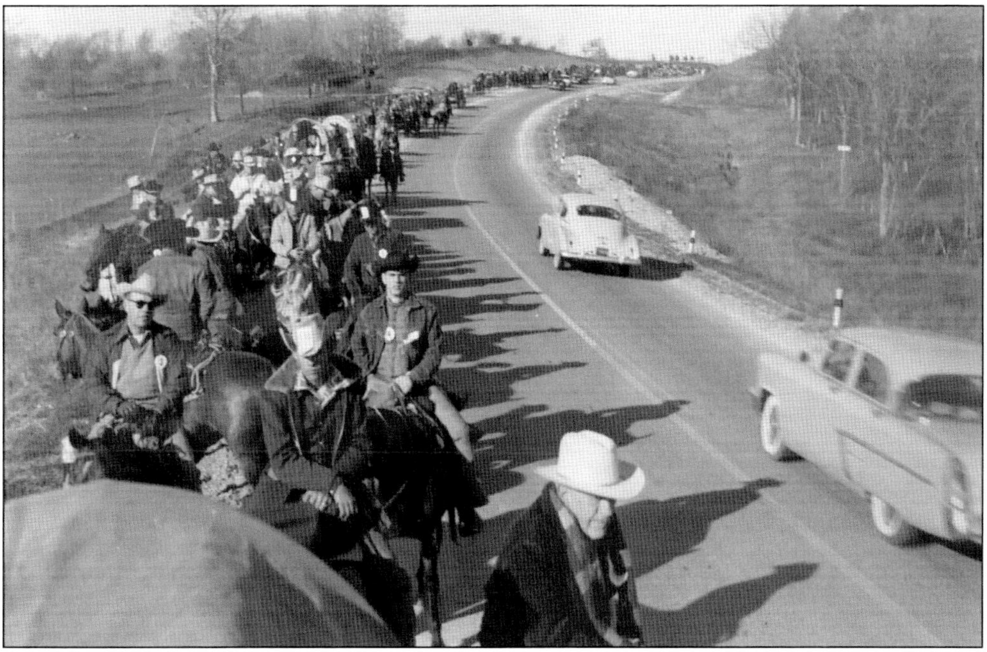

Riders in the third annual Salt Grass Trail string out along US Highway 290 on their way from Brenham to Houston. From a small start born from a bar bet, four riders grew to 100, then 300. The Salt Grass ride spawned a dozen other trail rides that ended with a parade through the streets of downtown Houston each winter. (Gloria Nix.)

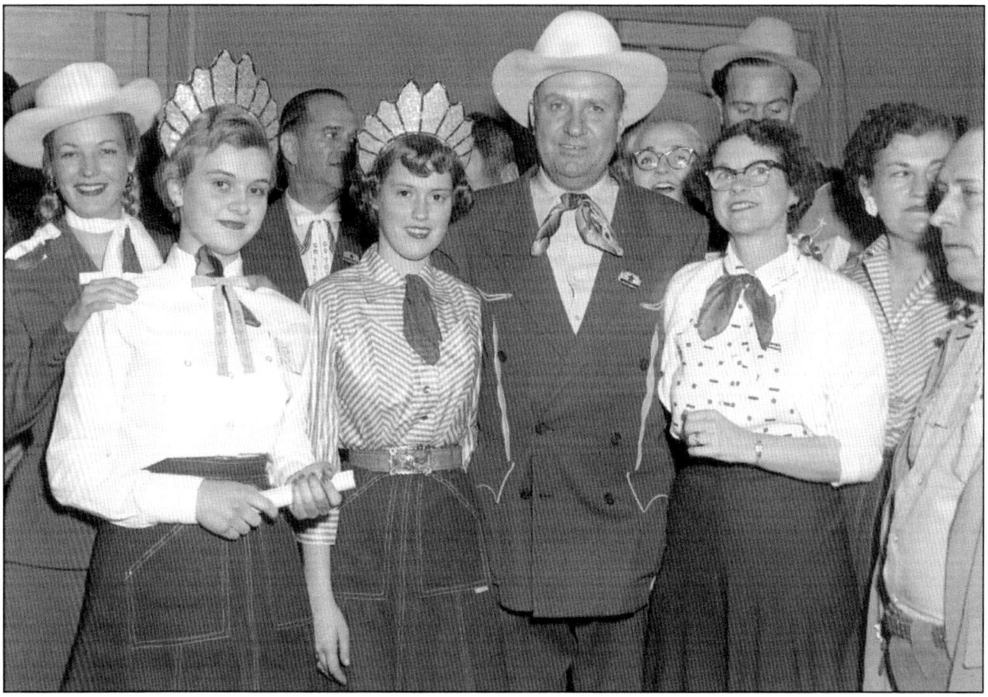

Cowboy star Gene Autry visited Brenham more than once to join Salt Grass Trail riders for the journey into Houston for the Fat Stock Show. In the early 1950s, he poses with members of the local Pilot Club. Bernice Hinze stands next to Autry with the flower hat.

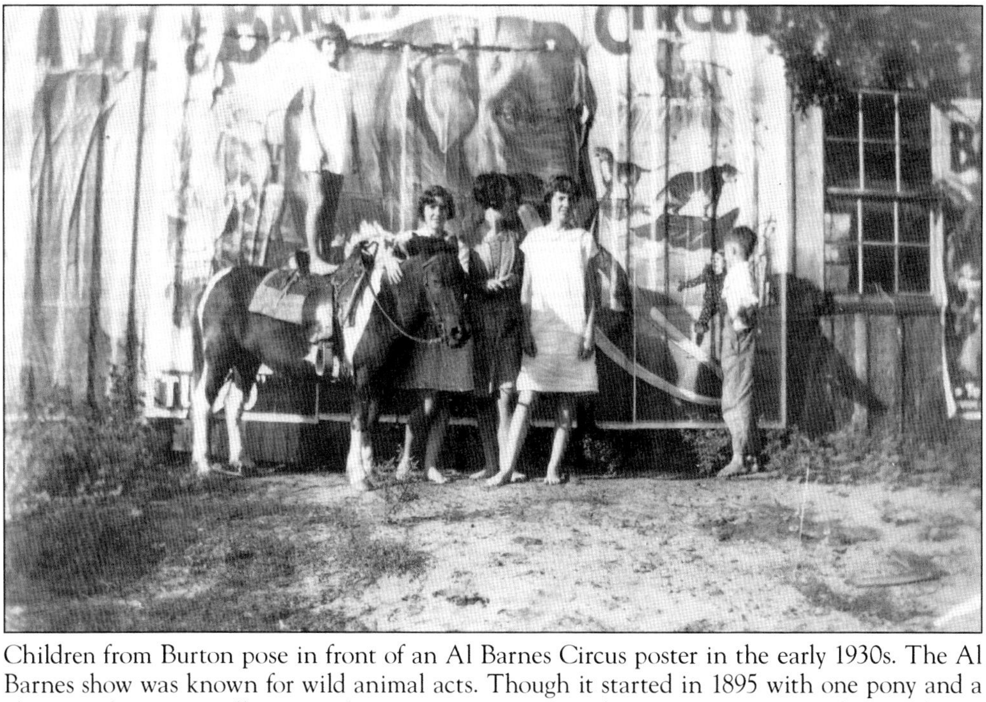

Children from Burton pose in front of an Al Barnes Circus poster in the early 1930s. The Al Barnes show was known for wild animal acts. Though it started in 1895 with one pony and a phonograph, it eventually grew to five rings. Circuses in Washington County were a long tradition, with the first coming to Brenham prior to the Civil War. (Debbie Lehrmann.)

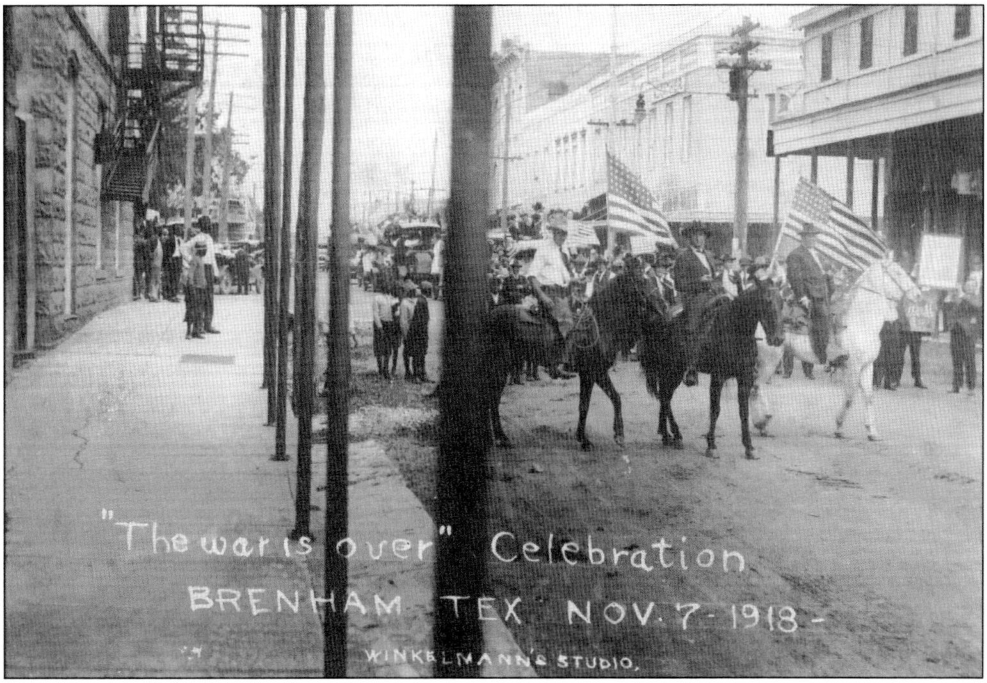

Brenham's Victory Day Parade in November 1918 was an epic celebration. Seemingly everyone in the county gathered downtown to mark the end of World War I. Though the armistice to end fighting took effect on November 11 at exactly 11:00 a.m., it was another 15 months before peace terms were signed. Battles continued until the final minutes, and over 2,700 men died on the final morning of the war. Like cities across the nation, the war had hit the area hard. More than 51 Washington County men died while on active duty in the Great War.

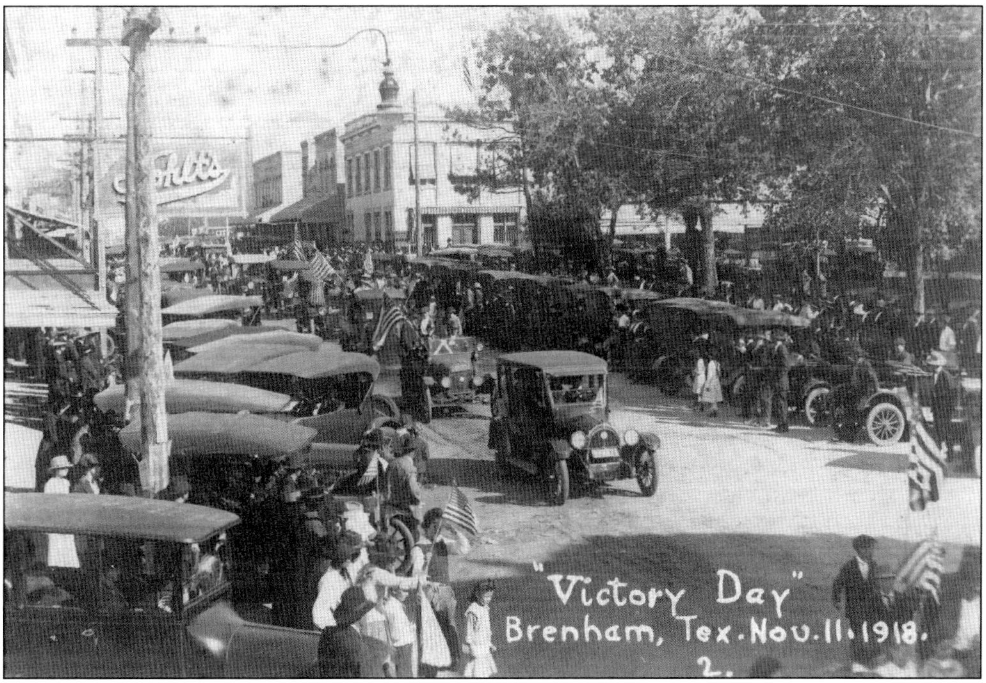

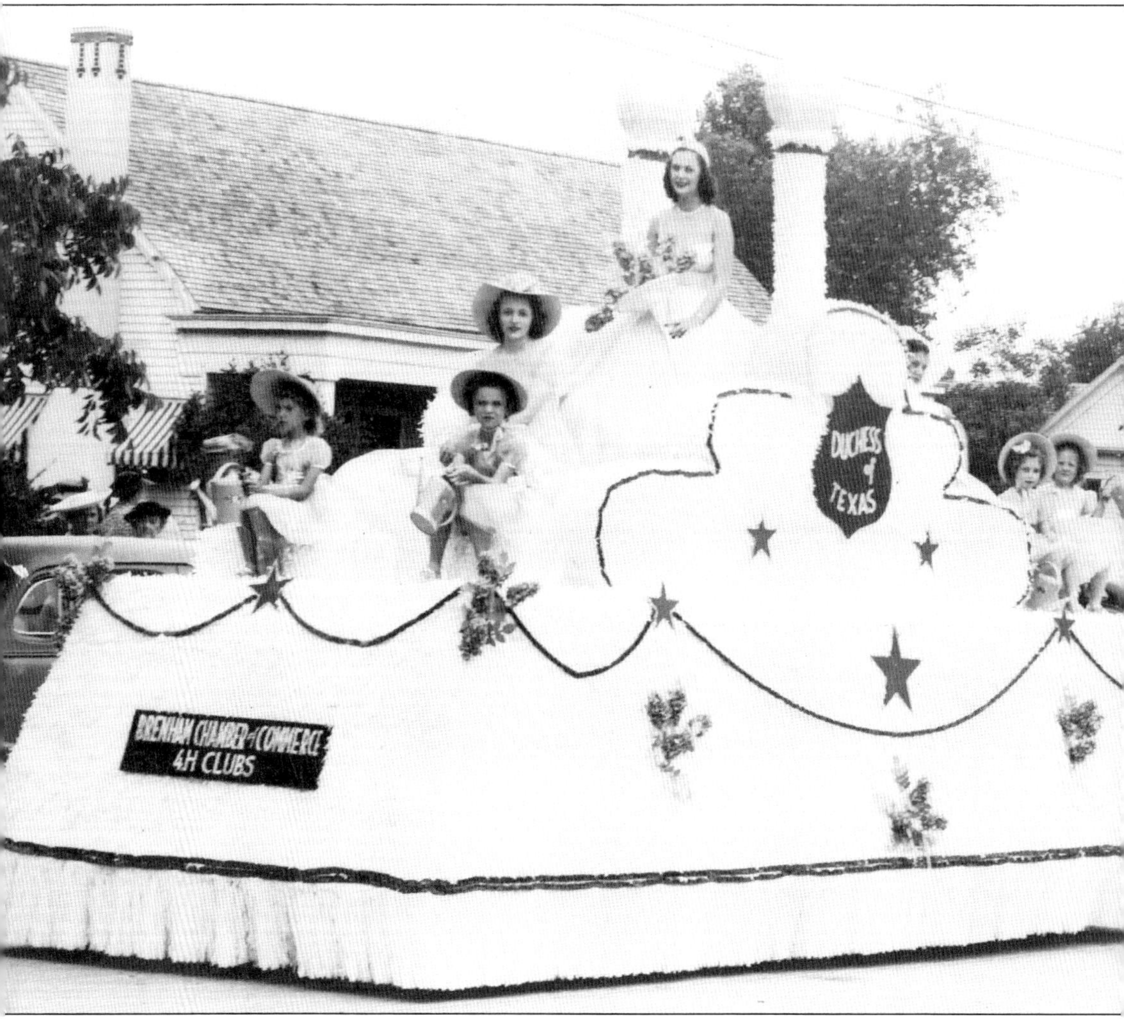

Pageants and spring festivals of all sorts reached a fever pitch across Texas on the eve of World War II. The long-established Maifest welcomed Molly O'Daniel, the daughter of the newly installed governor, in 1939. She had already served as honorary queen of Mardi Gras in Galveston and

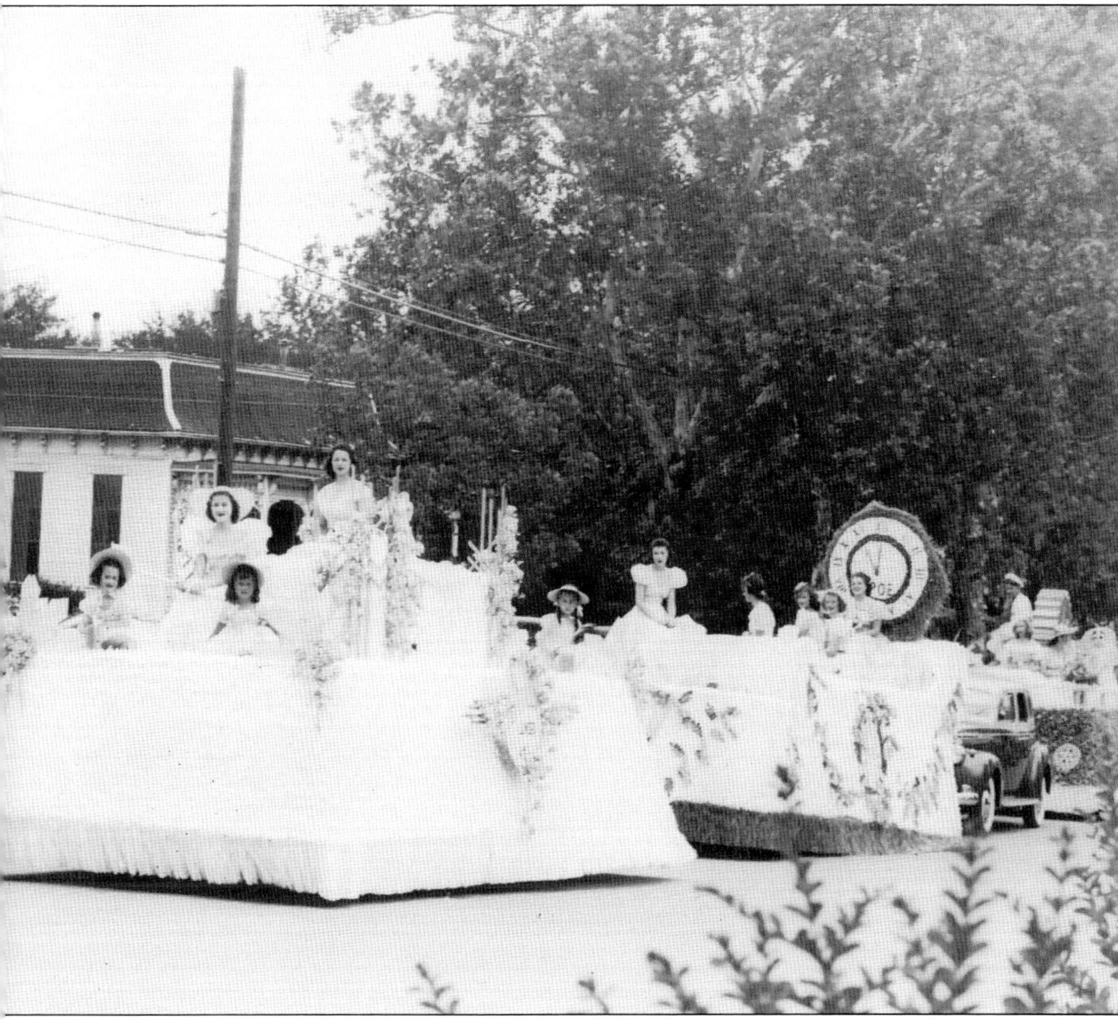

duchess of a festival in Navasota earlier that year. Other floats shown here hold Mary Stone and Marlene Searcy.

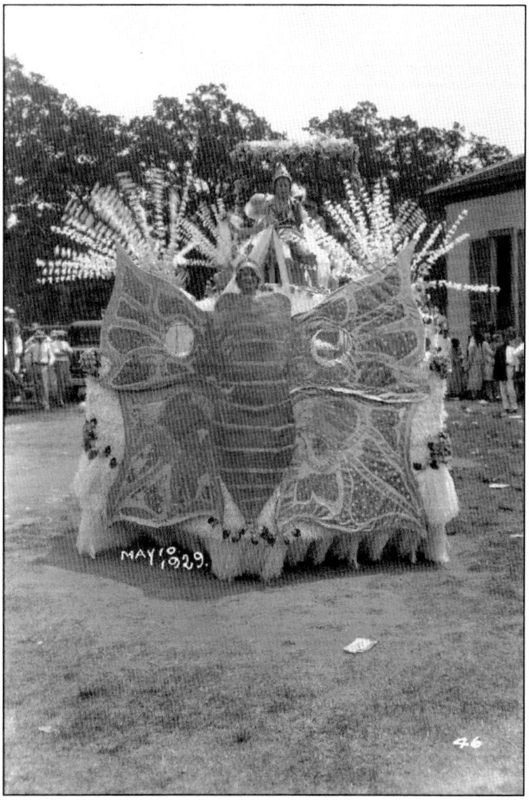

This moth float at the 1929 parade was one of many beautiful and elaborate floats that filled the period between when Maifest resumed in 1921 following World War I and before it was forced to pause again with the coming of World War II. Many Maifest aficionados believe those years to be the high point of Brenham's float building.

Automobiles had become much less of a novelty 10 years into the 20th century, but those with hard tops were still unknown. When this Maifest scene was captured around 1910, the vast majority of Brenhamites still traveled under horsepower from real horses. Just over a decade later, there were so many cars driven to Maifest that local Boy Scouts helped park them. (Brenham Fire Department.)

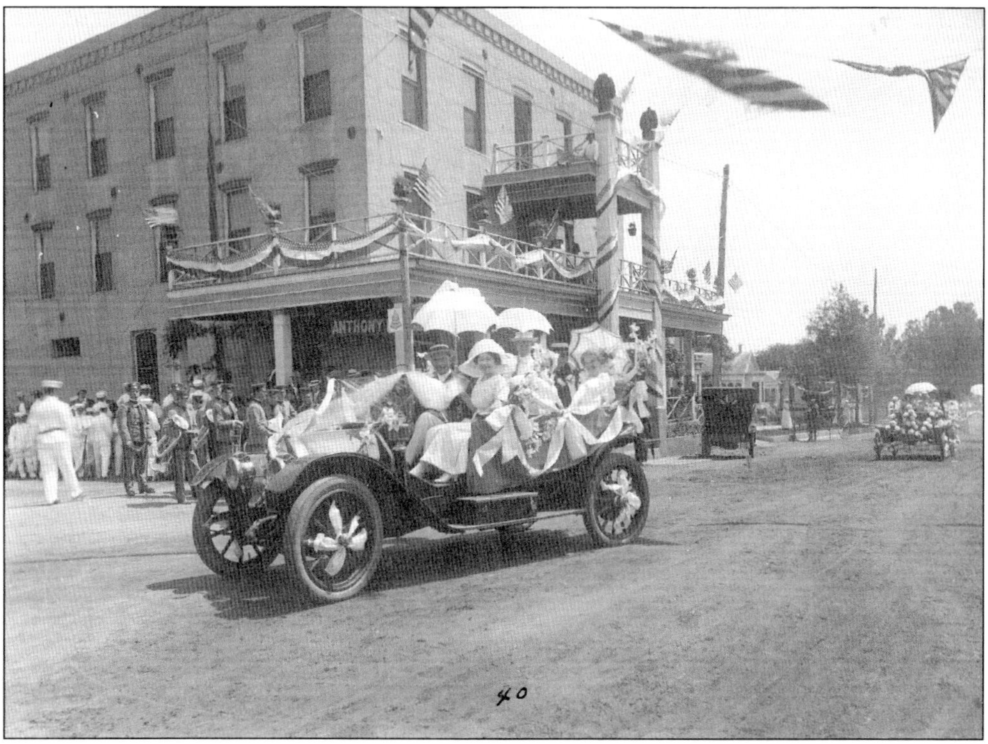

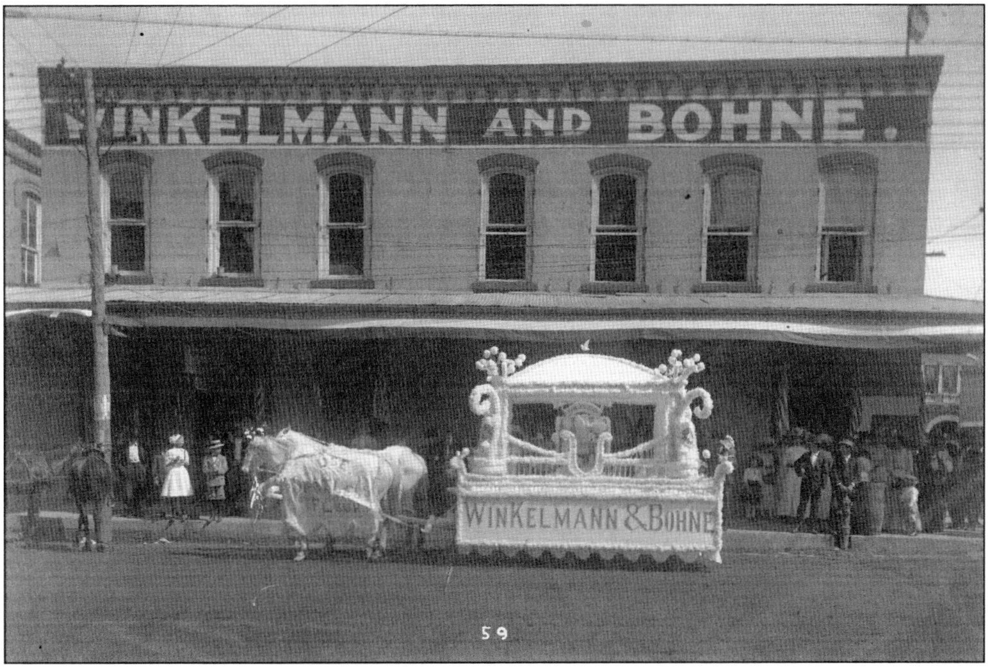

Parade-goers wear their finery in front of the Winkelmann and Bohne store on Main Street while viewing that firm's Maifest float. The partners had acquired Henry Hodde's grocery business upon Hodde's retirement in 1889 and added dry goods to the inventory. It was soon one of Brenham's largest mercantile concerns. After the demise of that large department store, J.C. Penney filled the space. (Brenham Fire Department.)

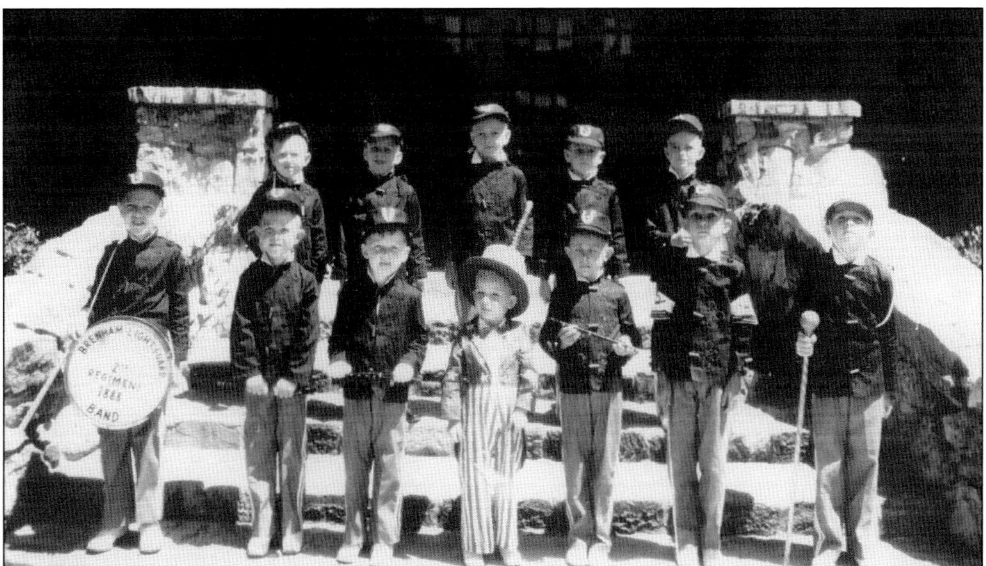

A collection of very young boys in uniform pose on the steps of the Brenham Library. The drum reads Brenham Light Guard 2nd Regiment Band 1888. That was the founding date of the 2nd Regiment Band, a men's military organization that was a staple in Brenham for many decades. These children wore the costumes decades later as part of Maifest.

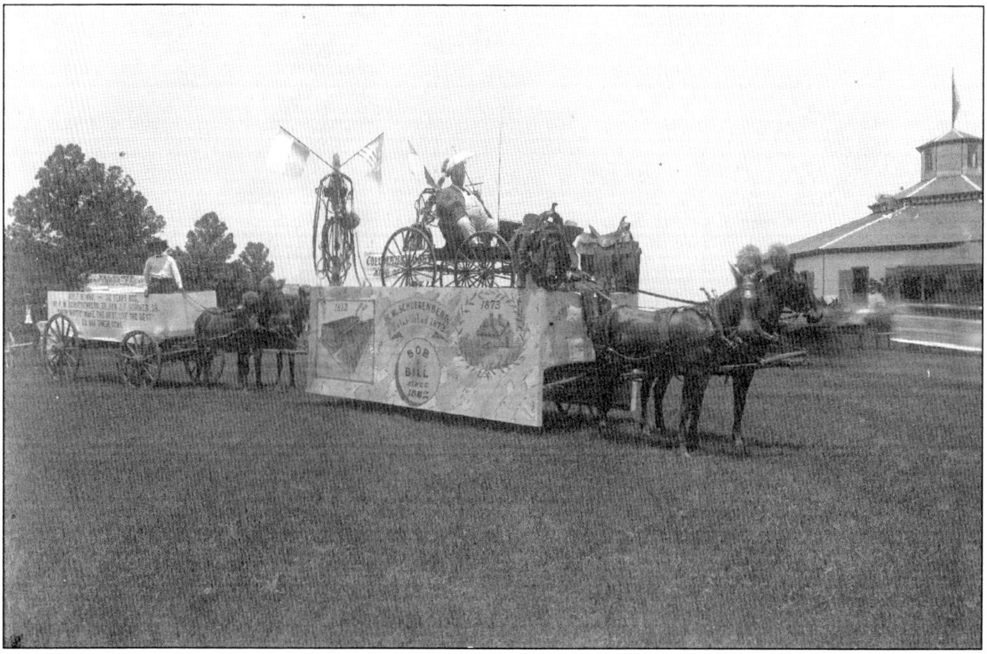

The F.W. Schuerenberg float is at Fireman's Park around 1912. Schurenberg's business started with a blacksmith operation, but he dabbled in a bit of everything. In the 1910s, the company was the licensed dealer in Washington and Austin Counties for Chalmers automobiles, a new high-end line of cars that would eventually be absorbed by Chrysler. (Brenham Fire Department.)

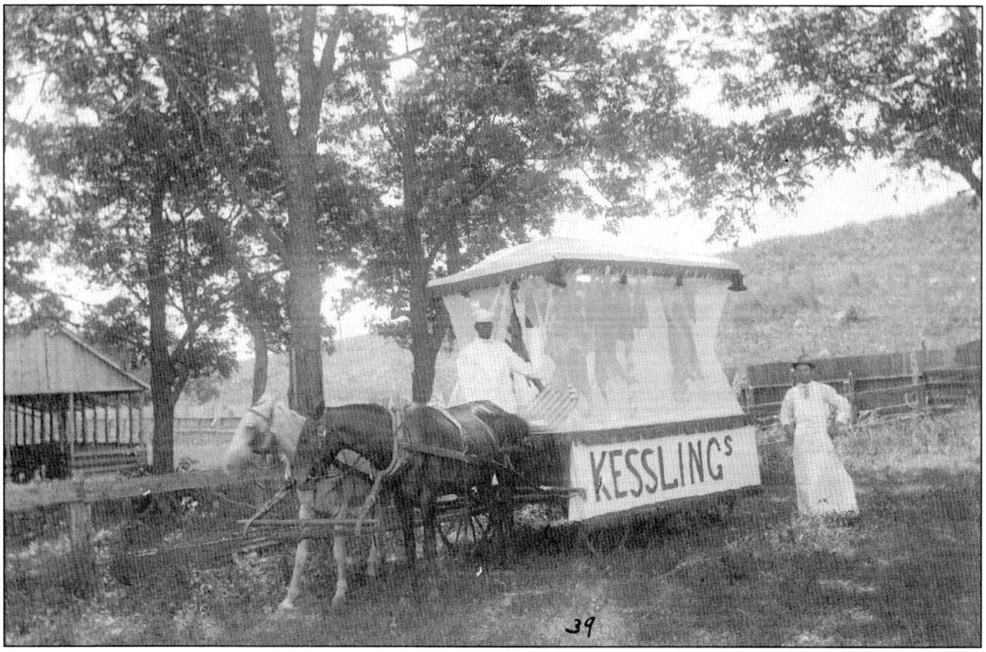

Adolph Kessling's Butcher Shop on South Ant Street created a float complete with real sides of beef behind insect netting. Kessling's offered the usual variety of meat in all sizes and had sausages made to order, but he also operated a small packing business, which local leaders urged him to expand in an attempt to encourage more hog raising. (Brenham Fire Department.)

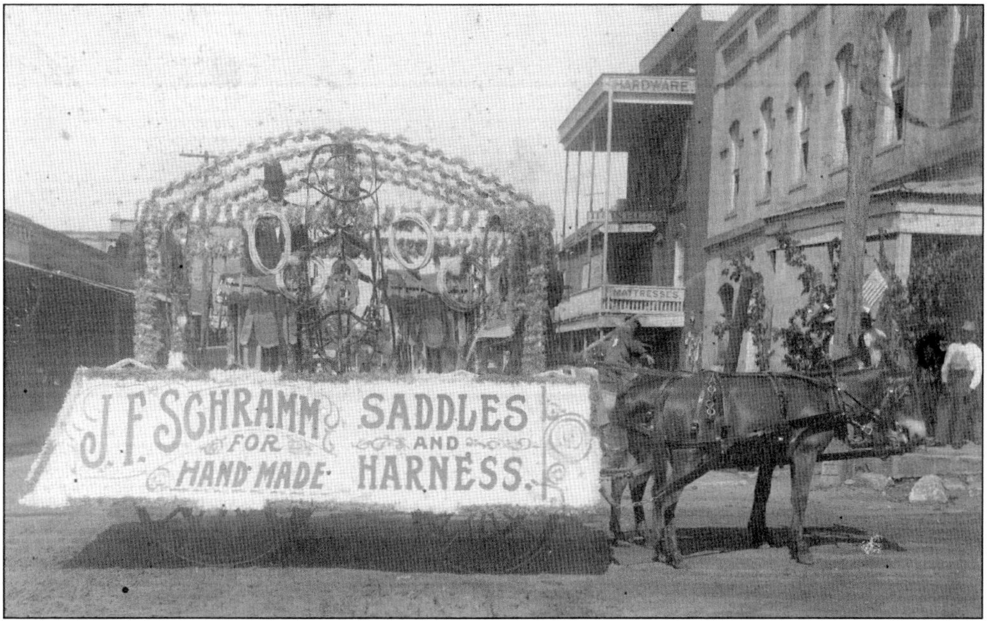

Joseph Frank Schramm advertised his saddles and harness by showing off his wares in the 1890s when his firm was new. The business continued to operate into the 1950s, producing quality leatherware. Schramm also looked forward into non-equine areas. Around 1918, with automobiles ascendant, he advertised Kor-Ker, a tire sealant guaranteed to stop leaks. (Brenham Fire Department.)

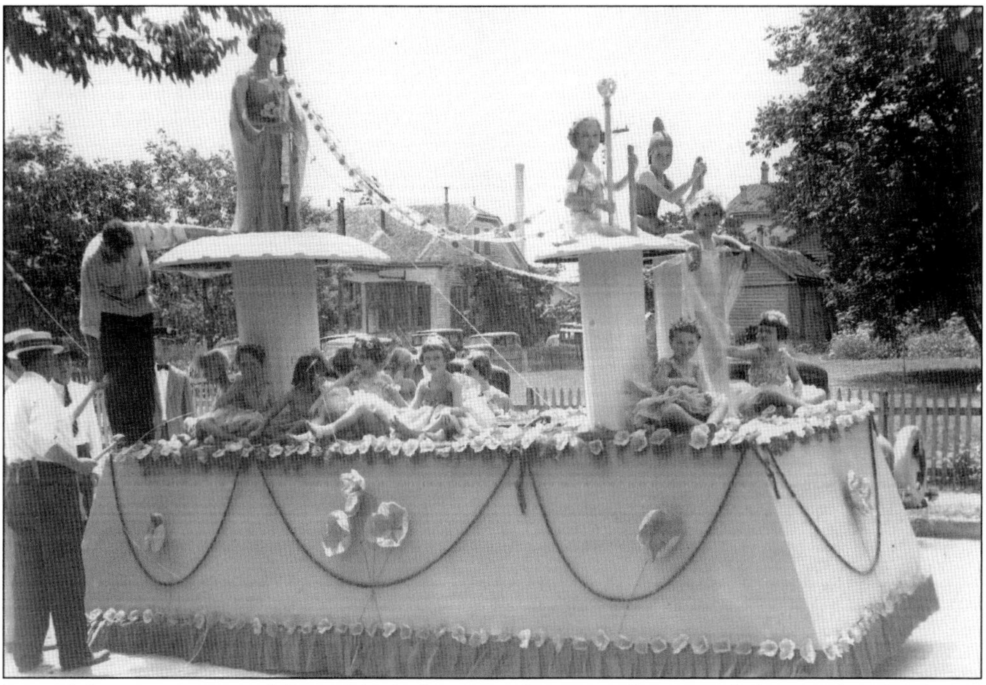

Part of the junior court of the 1936 Maifest stoically awaits the start of the parade. The theme was the Court of Wild Flowers, and the newspaper listed float assignments that placed the young celebrants into 27 vehicles. Queen Janice Hollemon presided over the Bluebonnet Court, and her king was Robert Schoenvogel. The celebration was extra large in honor of the Texas centennial.

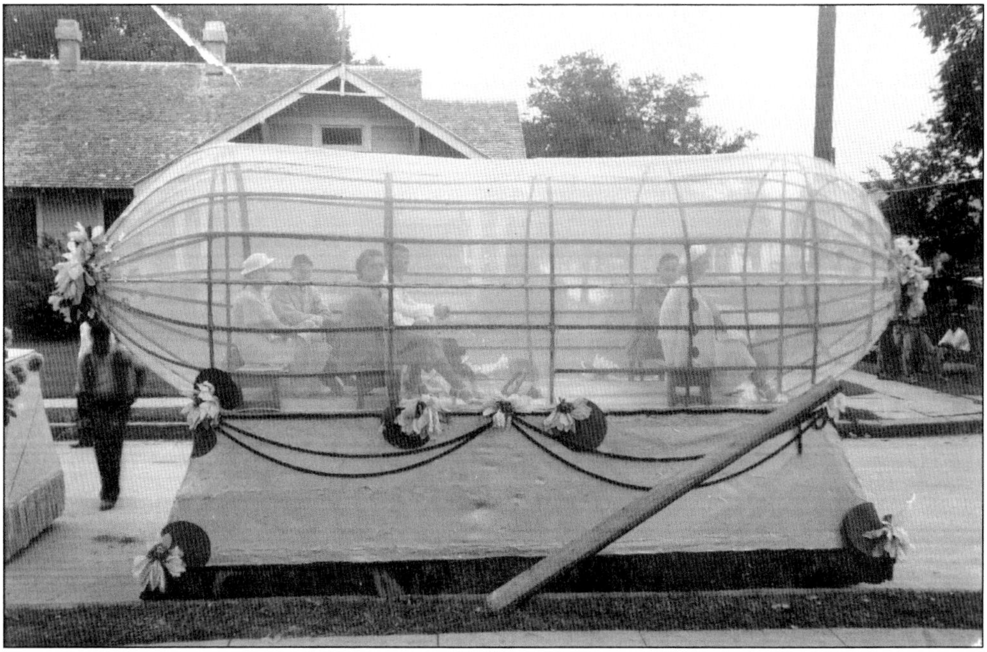

A show-stopping Eugene Tiemann–designed float in the 1935 Maifest Parade was this Zeppelin. The sheer fabric covering allowed the three passenger couples inside to see and be seen by the spectators. The gas-filled zeppelins were considered part of the future of air travel for two decades until the *Hindenberg* disaster ended their popularity with the public, just two years after this parade.

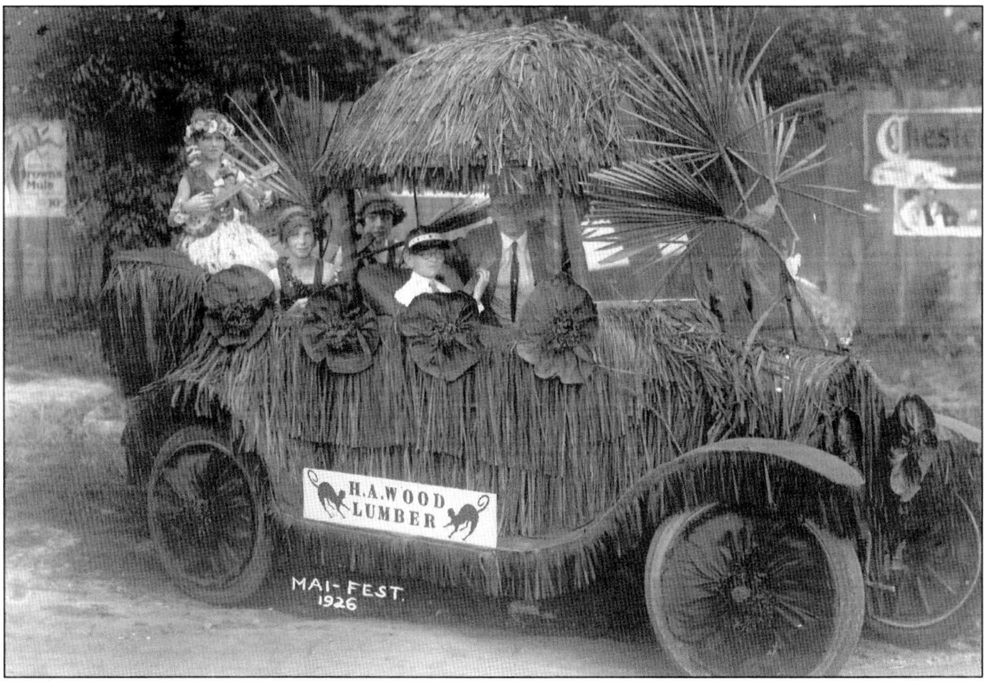

H.A. Wood's lumber company float opted for a Tiki theme in 1926 complete with a ukulele player perched atop the back seat. This was the final year in which there were only senior royalty. The following Maifest added a junior court, which became one of the festival's most popular traditions.

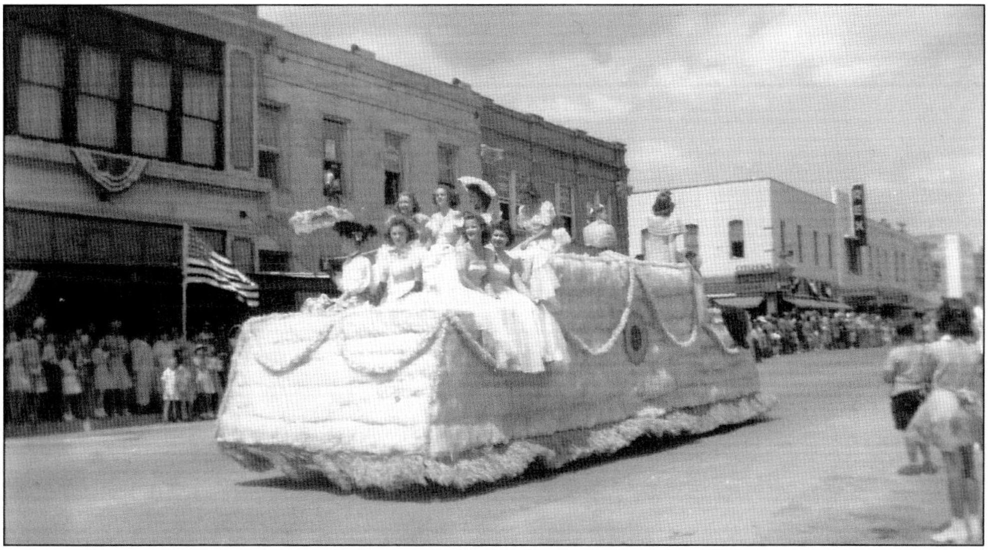

A float carrying a group of local women passes in front of Hohlt's Department Store on Main Street in this 1941 photograph. The United States entered World War II only half a year later, and Maifest was not held again until 1948. World War I had suspended Maifest for three years, and several Maifest kings saw service in the military.

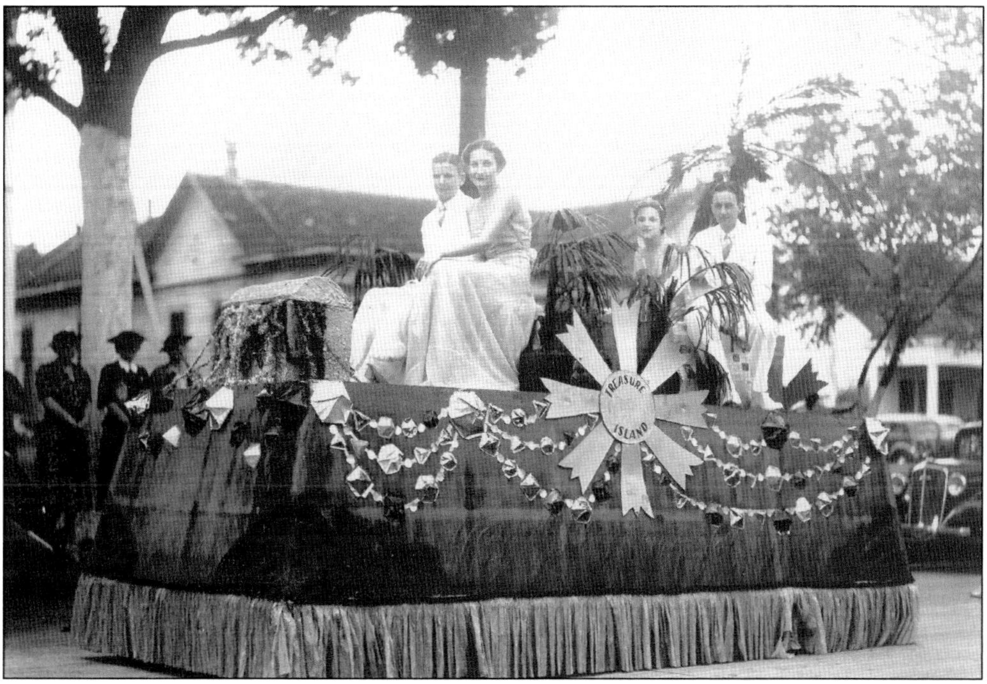

This *Treasure Island* float at Maifest in the 1930s presumably had smooth sailing through downtown. The first attempts at encasing an entire car inside a float did not always go so smoothly. Bunches of paper flowers sometimes cut off air to early engines, causing an automobile to stall out, and at least once, inadequate ventilation nearly overcame one of the hidden drivers. (Gloria Nix.)

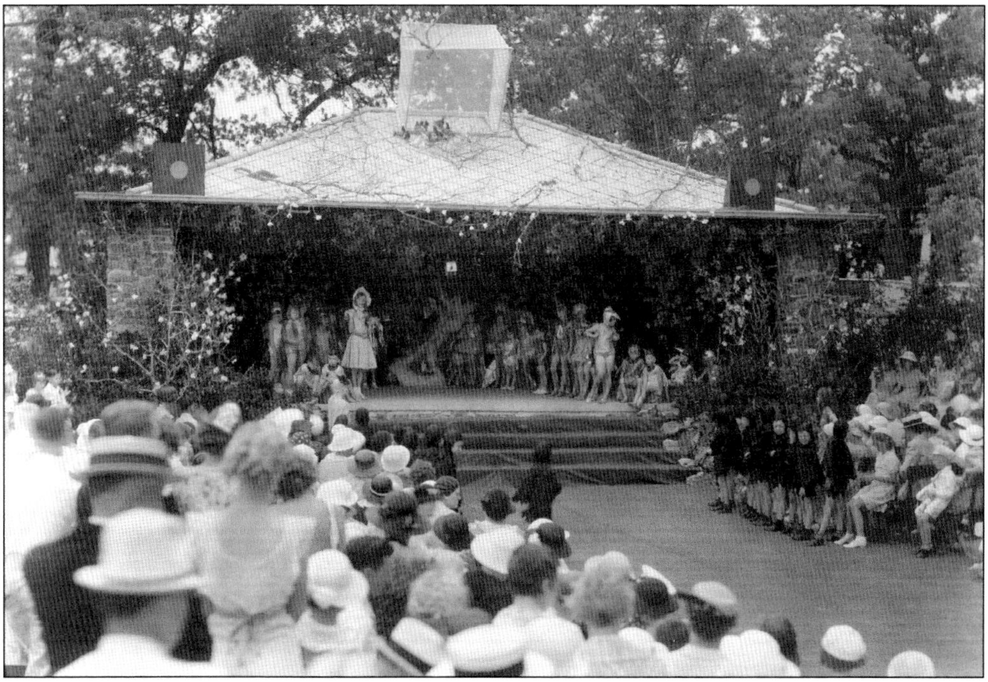

The junior coronation of Maifest in 1934 combined both great costumes and good weather to enjoy them. As part of the Court of the Feathery Kingdom, bird costumes were de rigueur. Two groups of children attired as blackbirds wait at the bottom of the steps in Fireman's Park.

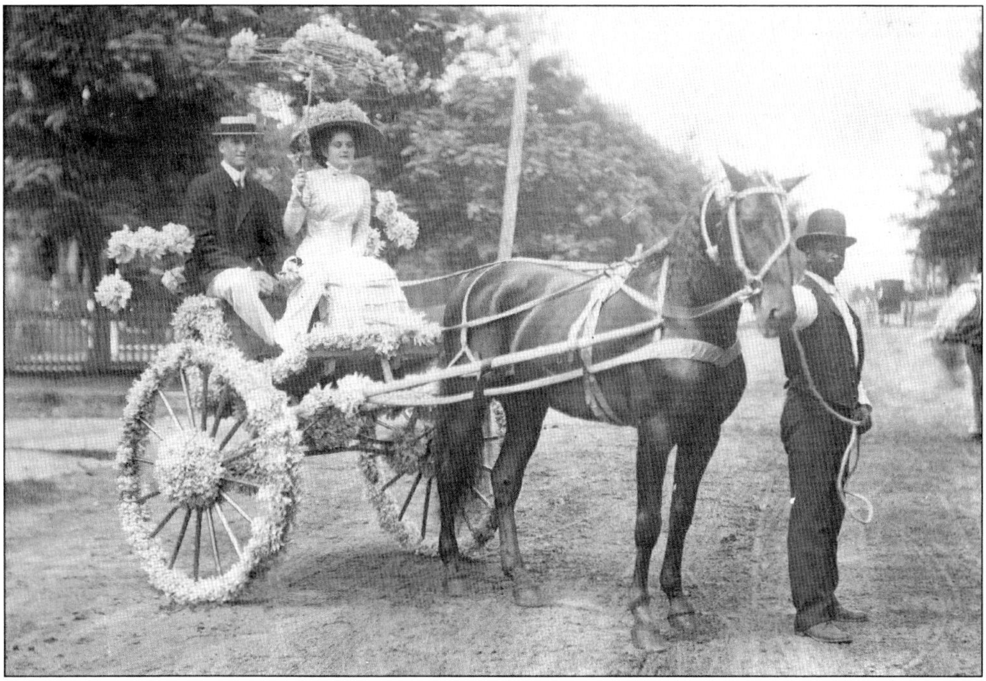

Maifest in the pre-automobile days meant lavishly decorated buggies. In this case, a gig was tricked out in flowers that seem to match the hat of Lila Shepherd, who was elected queen in 1910. The driver of the cart is her king and future husband, L.E. Rasberry.

The junior court for Maifest in 1928 was only the second junior court in the festival's history. Queen Mary Stone and King Frank Wood III reigned with Lady Nancy Green and Pages Billy Sloan and Ernest Reichardt Jr. in royal attendance.

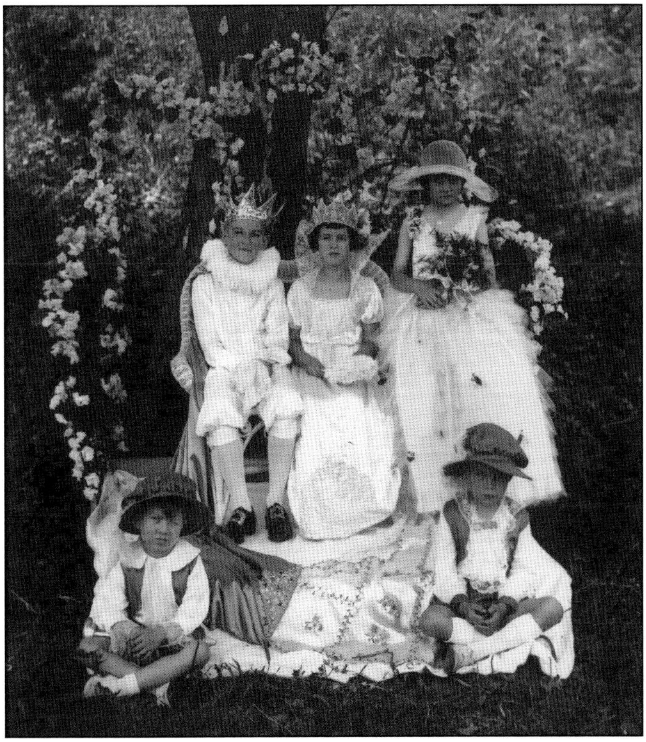

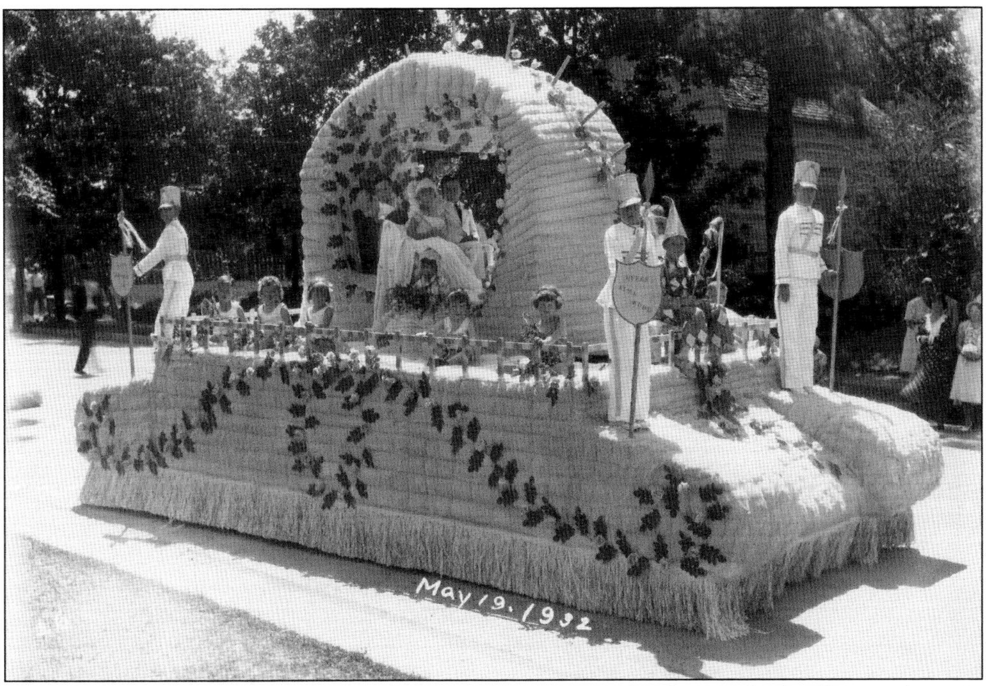

Junior queen Alma Wood Ferguson and her king, Ernest Reichardt Jr., rode this float in the 1932 Maifest Parade with a theme of Fete of Flowers. It was adorned with real cotton that had been quilted and dyed pink. Guards stood at attention on each corner of the float, and a court jester sat at the ready.

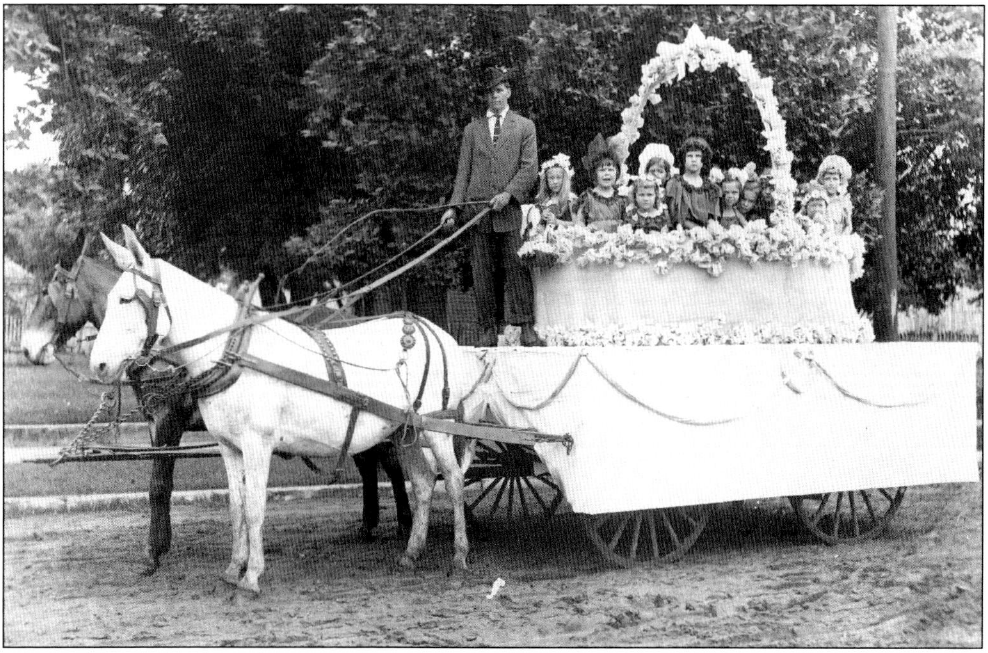

The Basket of Children theme was popular through the years. This horse-drawn iteration was in 1901. That year, a children's ball was held in the Fireman's Park Pavilion at 6:00 p.m. It followed a full afternoon of horse and cattle exhibitions.

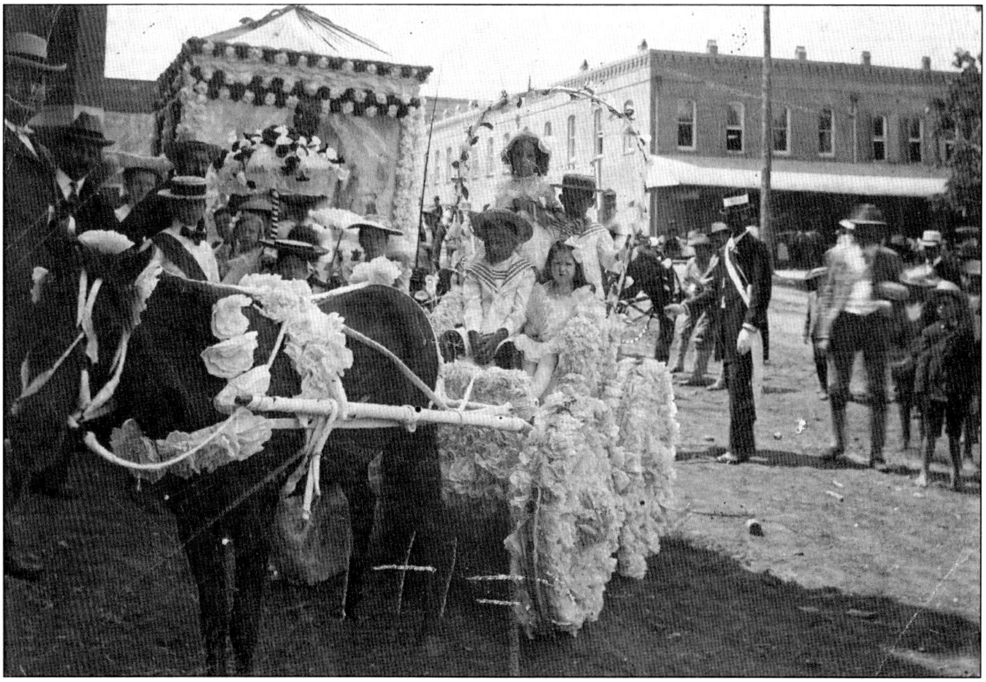

An early Maifest buggy festooned with paper flowers is attended by uniformed livery and parents downtown. The Winkelmann and Bohne Department Store is visible in the background. Though there was not yet a junior court, festively attired young Brenhamites were very much a part of the annual gala.

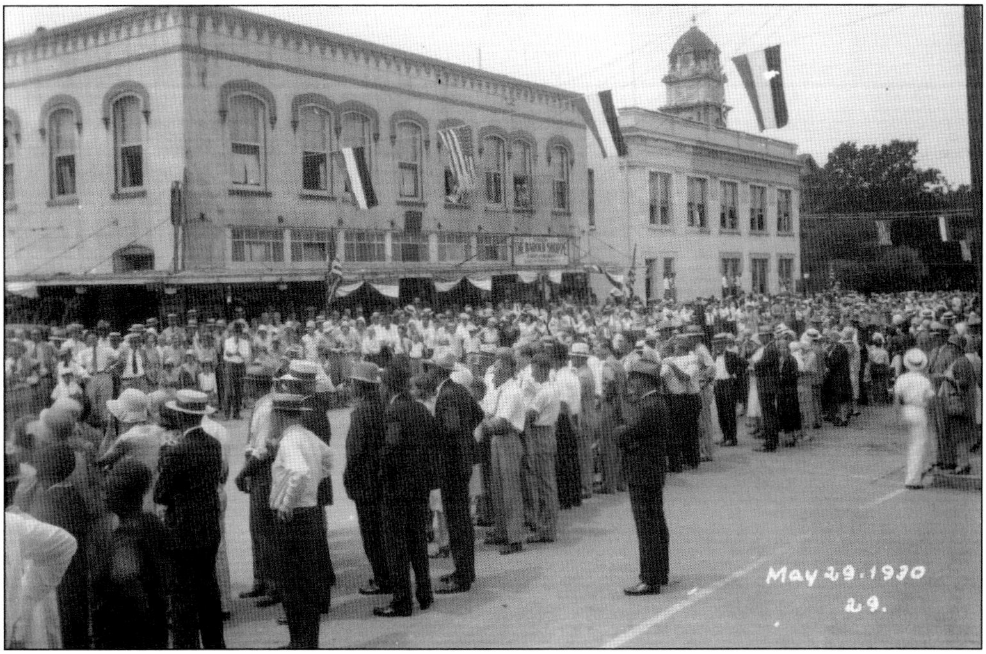

Parade crowds gather along Main Street near St. Charles Street in May 1930. The Harrold Shoppe for ladies and children was across the street, with the courthouse spire visible above the roofline. They would soon see Flora Ann Williams, queen of the Forget-Me-Not Court, atop a shimmering silver gondola, along with three local bands and an array of imaginative floats.

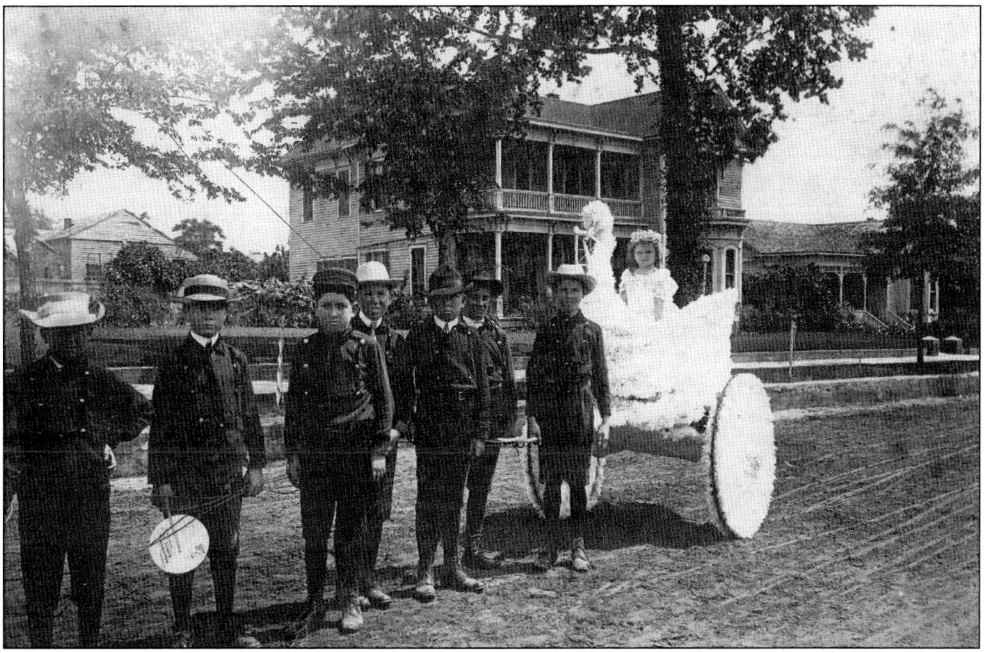

This white-gowned young lady in her private swan was borne by costumed attendants during a turn-of-the-century Maifest. The boys were appointed junior firemen for the day. Their queen with blonde ringlets was Martha Vernon Robertson. The photograph was taken in front of the Witte-Stone House on East Main Street, just past Market Street.

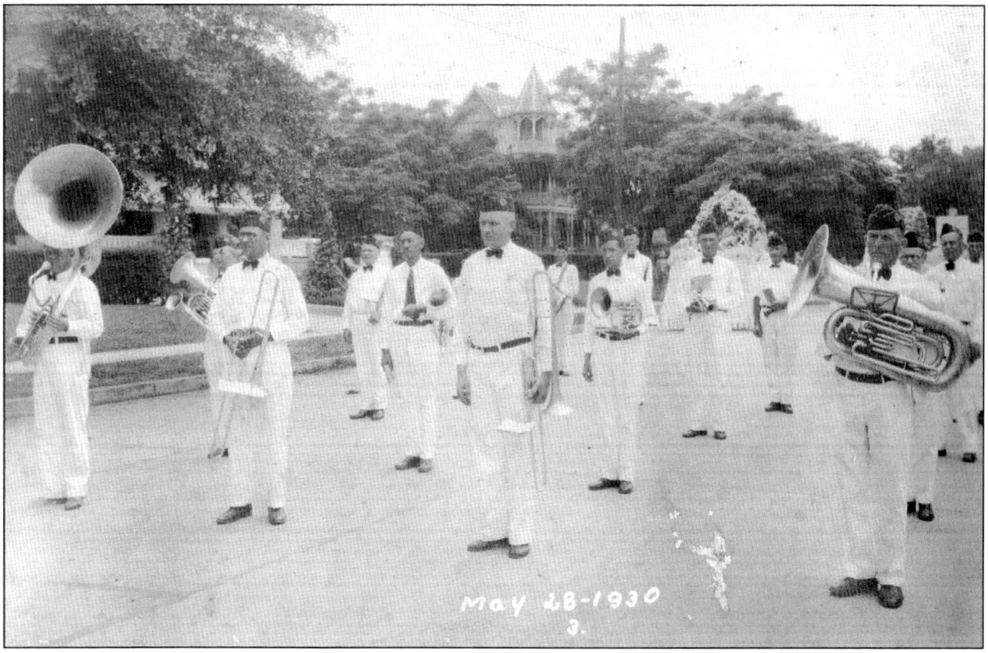

The Arabia Shrine Temple band from Houston, attired for a warm, sunny day, lines up on Main Street in anticipation of the parade start in 1930. It was Houston Day, with a special charter train and the first of a two-game baseball series between the Texas League Houston Buffs and Waco Cubs. Over 4,000 cheering Brenham fans watched each contest.

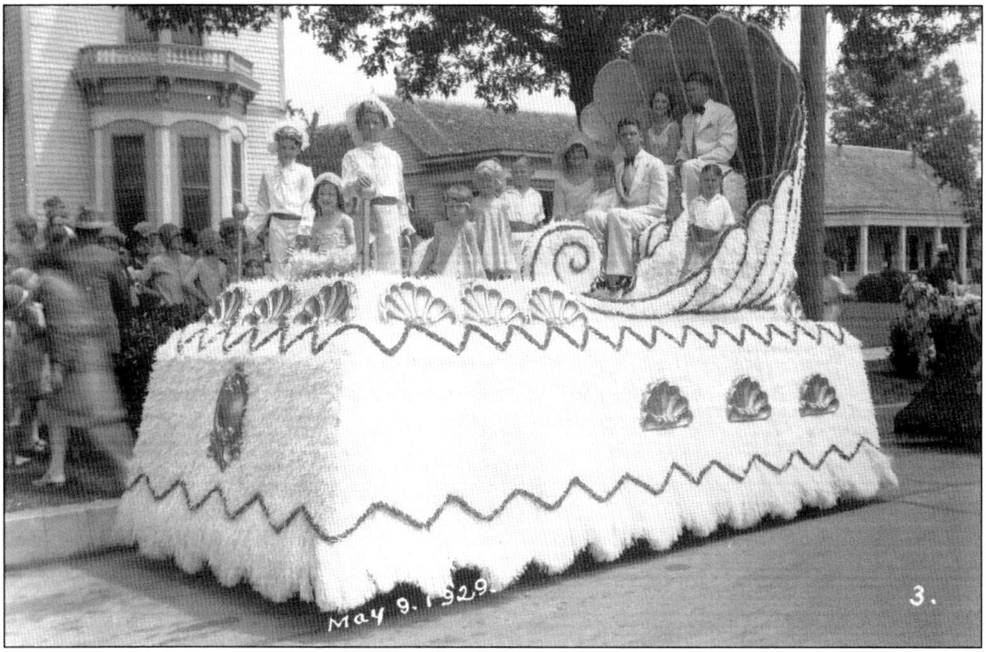

A fanciful clamshell float carries King Smith Mercer and Queen Ruth Hasskarl Robertson in 1929. Unlike today, Maifest parades and coronations at the time were midweek affairs, generally happening on Wednesdays and Thursdays. That year's rodeo featured Ruth Wheat, a Montana-born rider who had traveled coast to coast.

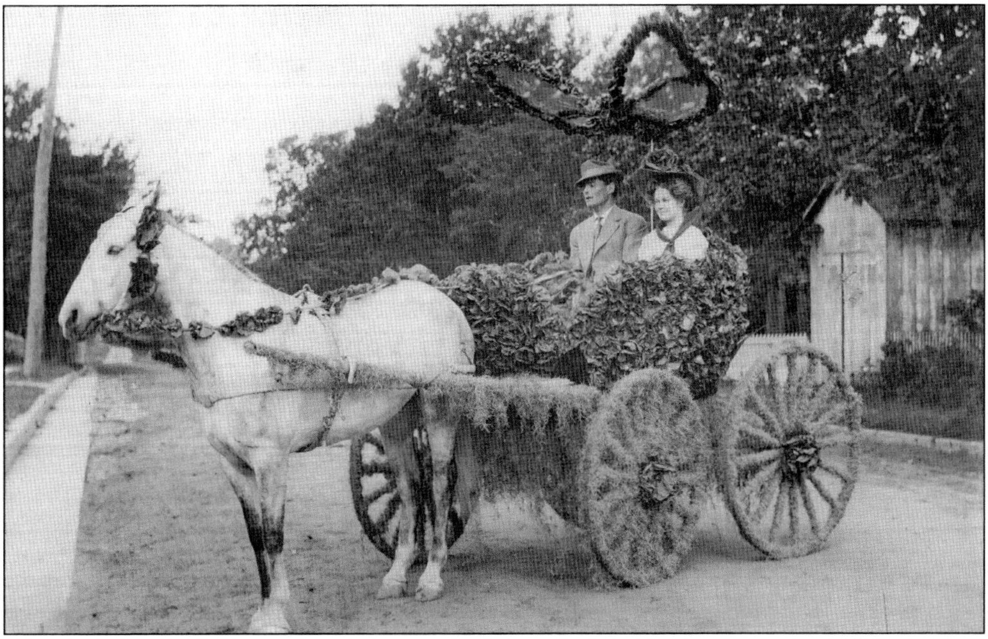

Adorned with Spanish moss and hundreds of paper flowers, a young couple sits beneath a giant butterfly on a quiet residential Brenham street. It was typical for the horses pulling the flats or buggies to also be freshly groomed and kitted out in decorations that sometimes matched their human's theme. At the very least, the reins and bridle were festooned with flowers.

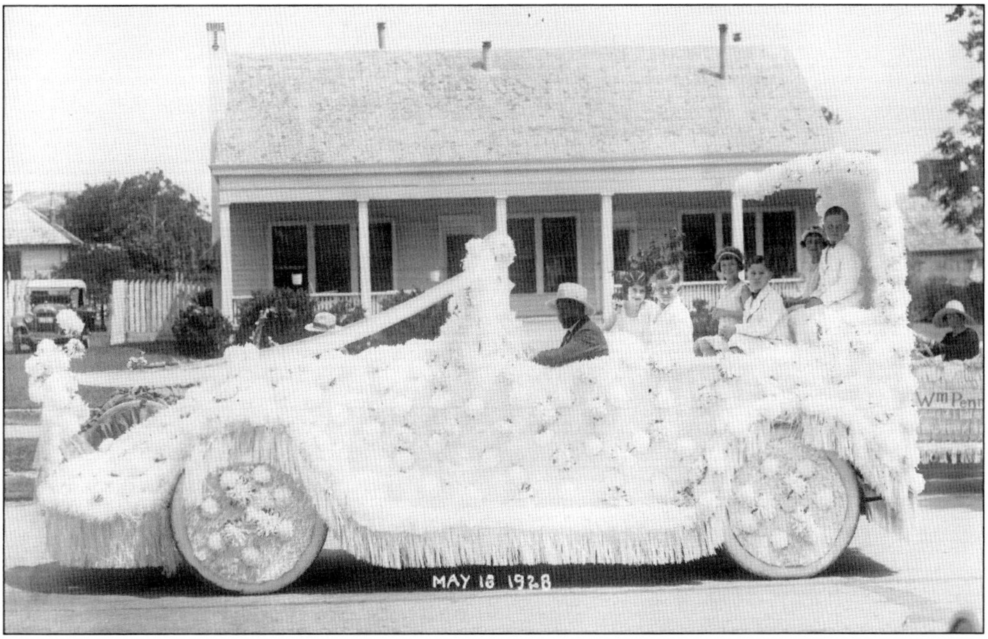

Junior royalty in 1928 prepare to be chauffeured through downtown. Though Maifest festivities were racially segregated, many African American men worked as drivers, and before that as horse stewards, on parade day to make sure things proceeded smoothly. Aside from farm labor, one of the few employment options open to black Brenhamites was domestic service, and some of these men and their wives worked for local families year-round.

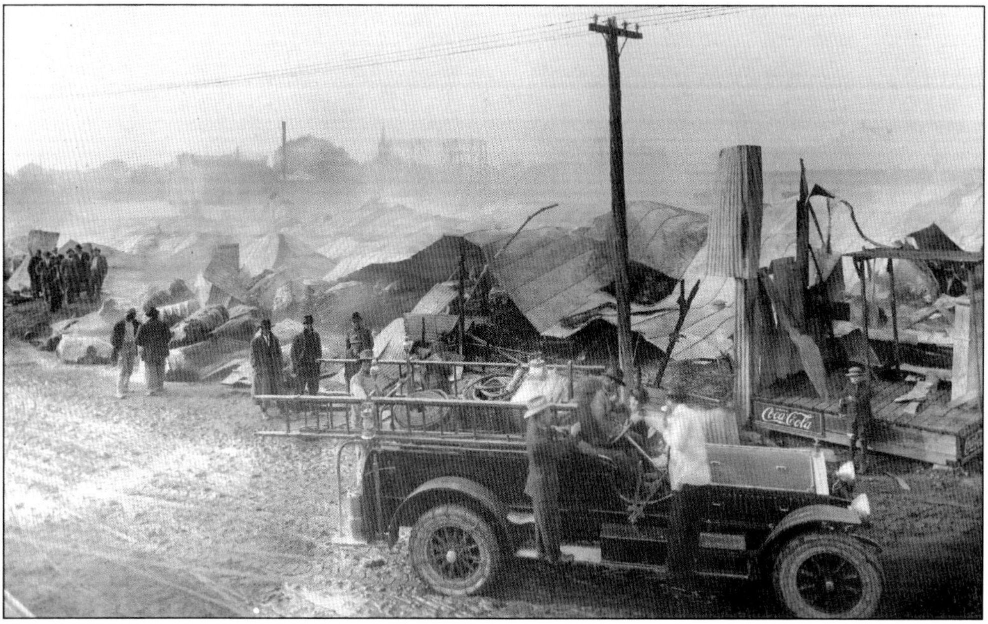

The Farmers Union warehouse went up in flames in November 1914. When firemen were slow in responding, Kate McGrady and Missy Wigand of the Brenham Telephone Company took it upon themselves to ring dozens of homes directly. Other than the concrete foundation, the large building was a total loss. The thousand-strong Washington County members of the Farmers Union vowed to rebuild.

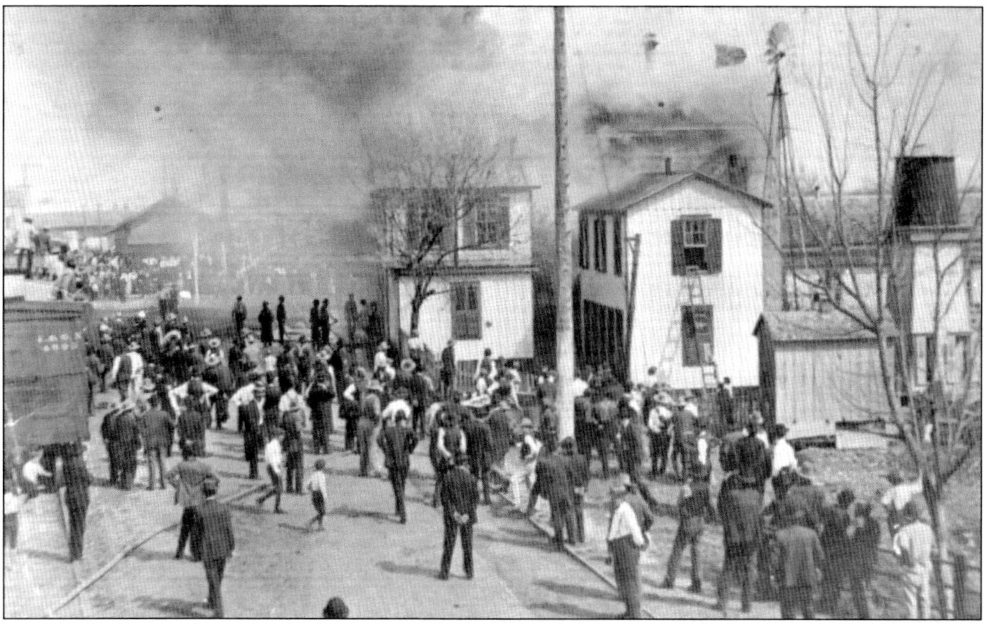

The Felscher Hotel, a large, working-class rooming house south of the railroad tracks on Baylor Street across from Beaumier Ironworks, also offered Brenhamites a daily fish and potato lunch in the pre–World War I years. On March 2, 1908, it caught fire. Volunteer firemen saved most of the structure. The only injury occurred when an onlooker was hit on the head by belongings tossed from a second-floor window.

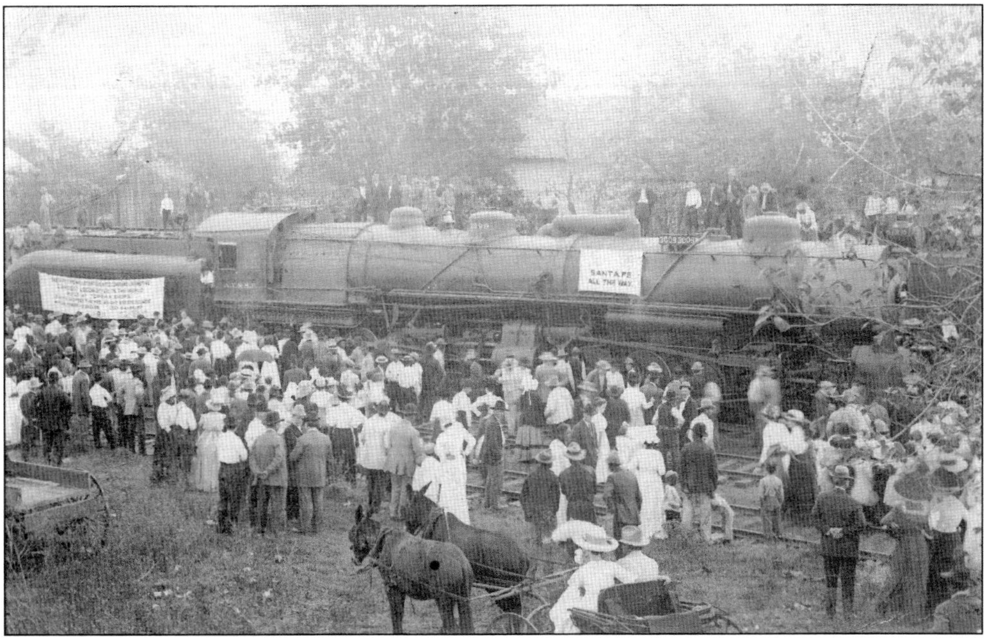

The Atchison, Topeka & Santa Fe Railroad's locomotive No. 3009 drew large crowds in Brenham in November 1911. The rare, articulated 2-10-10-2 Mallet design was billed as the largest locomotive in the world at the time. Unfortunately, their performance did not match the hype. No. 3009 was cut up less than six years later, and the pieces were used to build two smaller locomotives.

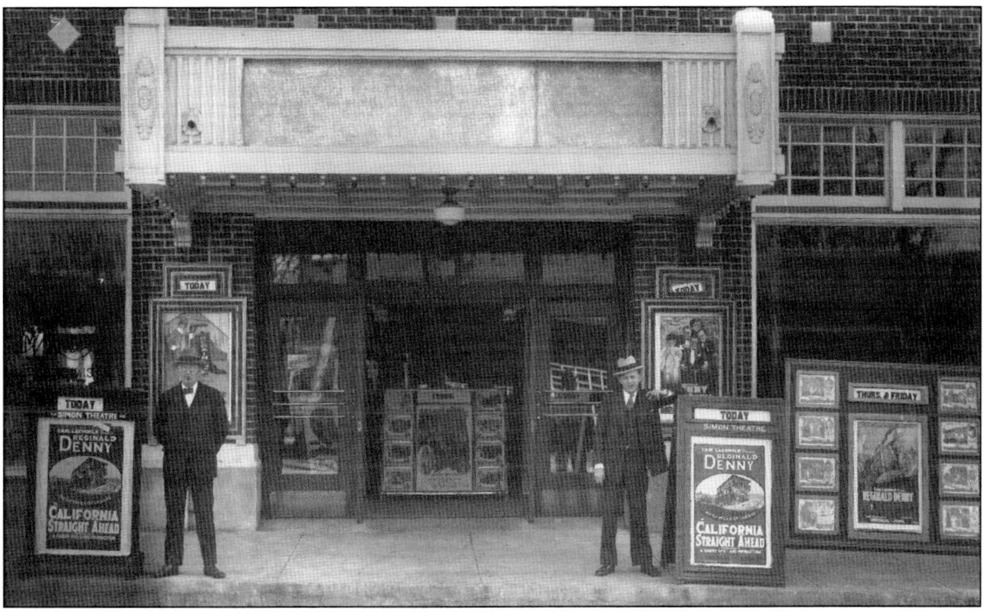

The Simon Theatre opened for its first show the day after Thanksgiving in 1925. It was the largest auditorium in town, holding 558 leather-upholstered chairs on the main floor and seats for another 235 in the balcony. For 35¢, adult moviegoers on opening day saw *The Merry Widow*, a silent film with organ accompaniment, plus comedy and news short reels.

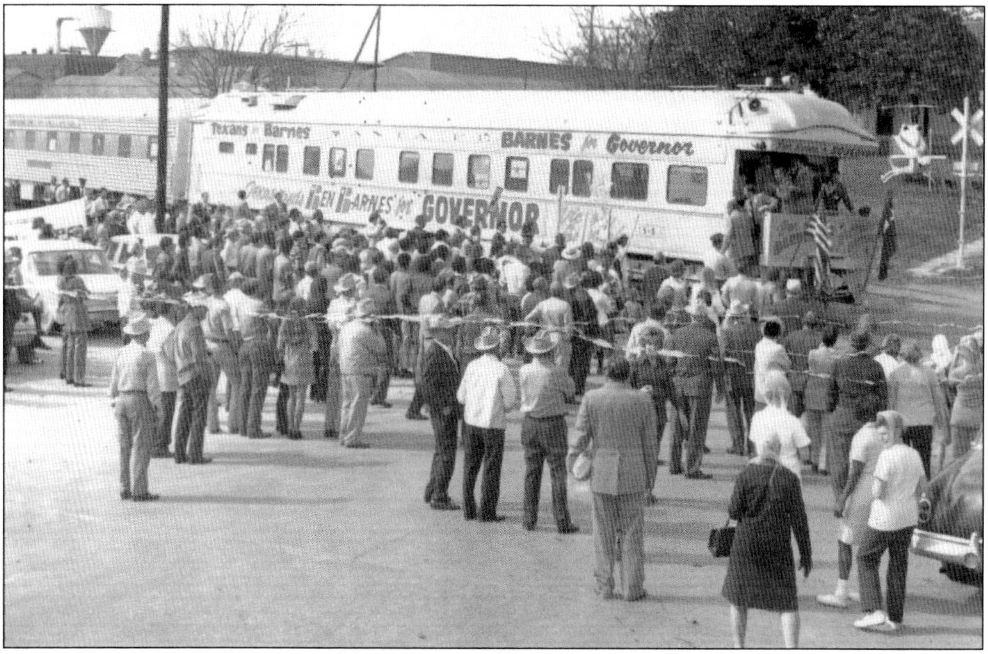

A crowd gathers to hear Ben Barnes on a whistle stop campaign for governor in 1972. Though he bested incumbent Preston Smith, Barnes still finished a distant third in the Democratic primary, losing to Dolph Briscoe. Both Barnes and Smith had been stained by the wide-ranging Sharpstown bank scandal of the previous year. (Debbie Lehrmann.)

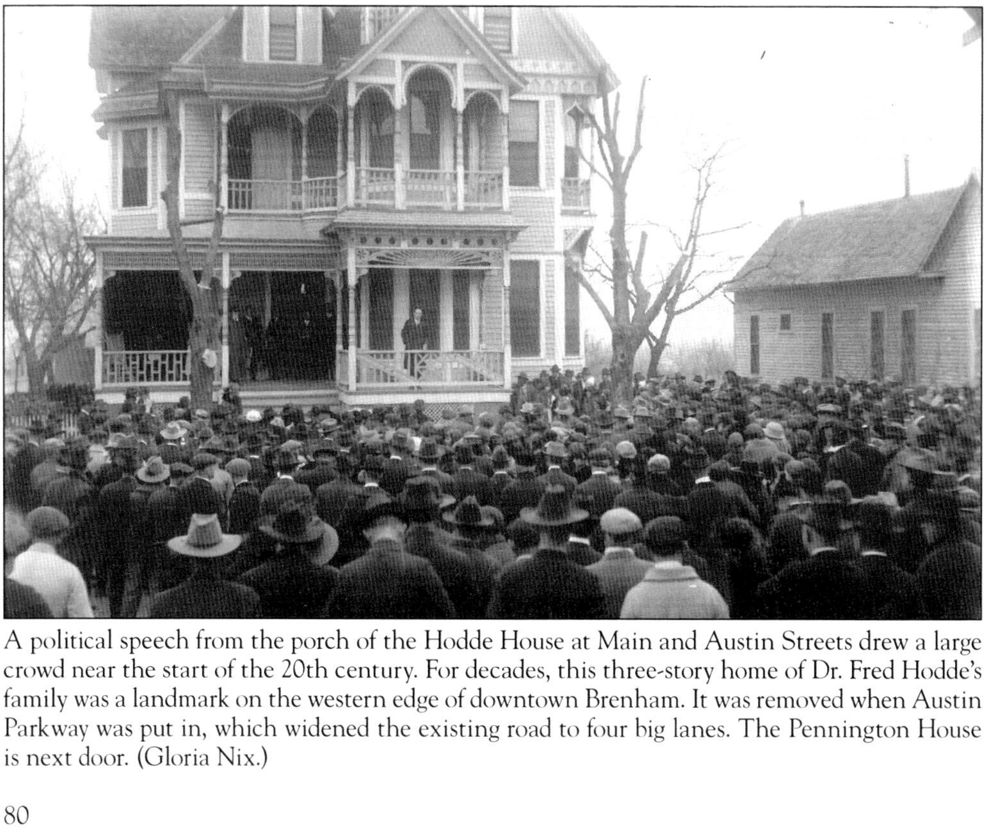

A political speech from the porch of the Hodde House at Main and Austin Streets drew a large crowd near the start of the 20th century. For decades, this three-story home of Dr. Fred Hodde's family was a landmark on the western edge of downtown Brenham. It was removed when Austin Parkway was put in, which widened the existing road to four big lanes. The Pennington House is next door. (Gloria Nix.)

Four

WORK

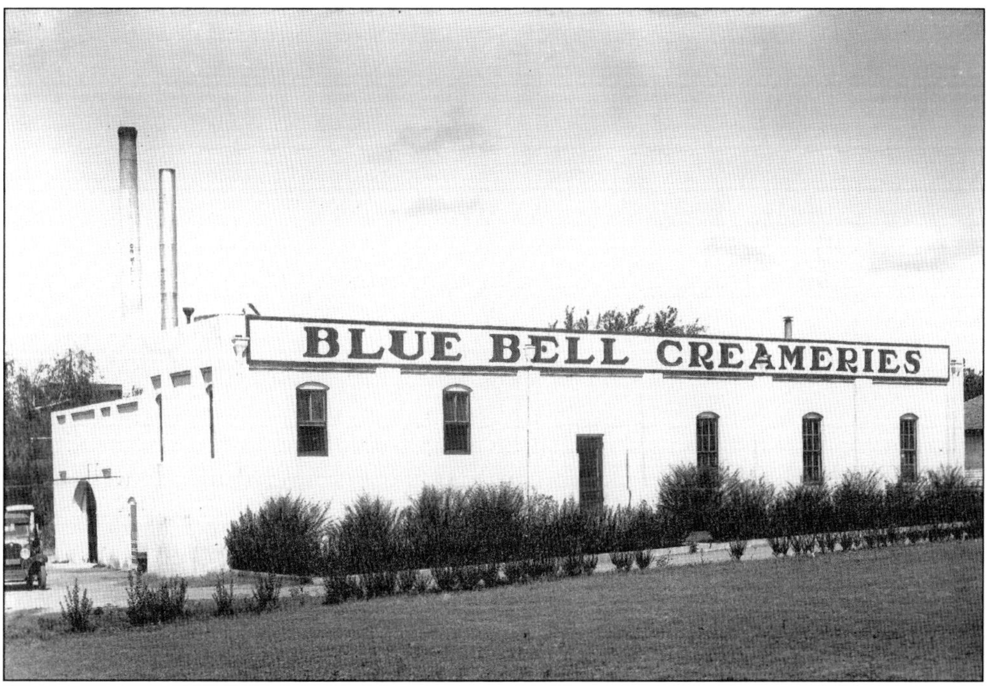

The advertising campaigns of Blue Bell Creameries have done as much to circulate the name of Brenham as anything else. The company's first product was butter, but the stockholders, several of the city's top citizens, quickly discovered that the profits lay with ice cream. This brick building, later plastered and painted white, was the sole plant until 1972.

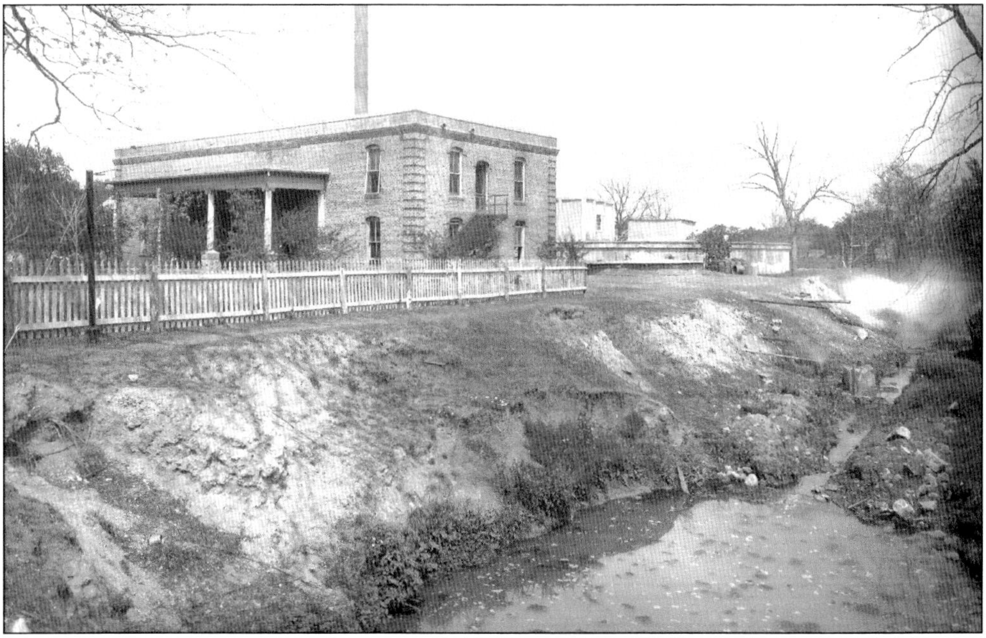

The old city utility building at 1105 South Austin Street was a major part of the Brenham story. A privately owned Brenham Waterworks Company handled the initial supply, but it was bought by the city in 1894 for $40,000. In 1924, operations were expanded to include a purification plant and reservoir at the rear of the property next to Hog Branch.

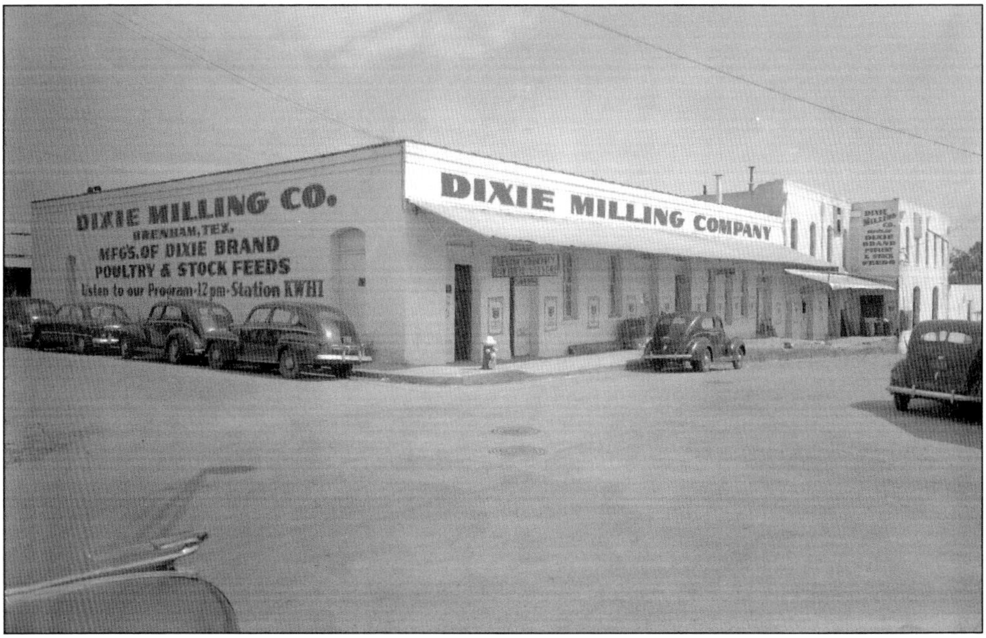

Dixie Milling Company had a large hatching operation that began in the 1920s. Thanks to that giant chicken farm, many Washington County farmers were furnished with free fertilizer. In November 1948, the company also opened this store in central Brenham with $100,000 worth of modern equipment to meet the needs of local livestock and poultry. (Briscoe Center for American History, University of Texas at Austin.)

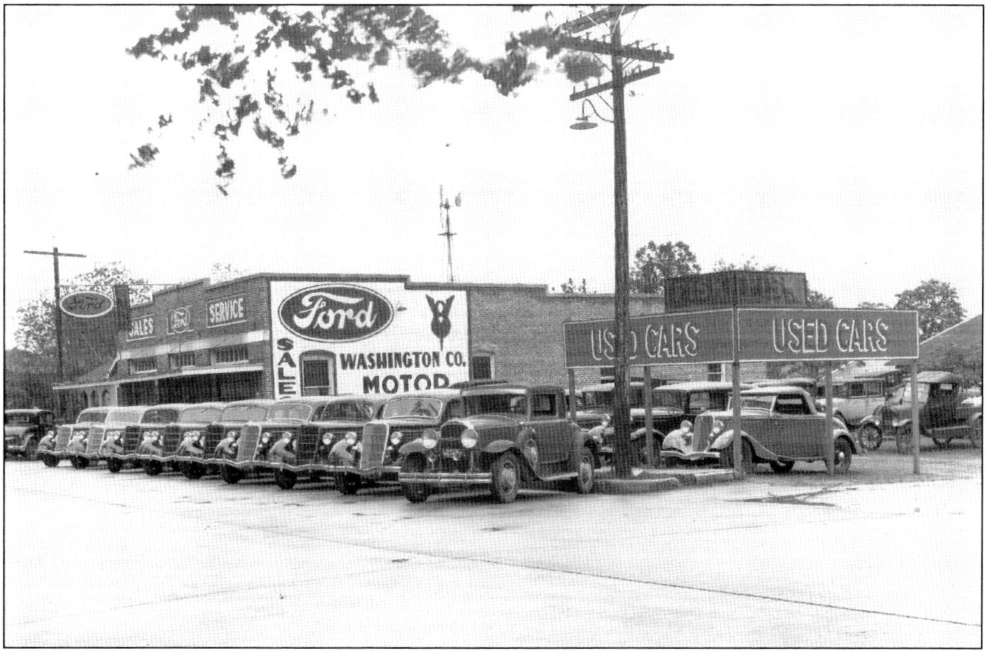

The recently opened Washington County Motor Company at Main and Clinton Streets offered Ford sales, parts, and service in 1935. In the first four months of that year, the dealership sold 80 new Ford V-8 cars and trucks and more than 120 used vehicles. Terms on a used car were a low down payment and installments as little as $2 a week.

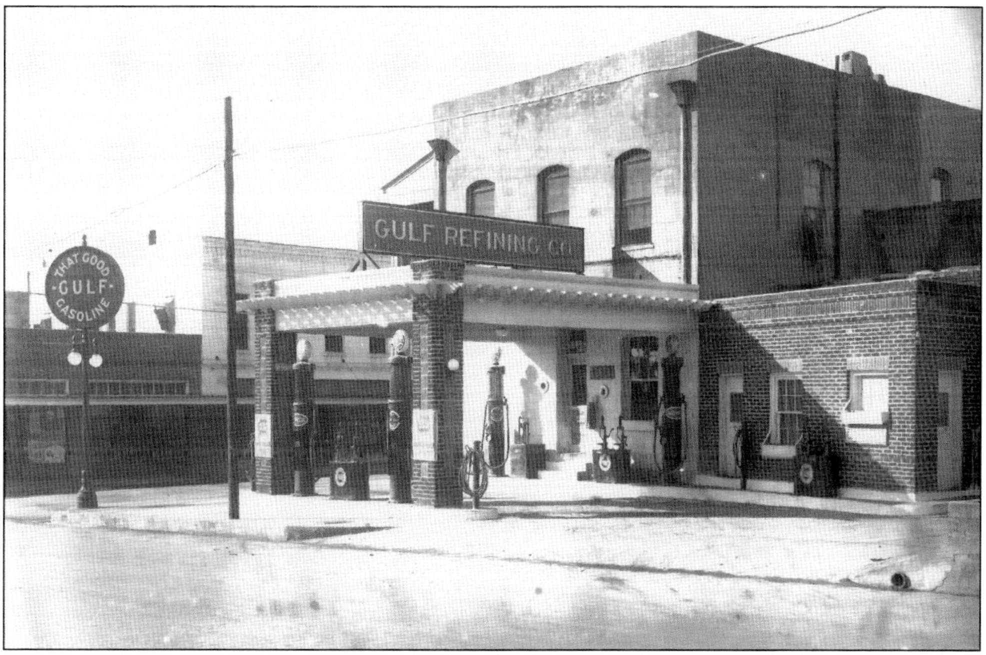

"That good Gulf gasoline" with "No nox" were slogans of the Gulf Oil Company products at the station that graced the northwest corner of Market and Alamo Streets. Other brands of gas were later sold at that same location before the station vanished entirely. For 50-plus years, there were multiple opportunities to buy gas in the heart of downtown, but none remain.

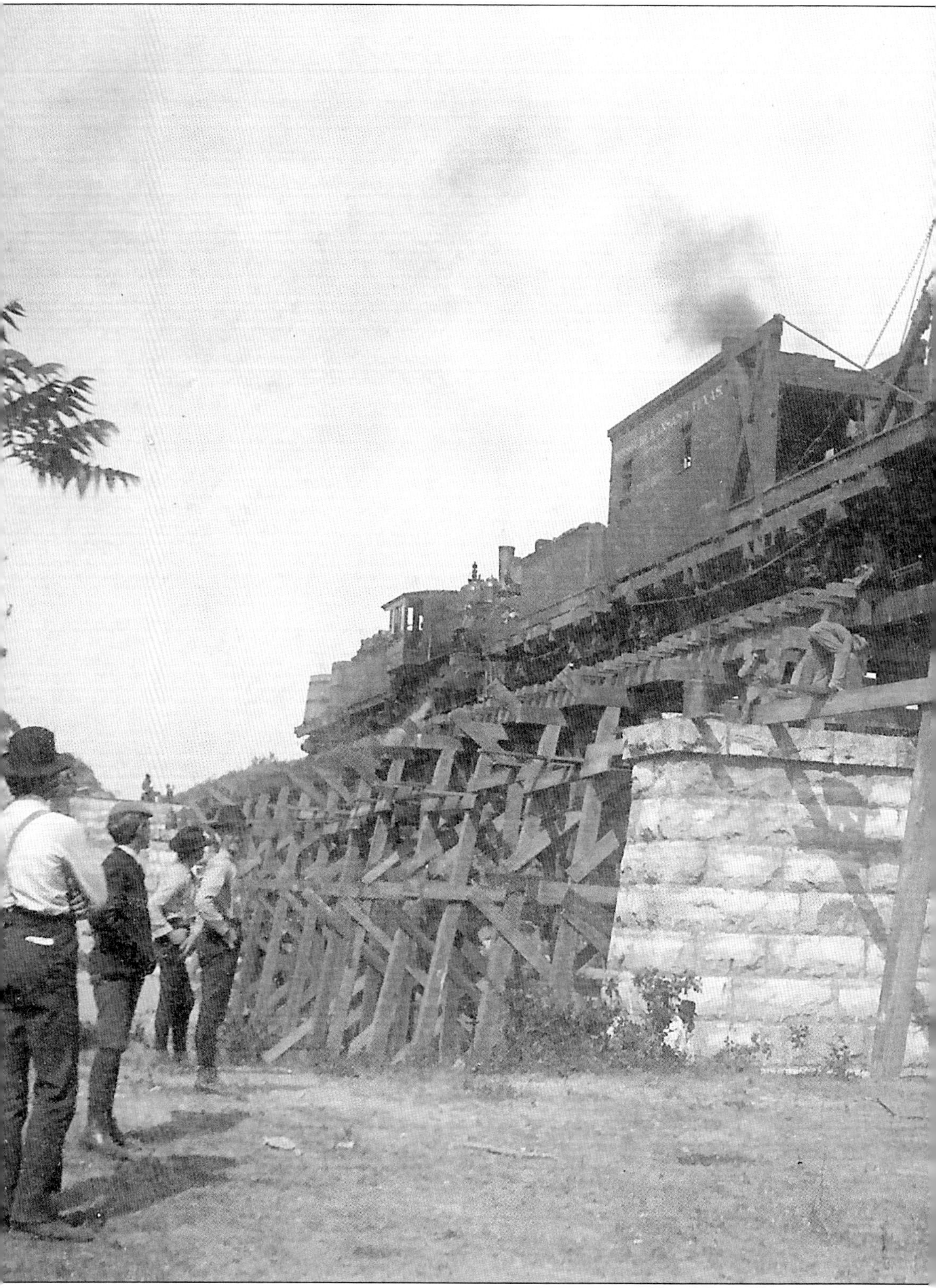

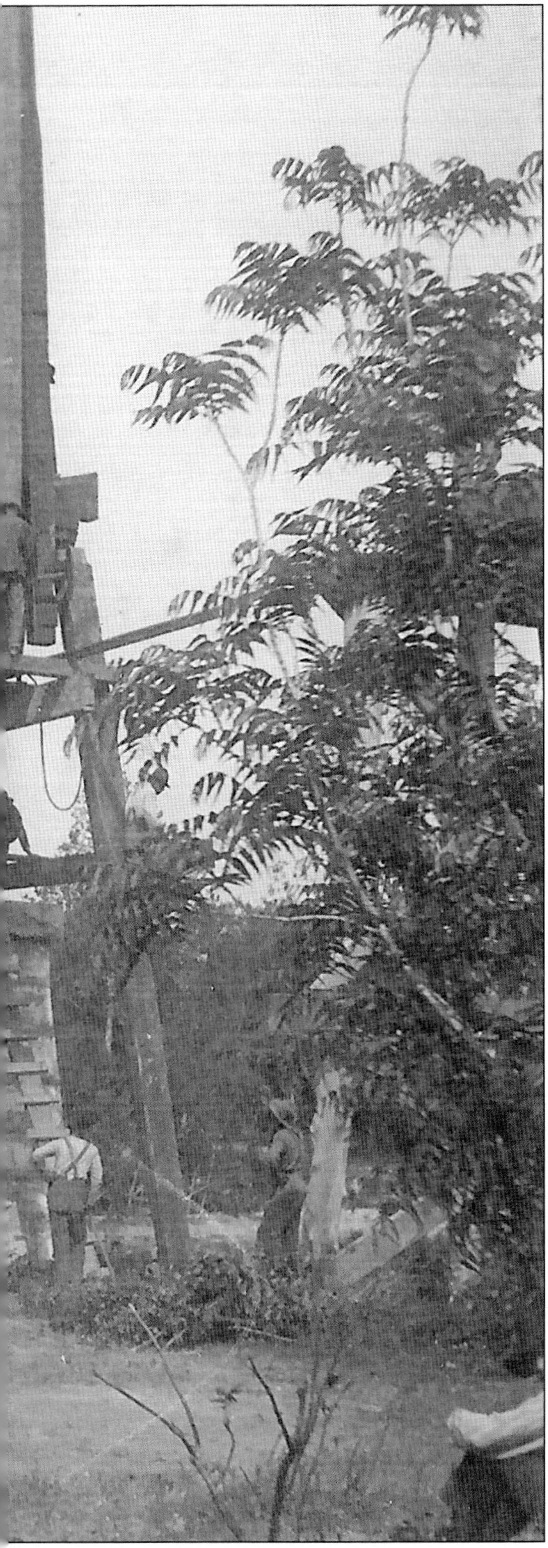

Construction of a railroad bridge takes place outside of town in the late 19th century. Brenham's early prosperity was the result of having two major railroads pass through the city. Leading figures from both Brenham and Chappell Hill understood the economic potential of the trains in the 1850s and set to work raising capital. Part of their investment came as pledges for enslaved labor to build the tracks. That line, the Washington County Railroad, tapped into the Houston & Texas Central on the eve of the Civil War and was eventually bought out by that railroad. The Gulf, Colorado & Santa Fe arrived in 1880 and ultimately became the busier line, still seeing daily train traffic.

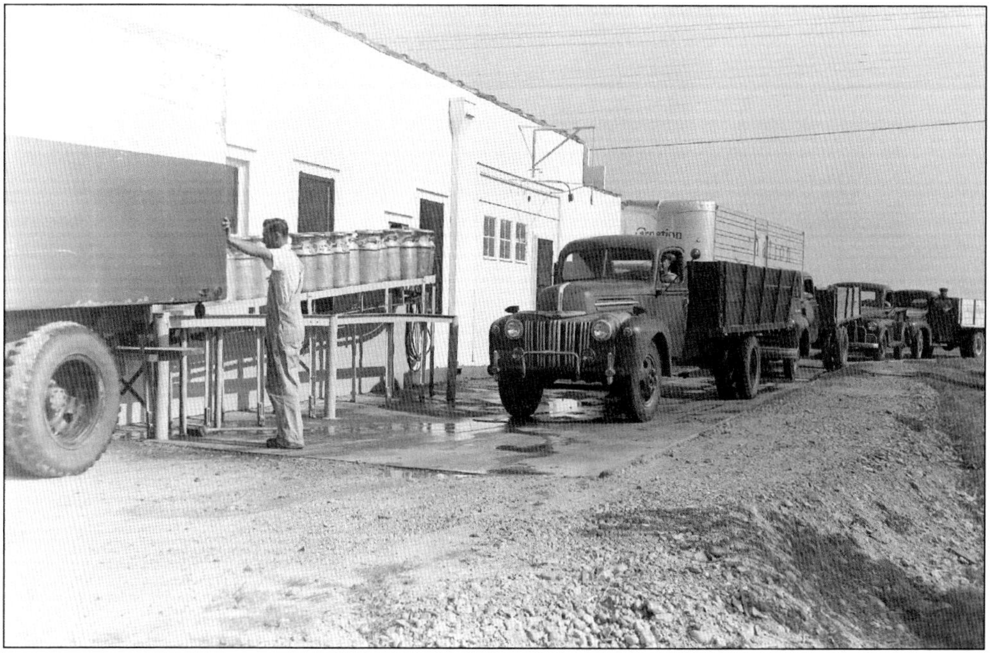

At one time, Washington County was home to scores of dairy farms. Some of those farmers lined up for a promotional photograph at the Carnation Dairy facility at 1801 West Main Street. The plant workers unloaded the numbered cans of raw milk, which ended up in Carnation bottles. (Briscoe Center for American History, University of Texas at Austin.)

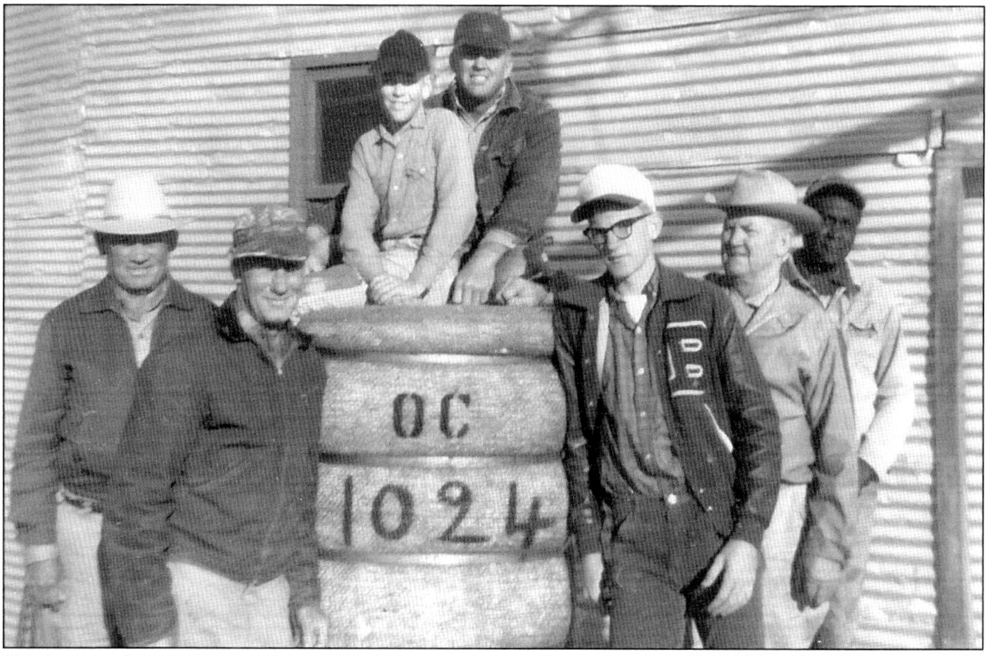

Workers and customers gather at the Sommer Gin in the northeast part of Washington County in 1961. From left to right, Christoph Klussmann, Herbert Emshoff, Stanley Sommer, Floyd Sommer, Lester Mertins, Fred Sommer, and Plas Eldridge pose with Otis Conner's bale No. 1024. It marked the most bales of cotton ever ginned at the family operation in a year. (Stanley Sommer.)

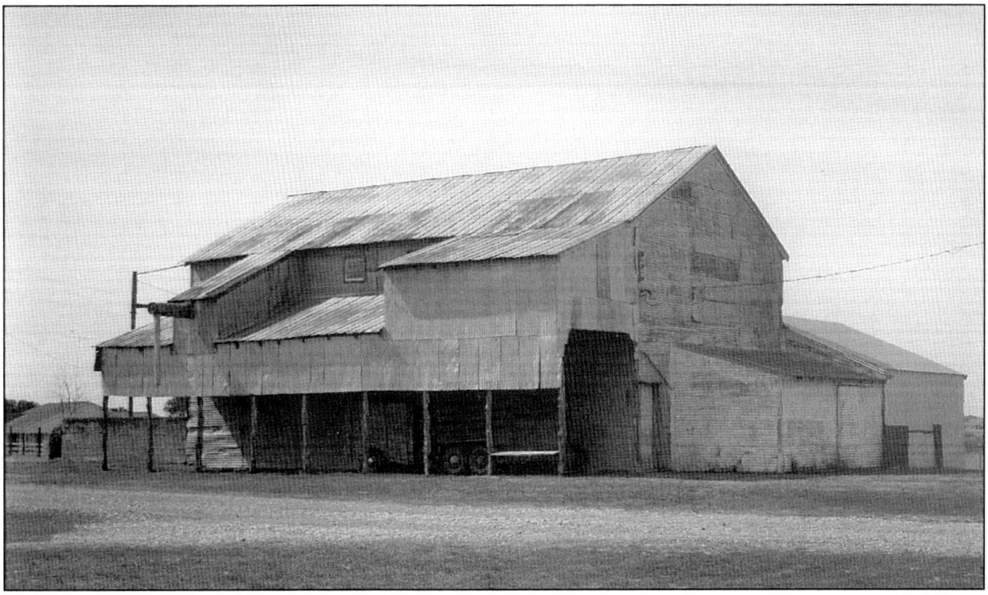

The Sommer family operated a cotton gin in the William Penn community of northeast Washington County for 132 years. It was one of many privately owned ginning operations in the county. After cotton production peaked locally in the 1930s, the number of competitors grew fewer and fewer. Today, the Sommer Gin and the Cotton Gin Museum at Burton are the only two intact in the county. (Stanley Sommer.)

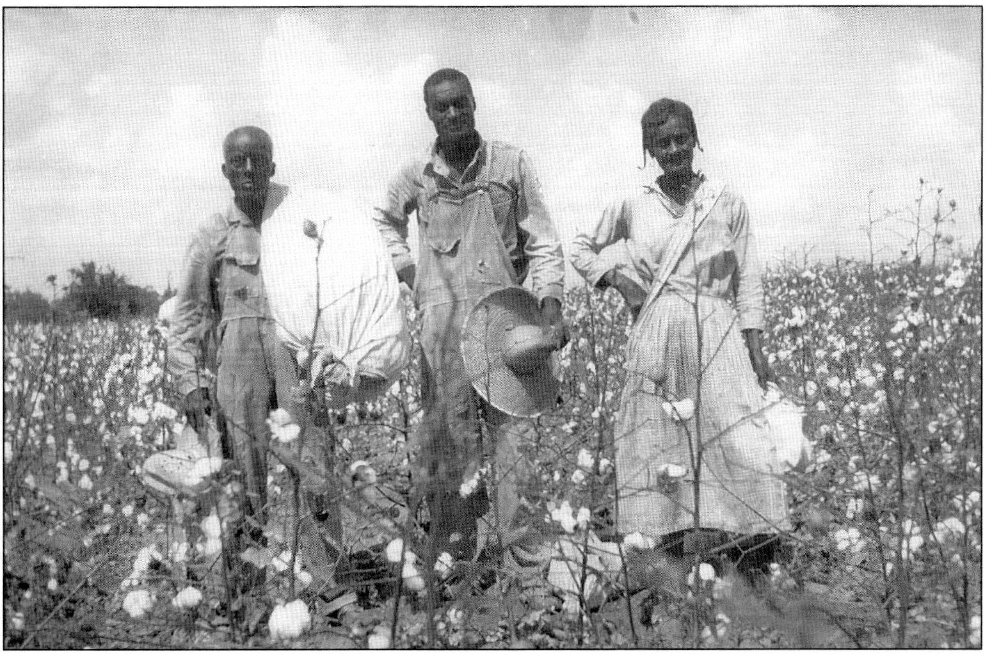

The Miller family stand in cotton fields where they worked and lived on the Sommer farm near William Penn. Tommy Miller's parents had sharecropped on the same farm. Hundreds in Washington County worked another family's land for a share of the crop's profit. Those who found the situation agreeable stayed for years. In other cases, some sharecroppers moved often in search of a living wage. (Stanley Sommer.)

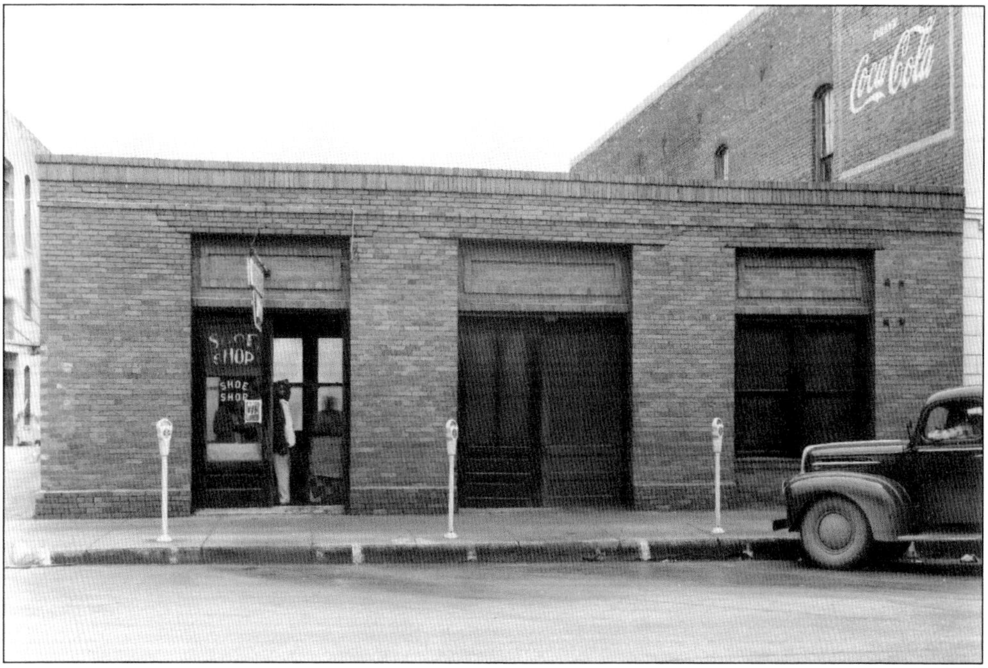

This small shoe shop on Alamo Street was one of many of Brenham's African American–owned businesses that were part of a parallel economy during the days of Jim Crow segregation. In front of the shop are some of the gleaming new parking meters that were installed downtown in the summer of 1949 from Market to Austin Streets and Vulcan to Commerce Streets.

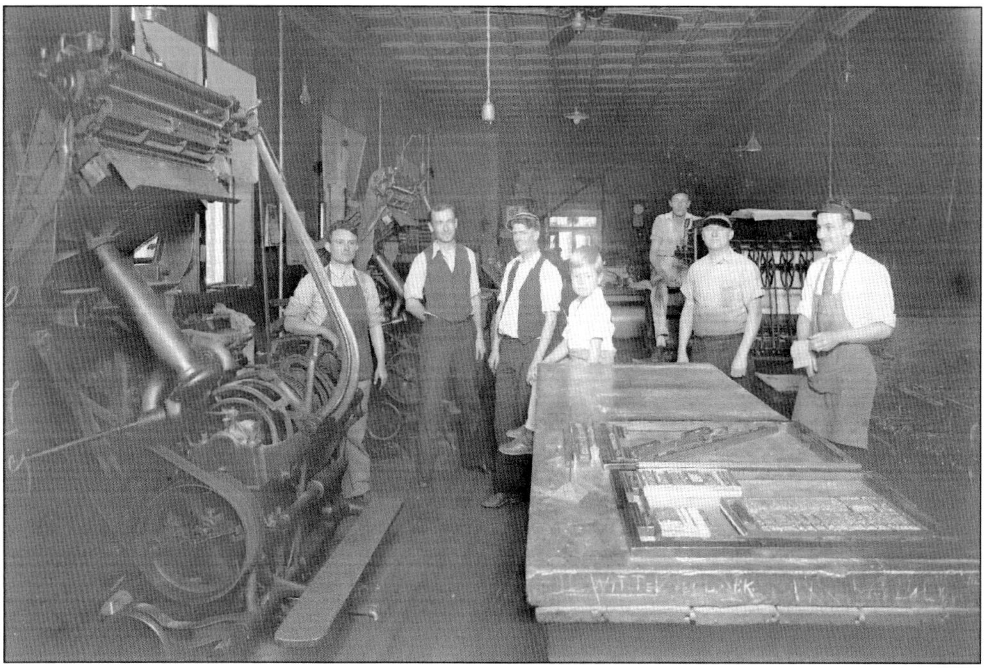

Printers and composers for the *Brenham Banner* happily show off their equipment in the early 20th century. The paper had two big electric presses to serve its customers, who in 1910 could purchase a subscription for $1 a year, paid in advance. Graffiti on the composing table tells a tale of long use.

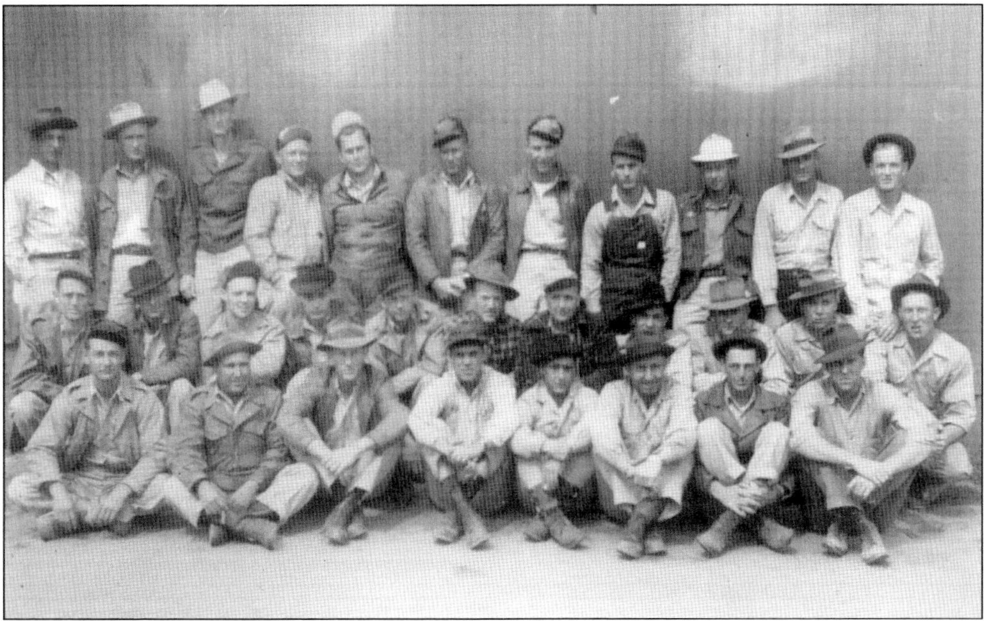

When World War II ended, millions of veterans returned home in need of work, including hundreds in Washington County. Some of their former jobs had been filled by women, who were often then displaced from the workforce. This group of veterans found work with Brenham Rural Line Construction, a forerunner of Bluebonnet Electric Co-op. These newly created jobs brought electricity to much of the county for the first time. (Ben Seeker.)

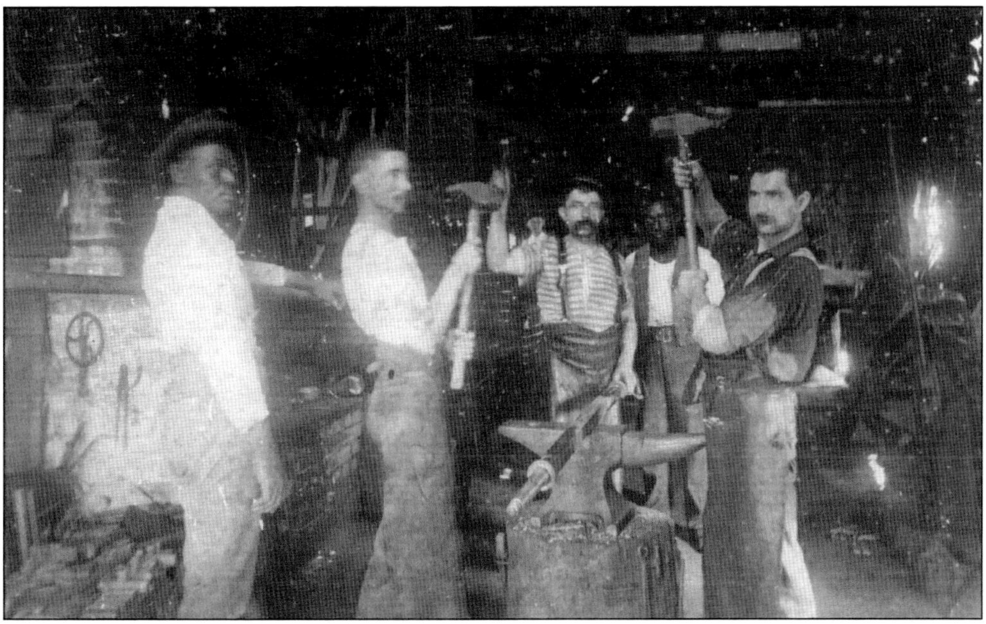

Frederick W. Schuerenberg's blacksmith operation reached a peak under sons William and Robert, but the advent of combustion engines hit it hard, ending some lines of equipment. Still, the blacksmith portion of the business remained viable for decades. The transition to fossil fuel-powered transportation was not instantaneous, and it was common to see horse- or mule-drawn vehicles in Washington County all the way to World War II.

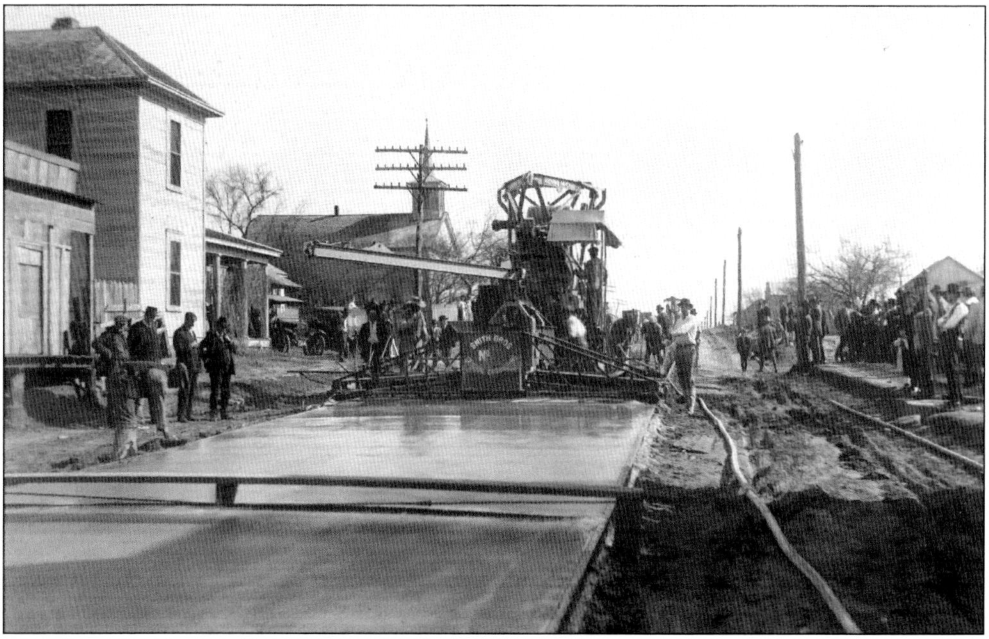

Crews pave a portion of highway through Chappell Hill in March 1922. With their own projects planned, citizens from Brenham traveled the dirt roads to observe the paving machine in action. Among the visitors was a reporter from the *Brenham Banner-Press* who carefully described the concrete-mixing machine and the second contraption that followed behind it to smooth the surface. (Texas Department of Transportation.)

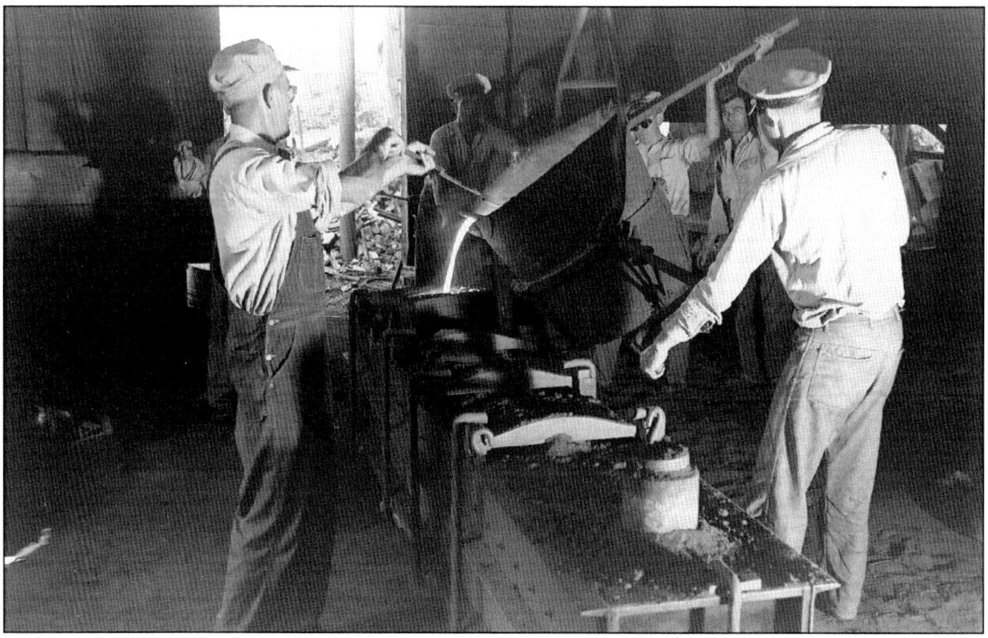

Beaumier Ironworks dated to the 1880s and manufactured a wide variety of made-to-order casts for iron products, but the name also shows up on steam engines, various motors, boilers, and other large industrial equipment. The company also offered machinery repair. For decades, even City of Brenham manhole covers carried the Beaumier name.

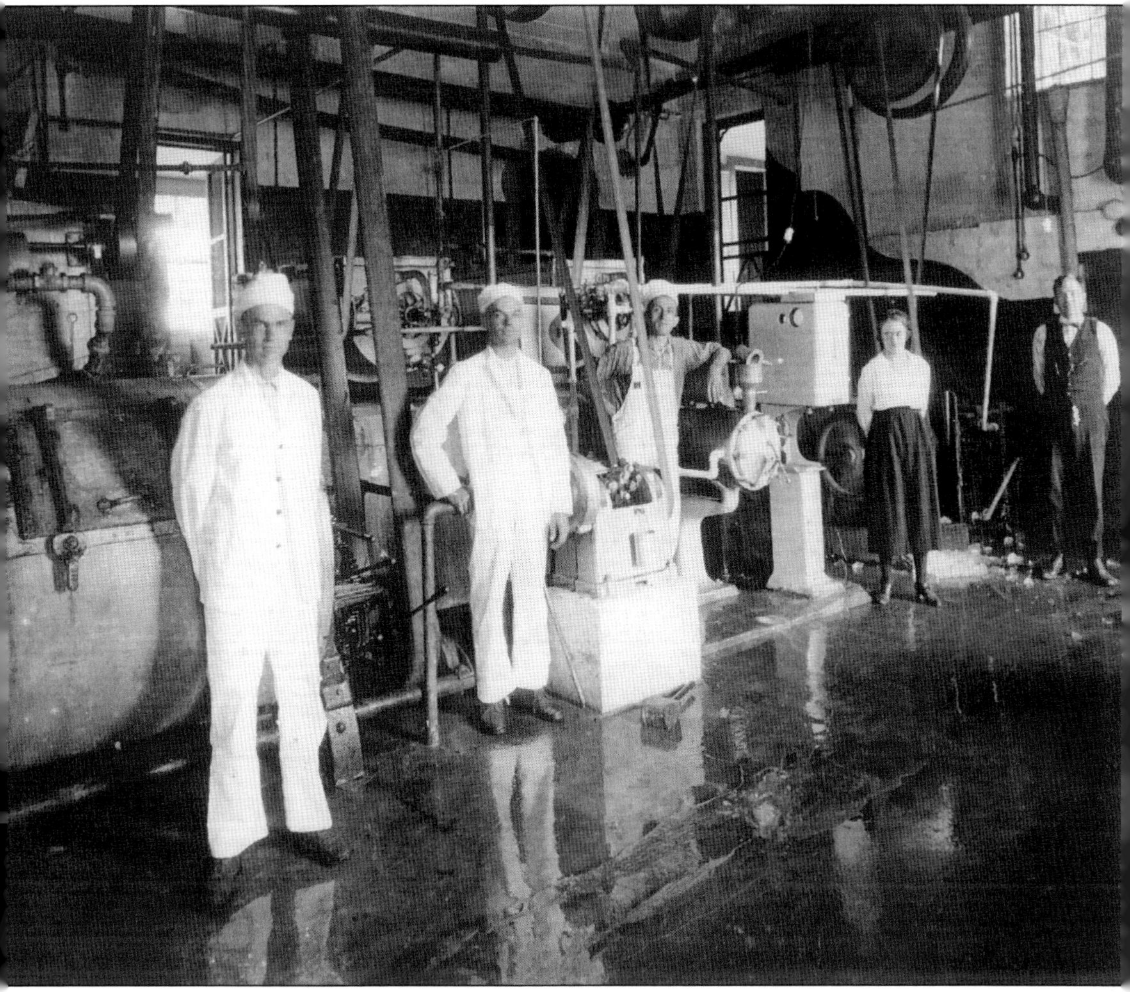

This photograph taken inside the Blue Bell ice cream–making operation in the early 1920s shows E.F. Kruse at the far right. Kruse, trained as a teacher, took the manager job in 1919 and gradually improved business practices, the physical plant, and public relations. The company had seen early success under the pre–World War I management tenure of H.C. Hodde who added ice cream to the creamery's repertoire in 1911 and then oversaw relocation to an empty cotton gin building. He also made the addition of ice cream machinery, tubs, freezers, and an ice cracker. After a wartime slump, Kruse's steady hand and solid work ethic turned local butterfat into vanilla, chocolate, strawberry, buttered pecan, and success. Marketing made a difference. That included giving free ice cream samples to the local newspapers and placing Blue Bell floats in the Maifest Parade. Kruse stayed at the company's helm until his death in 1951.

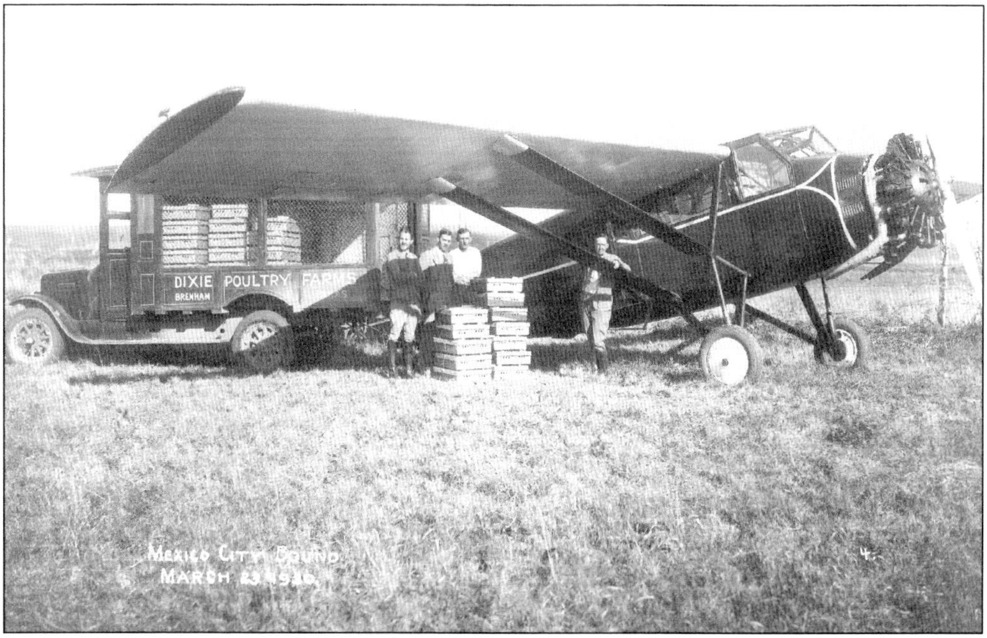

H.H. Drumm of Dixie Poultry Farms appreciated a good promotional idea. It was one of the largest chicken operations in Texas during the 1920s, with capacity for hatching half a million eggs and a brooder for 150,000 baby chicks, which were sent to numerous states. Drumm bought many of the eggs from local farmers and hatched them. When these Dixie chicks were bound for Mexico by air, it provided a chance to pose with the plane. (Gloria Nix.)

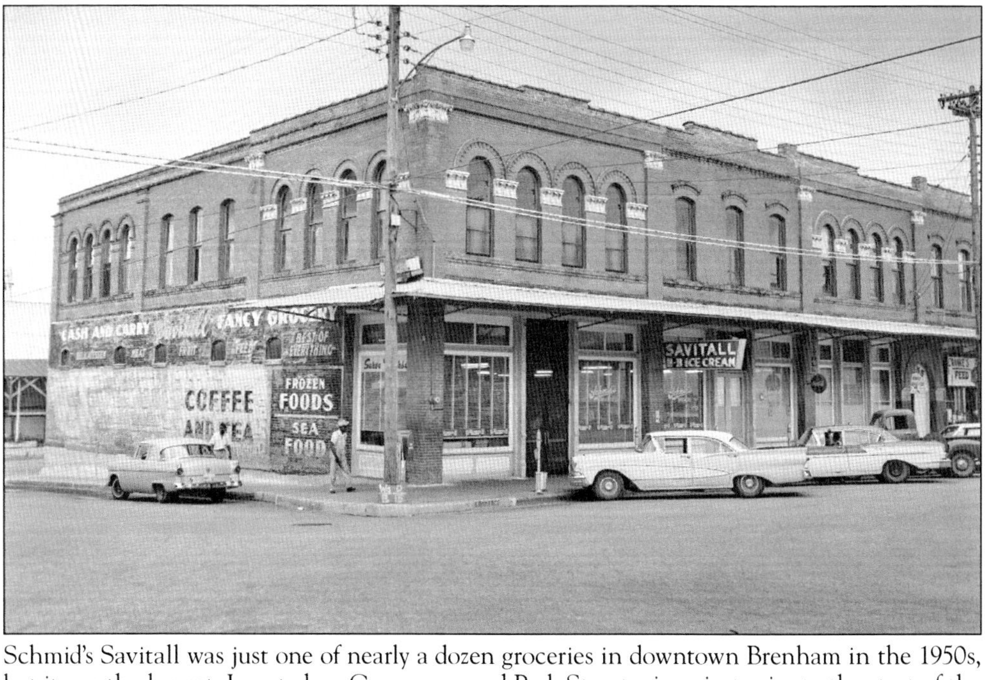

Schmid's Savitall was just one of nearly a dozen groceries in downtown Brenham in the 1950s, but it was the largest. Located on Commerce and Park Streets since just prior to the start of the 20th century, it boasted over 21,000 square feet of floor space and 134 feet of "costly plateglass windows and door" along the street frontage, according to the *Brenham Daily Banner*.

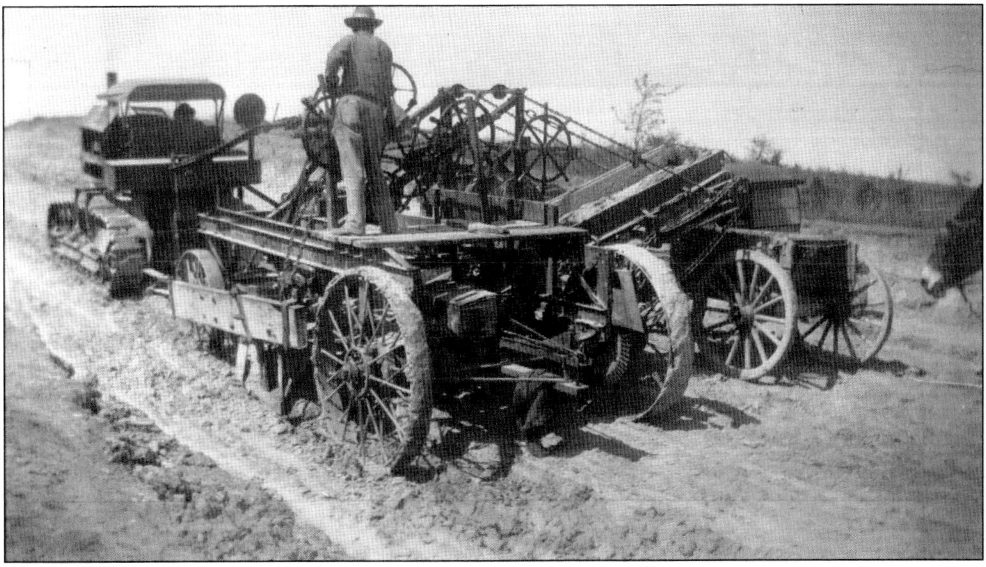

A highway department road grader operates on a hill, taming a stretch of highway that is now State Road 105 east of Brenham toward Navasota. This road was proposed in 1925 as Highway 105 that would run to Cleveland, Texas. A year later, a route change transferred it to State Highway 90. In 1973, that section was again designated part of 105. (Texas Department of Transportation.)

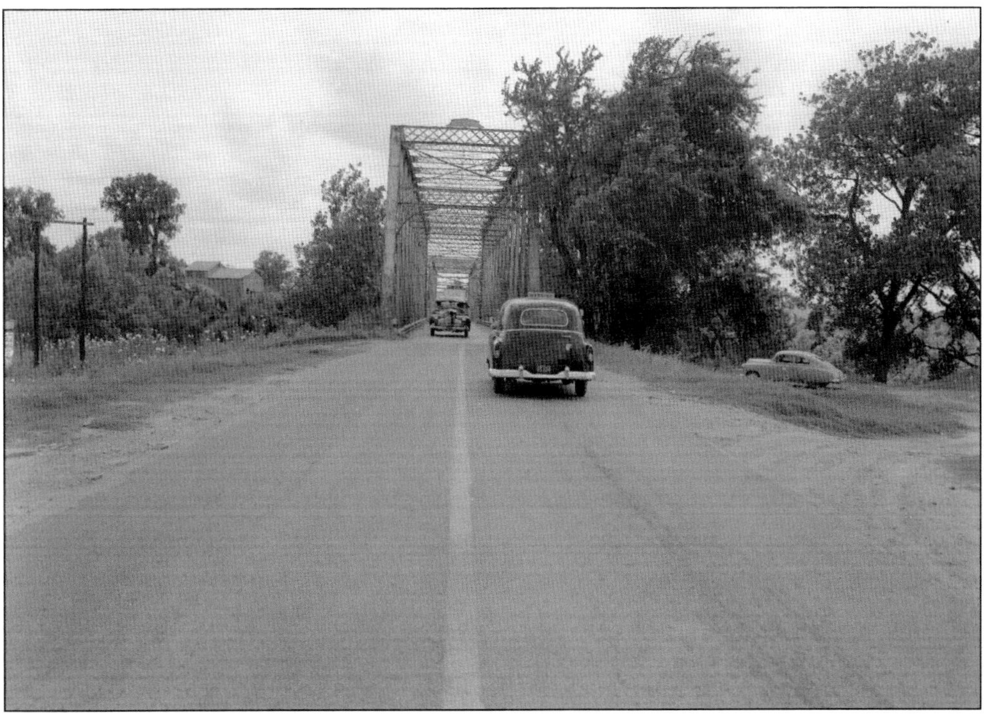

The bridge across the Brazos River at today's US Highway 290 did not open until the late 1920s. The ferry it replaced handled only three automobiles per trip. It was originally hand-pulled, but in later years, a small motor did the work. The banks were sometimes too steep for the weaker, older cars to drive up after a crossing. (Texas Department of Transportation.)

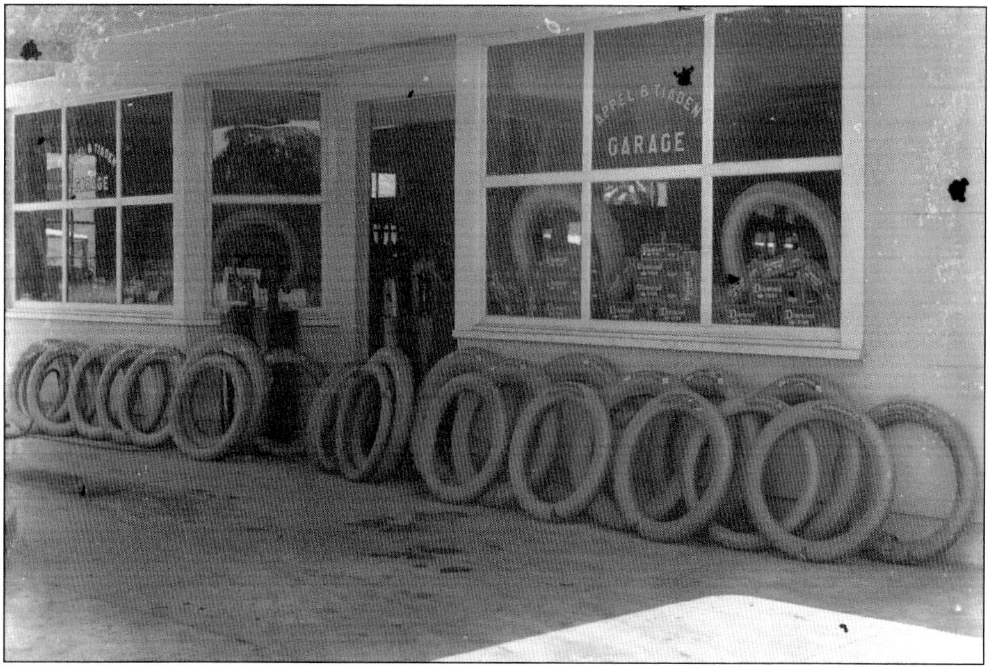

A display at the Appel Tiaden Garage shows off Diamond cord tires. There were Diamond brand inner tubes for those tires available inside. The garage was on South Austin Street not far from Schleider Furniture. A poster for Dan Moody, Texas governor from 1927 to 1931, graces the window.

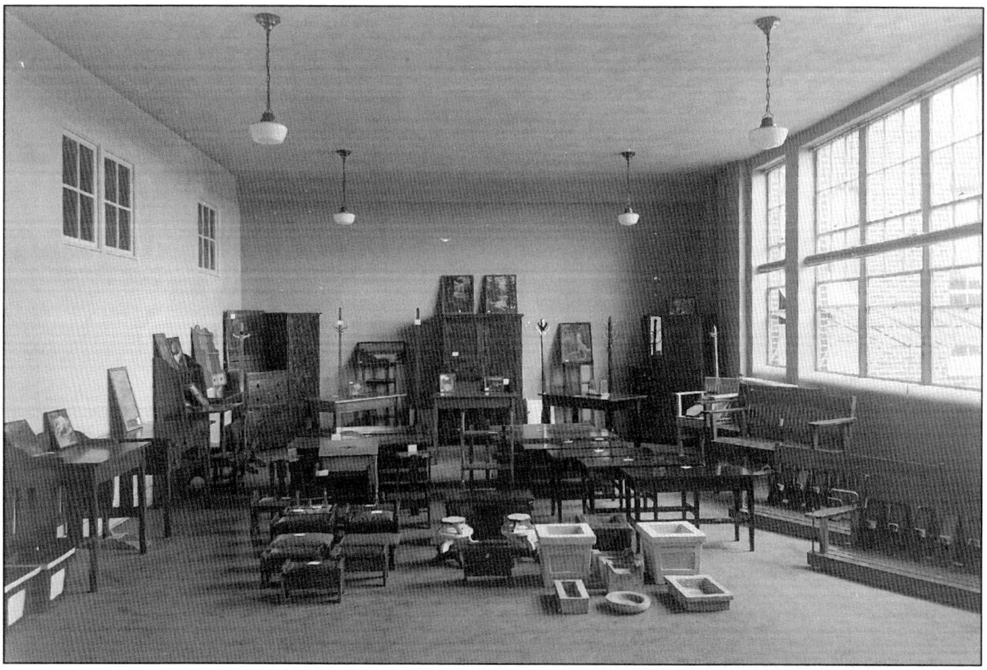

The Brenham High School Manual Training program, also known as shop classes, reflected a nationwide trend for vocational education in the early 20th century. Carl Niebuhr was the teacher who oversaw the boys who fashioned these tables, dressers, chests, swings, benches, chairs, and coat racks around 1930. (Brenham Independent School District.)

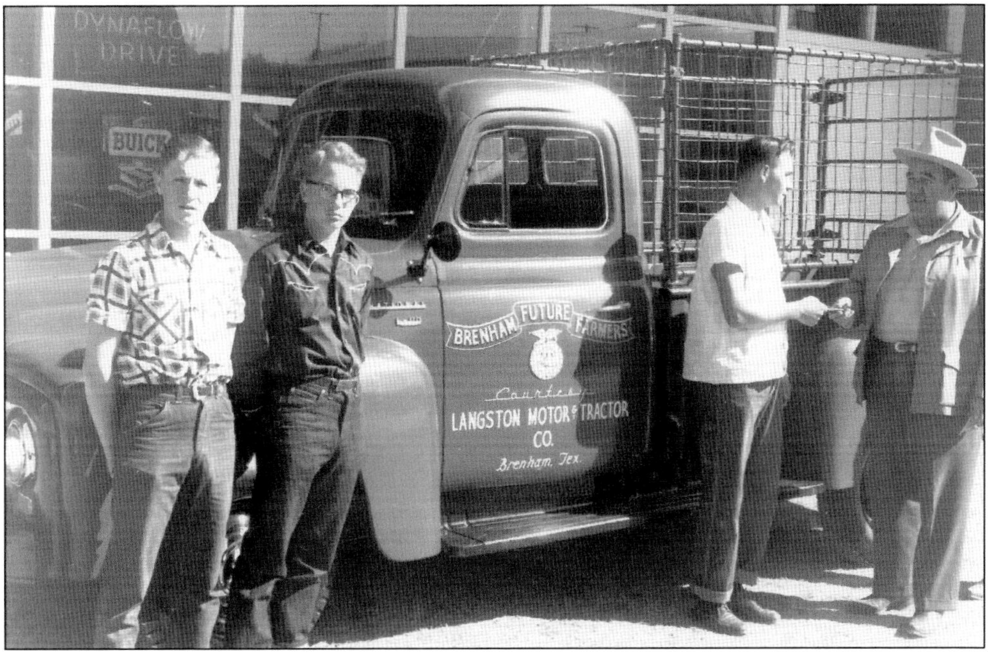

Brenham's Langston Motors supplied a courtesy pickup to the local Future Farmers of America chapter. The FFA and 4-H grew out of earlier corn clubs that were designed to teach agriculture and ranching to rural youth. The movement was popular across the United States and utilized schools, extension agents, and regional universities for agriculture education. (Washington County Fair.)

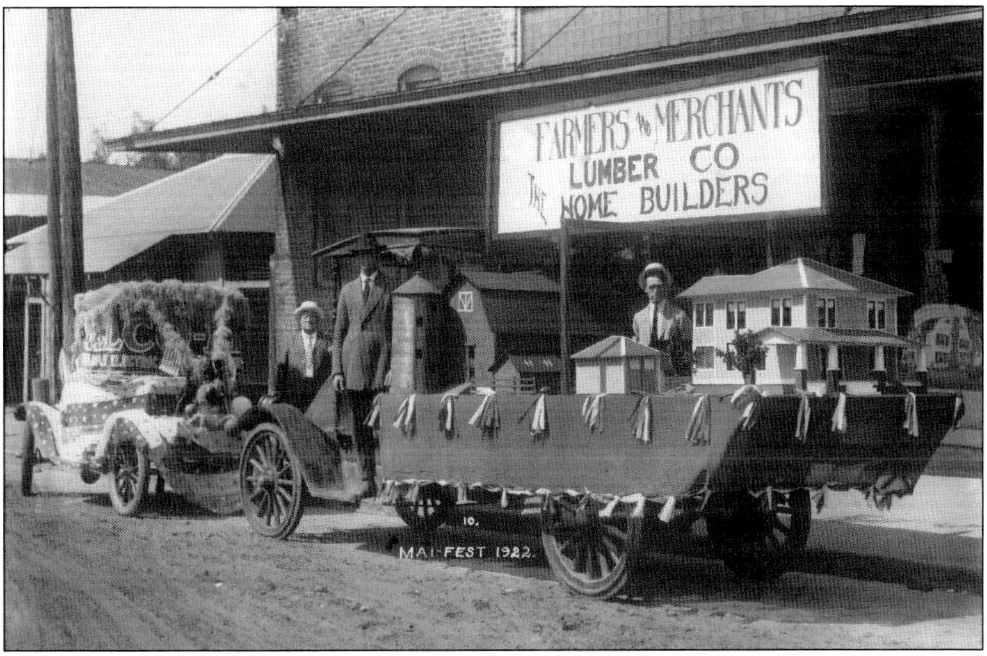

In 1922, the Farmers and Merchants Lumber Company showed off models of the types of homes and farm buildings that its products could make possible. T.A. Low, who also served as Brenham's mayor, was the driving force behind the company. It started in 1889 as a partnership, but was taken over by Low a decade and a half later.

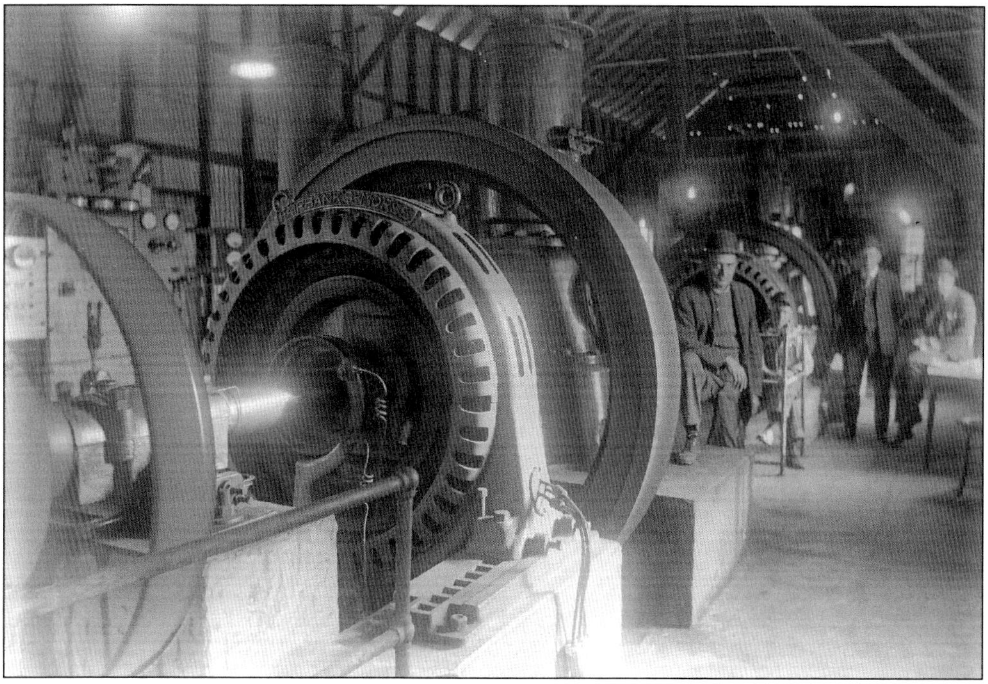

Brenham was not without manufacturing. These large engines, generating as much as 300 horsepower each, were most likely at the Brenham Cotton Compress. It was a complex of more than half a dozen buildings that ran southwest from the junction of the city's two railroads. Cottonseed was big business for decades, with the oil used for soap, shortening, and several vegetable-based food products for humans and cattle.

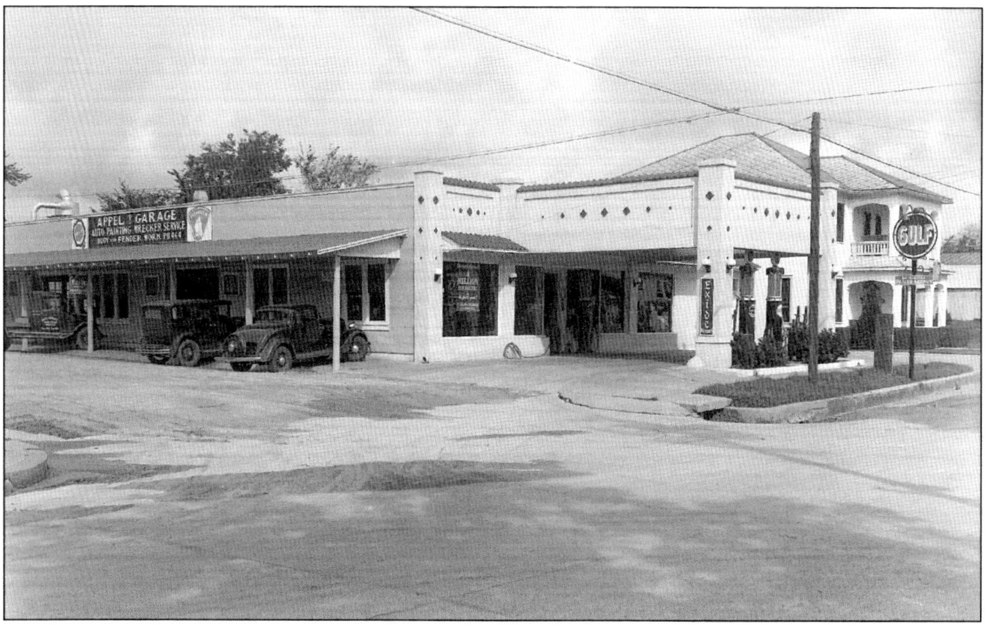

Appel's Garage and Gulf Station at 504 South Austin Street offered a variety of services including body and fender work. One of its wreckers sits under the awning at left. To the right is the funeral home and chapel run by Leon Simank, which handled a different type of body work.

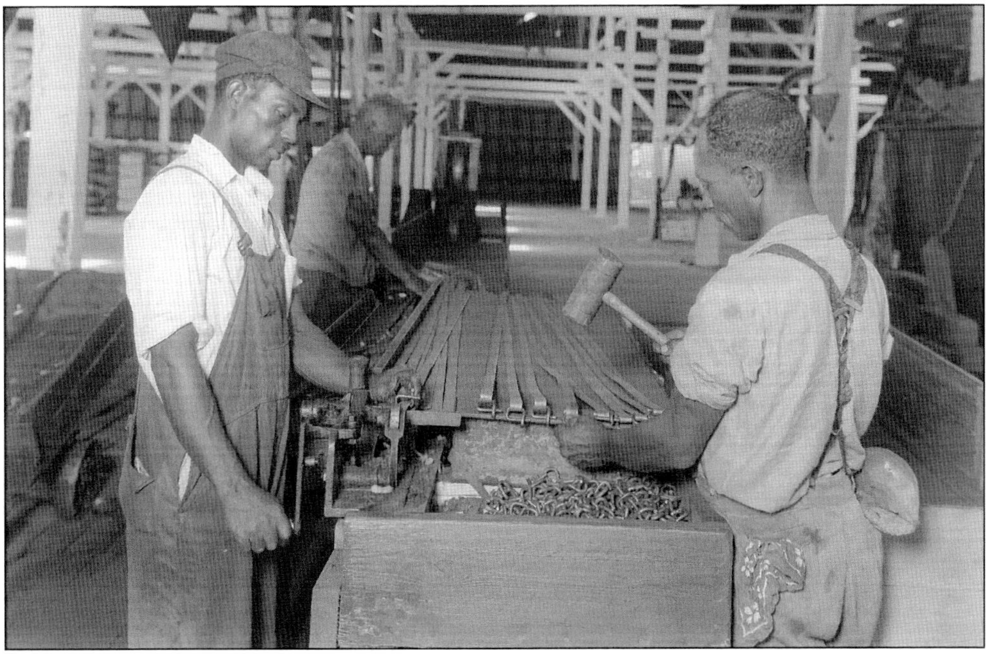

Cotton was still big business in Washington County in the first half of the 20th century, and its journey from the field to shipment passed through multiple enterprises. The last part of the ginning process pressed the cleaned cotton into tight bales, wrapped it in burlap, and secured the bales with metal strapping. These men made those bands at one of Brenham's several cotton warehouses.

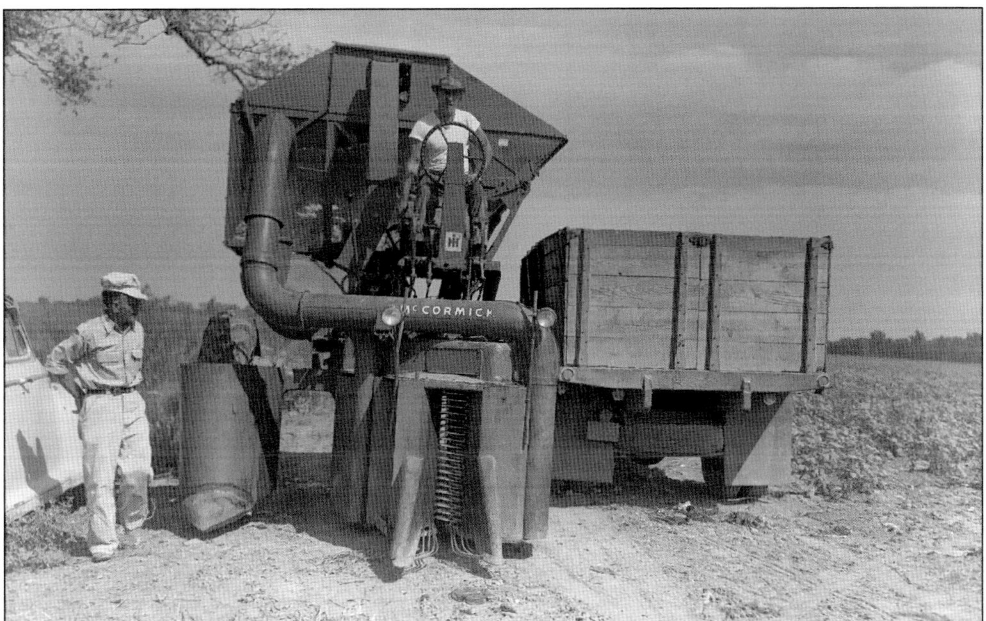

Picking cotton by hand was backbreaking and skin-cutting labor, but the sharecropping system provided a seemingly endless supply of cheap labor. Farmers who could afford mechanized pickers were truly living in high cotton in more ways than one. Harvesters like this McCormick in 1953 could do the work of more than 50 people, and they forever changed cotton farming.

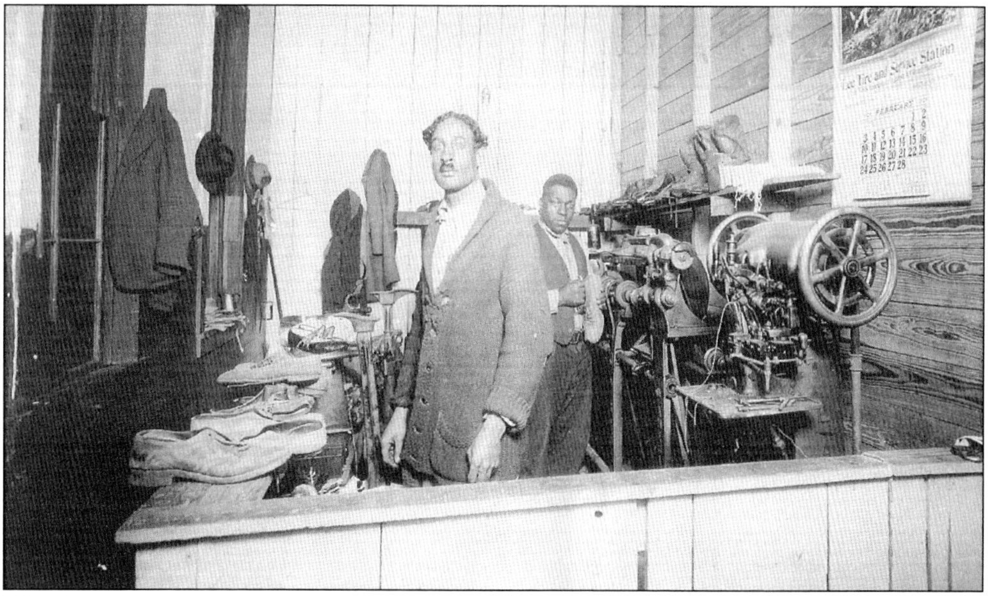

Elbee Newsome Sr. was photographed in his shoe shop in February 1929, as the wall calendar confirms. He was a World War I veteran, serving in France with the segregated 701st Engineers Stevedore Battalion. Newsome's business was one of dozens owned by African American Brenhamites, mostly along Alamo and Commerce Streets. He and his family lived in the Post Oak Addition.

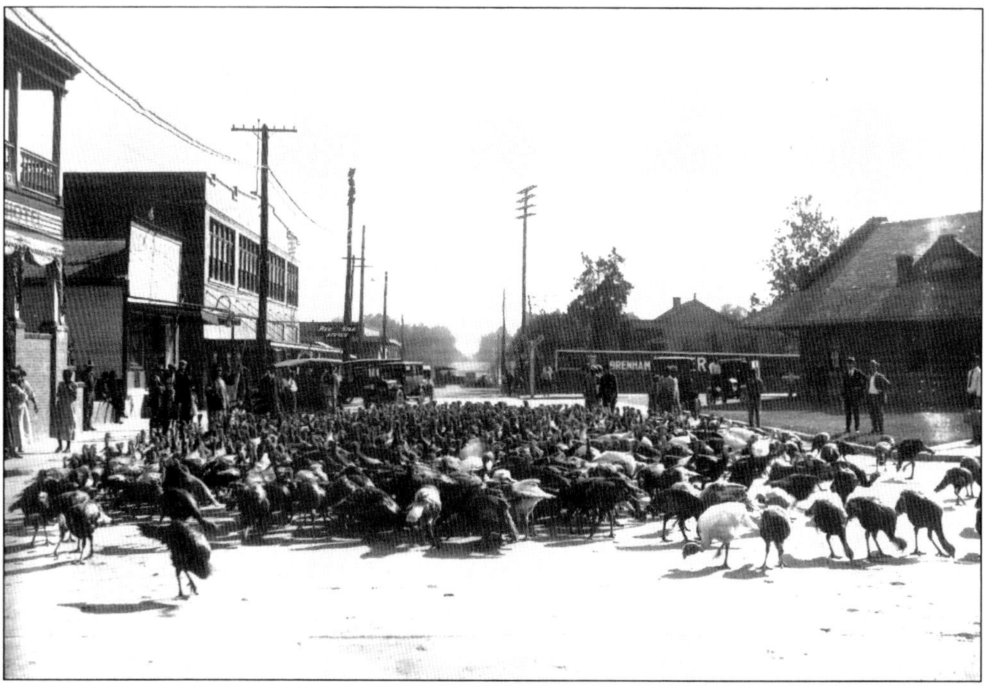

Turkey farming was extremely popular in Texas during the first part of the 20th century. These gobblers crowd Austin Street near the passenger depot at right. By the mid-20th century, farmed turkeys had been selectively bred to rapidly convert feed into more breast and leg meat. These top-heavy turkeys could no longer "trot" down Texas streets.

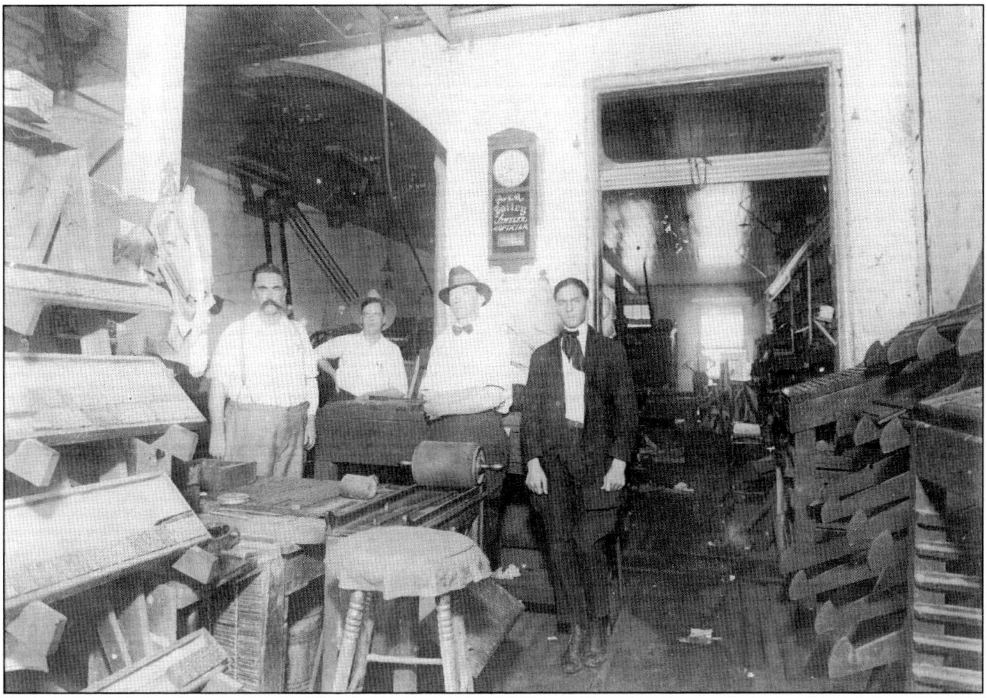

The Paul Mundelius Print Shop operated for several decades in Brenham. Mundelius immigrated from Germany as a preteen in 1872, joining his father who had come before him. By 1920, a third generation of Mundelius men were part of the business, handling a variety of jobs from printing the *Brenham Weekly Messenger* newspaper to local show posters and baseball game tickets.

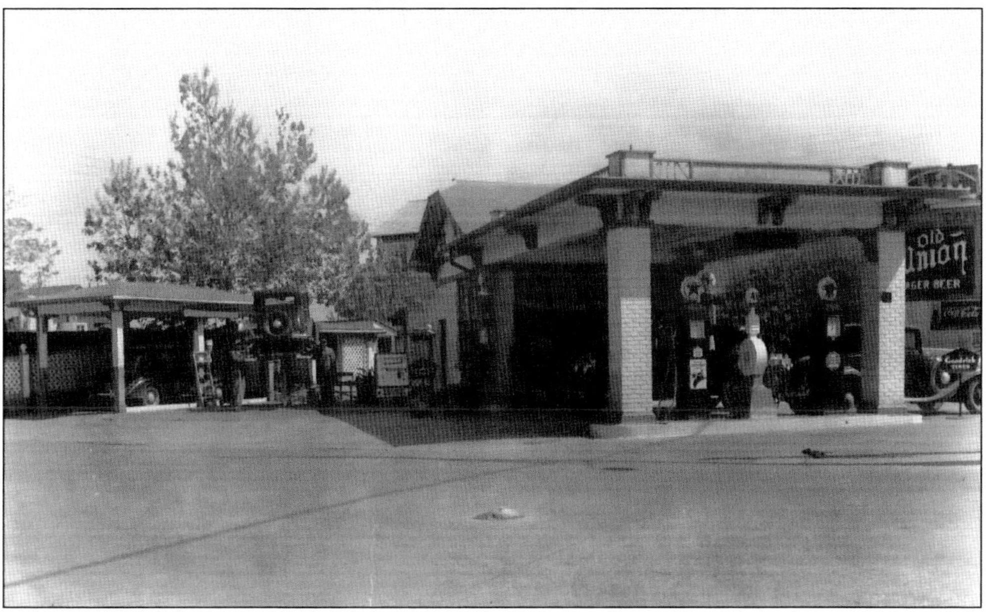

The Mitchamore Service Station in 1936 had an open air lift at 213 South Austin at Commerce Street. It was a prime stretch for Brenham gas stations in the pre-bypass days when the major highways of US 290, State Road 36, and others met in the center of downtown. The Mitchamore family lived in the house behind the station.

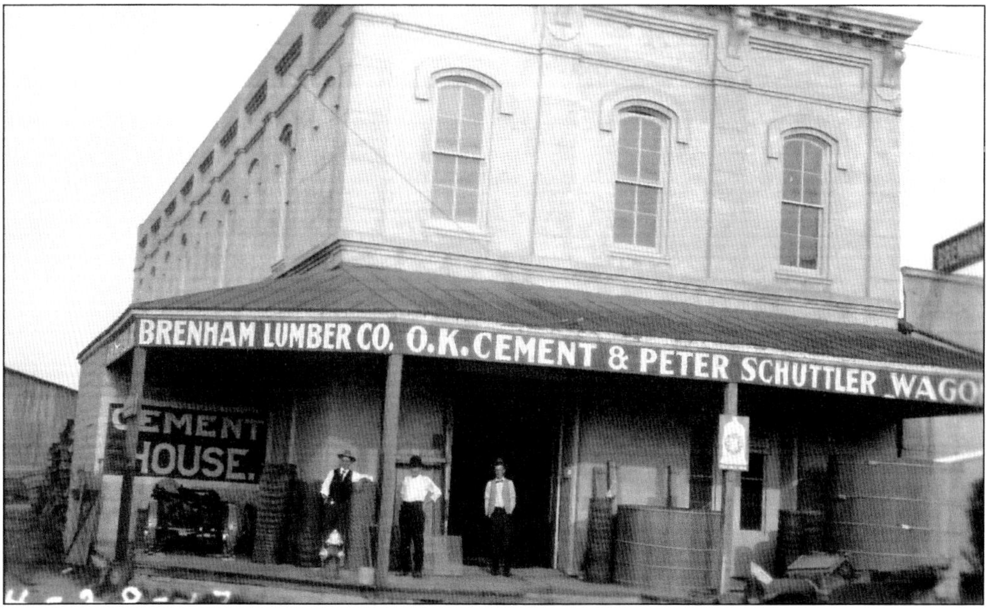

The O.K. Cement Company was one of a trio of business names that shared accommodations at Brenham Lumber Company. The Wood family advertised cement and wagons along with iron roofing and ready-made doors and windows. In 1915, the Woods advertised that they sold 22 train carloads of cement.

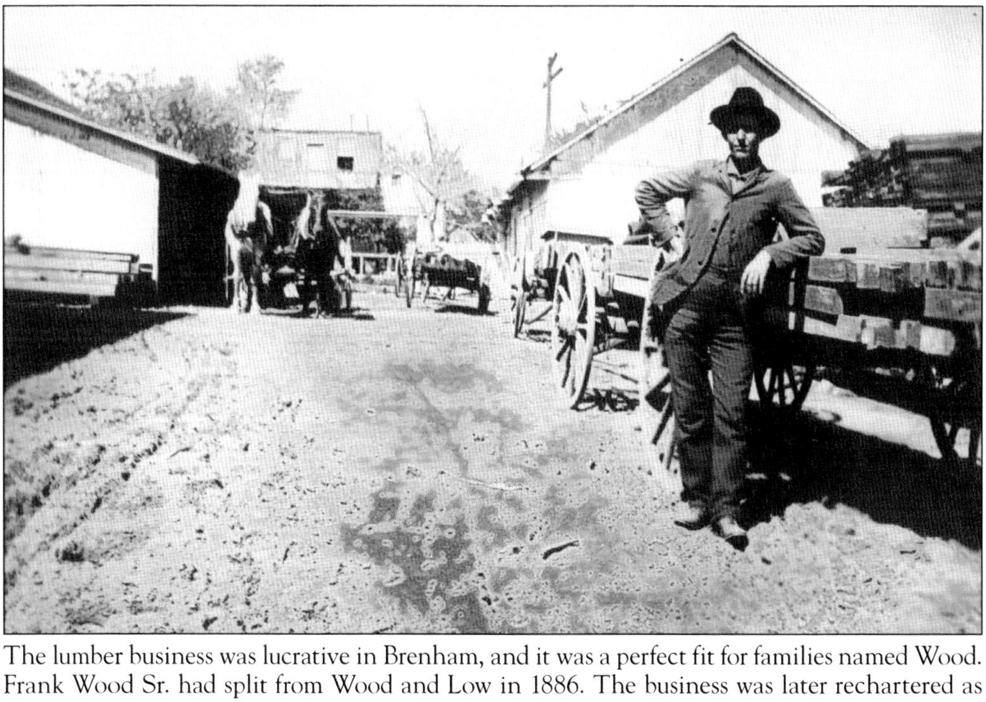

The lumber business was lucrative in Brenham, and it was a perfect fit for families named Wood. Frank Wood Sr. had split from Wood and Low in 1886. The business was later rechartered as Brenham Lumber Company under the management of Howard Wood and his brother, amateur photography buff Frank Wood Jr. Their lumberyard fronted on today's Commerce Street, near the Houston & Texas Central tracks.

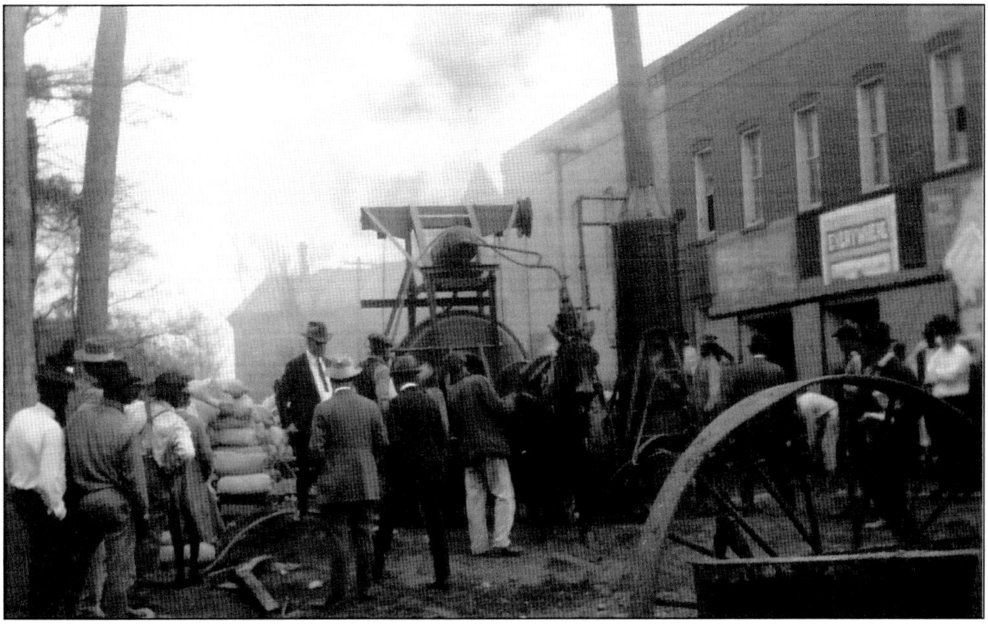

This smoking horse-drawn concrete mixer drew quite the crowd in February 1922. The technology of a portable mixer, however difficult to move, was barely a decade old. It had transformed the way American streets were paved, largely replacing earlier methods such as cobblestones, bricks, wood blocks, and planks. Streets slated for paving then included short stretches of Market, St. Charles, and Quitman (now Commerce) Streets.

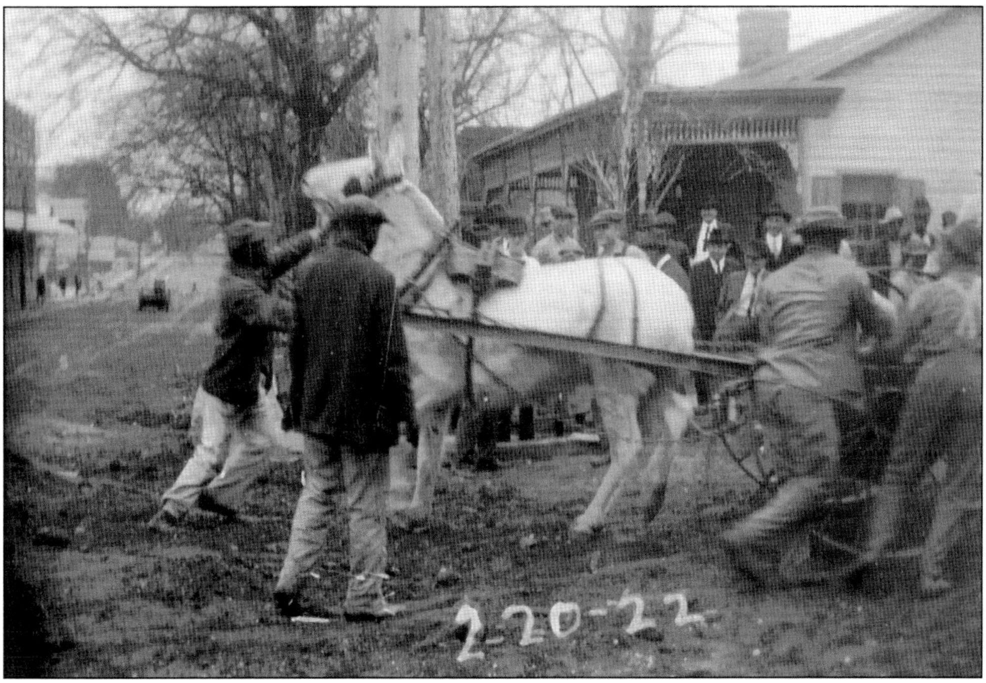

Men work to contain horses hooked to street paving equipment. A quick glance at the roadway shows the dire need. In 1922, the City of Brenham carried a liability of almost $40,000 in the form of a street-paving bond. It was the largest municipal debt by a wide margin.

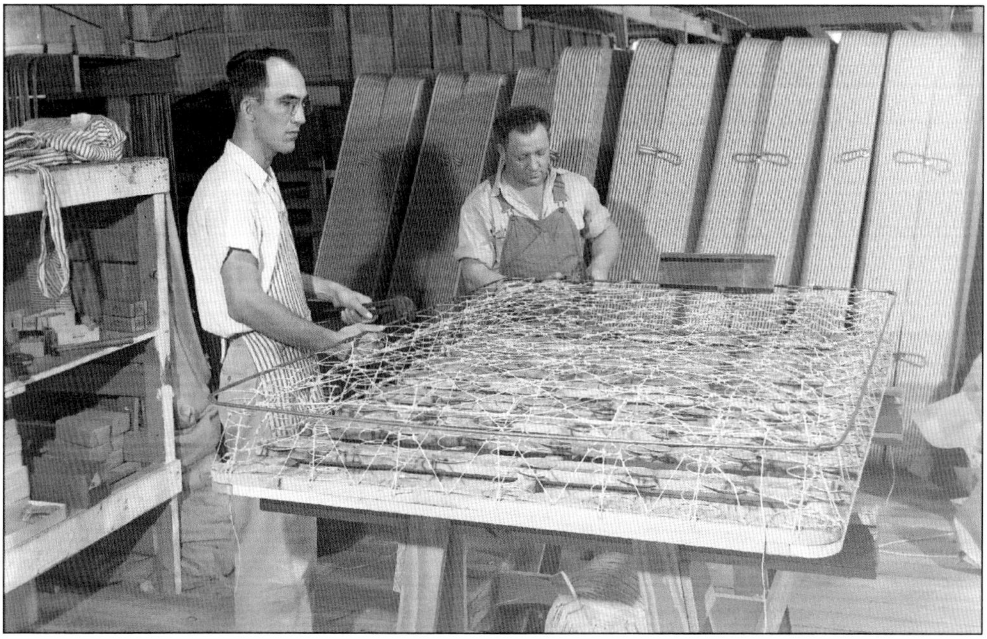

The Sealy Mattress Factory remains a thriving Brenham business today. This photograph from 1951 captures two employees handmaking a box spring. There were about 40 employees at the time, and they also made custom bedding and "fine upholstered living room furniture." The company was founded in nearby Sealy, Texas, in the 1880s, and was the first mattress company to sell manufacturing licenses. (Briscoe Center for American History, University of Texas at Austin.)

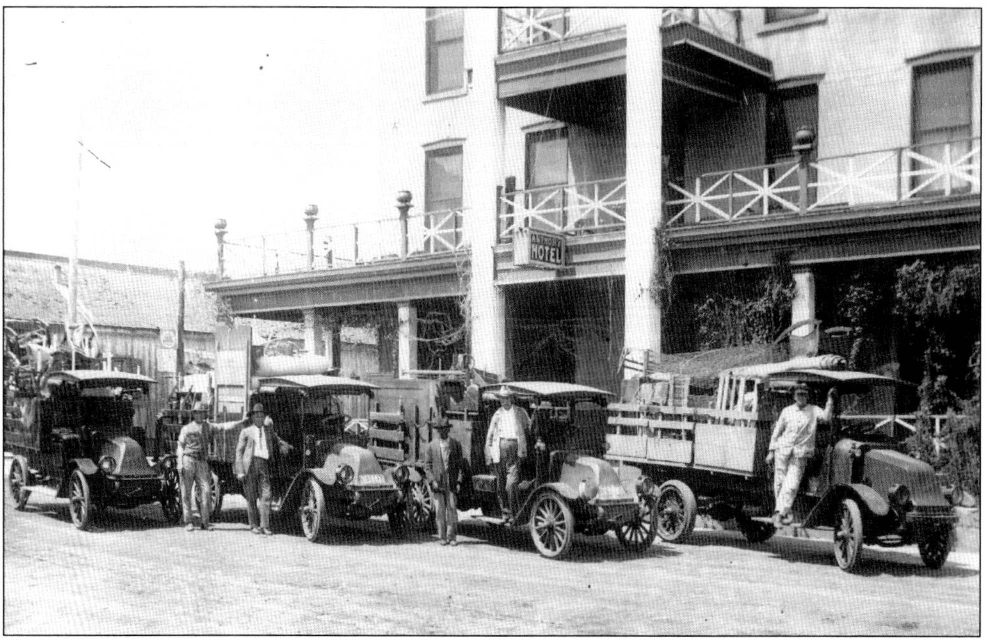

Four International trucks, about 1919 models, configured for hauling, are lined up in front of the Anthony Hotel and filled with furniture, box springs, mattresses, and other sundries. About this time, locals and visitors alike were cheered to hear that J.H. Lewis was back from World War I military service and ready to resume his job as manager at Brenham's top hostelry.

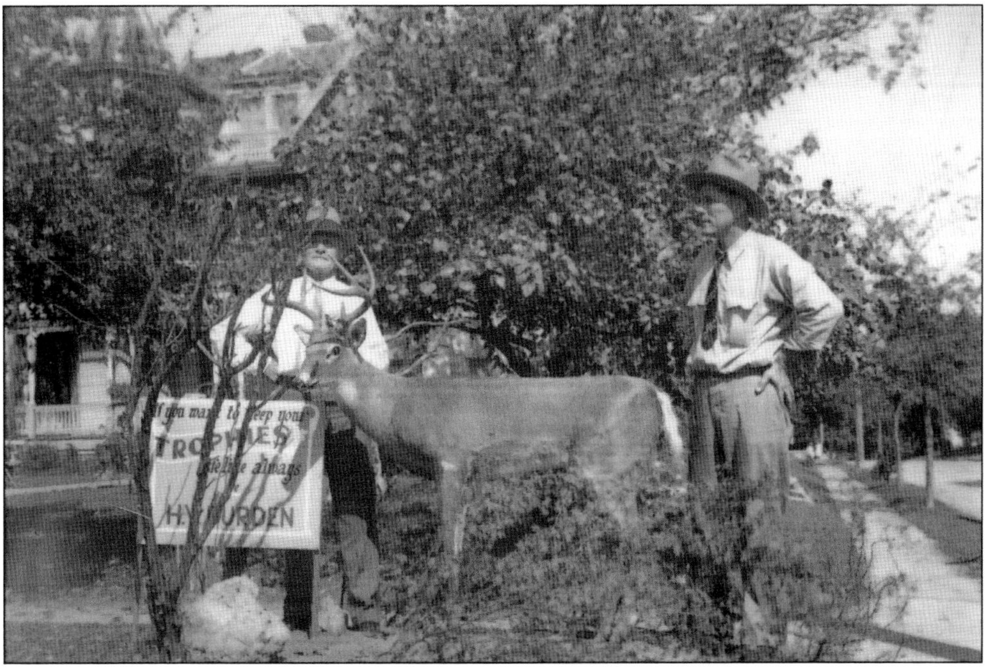

Hugo V. Durden Jr. operated a taxidermy business on Washington Street in Brenham. Deer heads were the most popular, but the entire animal was an option. Opening in 1930, Durden, who advertised as an "artist with a reputation for perfection," was still going strong in the mid-1960s.

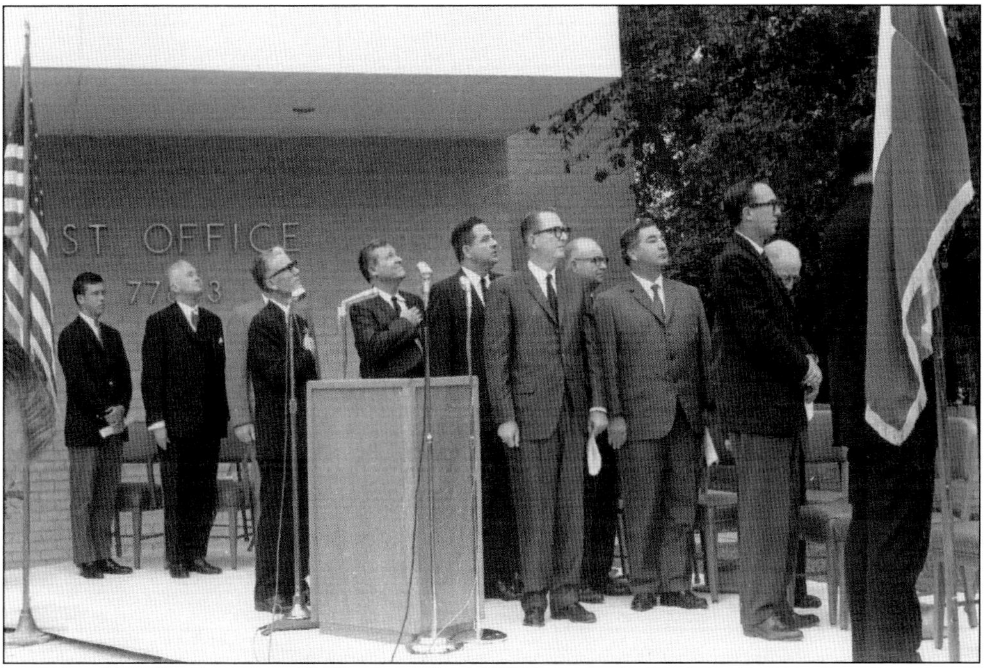

Postal and government officials honored America at the dedication of the new post office on Market Street on September 25, 1965. Local postmaster Wilson Munz stands under the letter C. Washington County's state representative Gus Mutscher is wearing a black jacket immediately left of the flags.

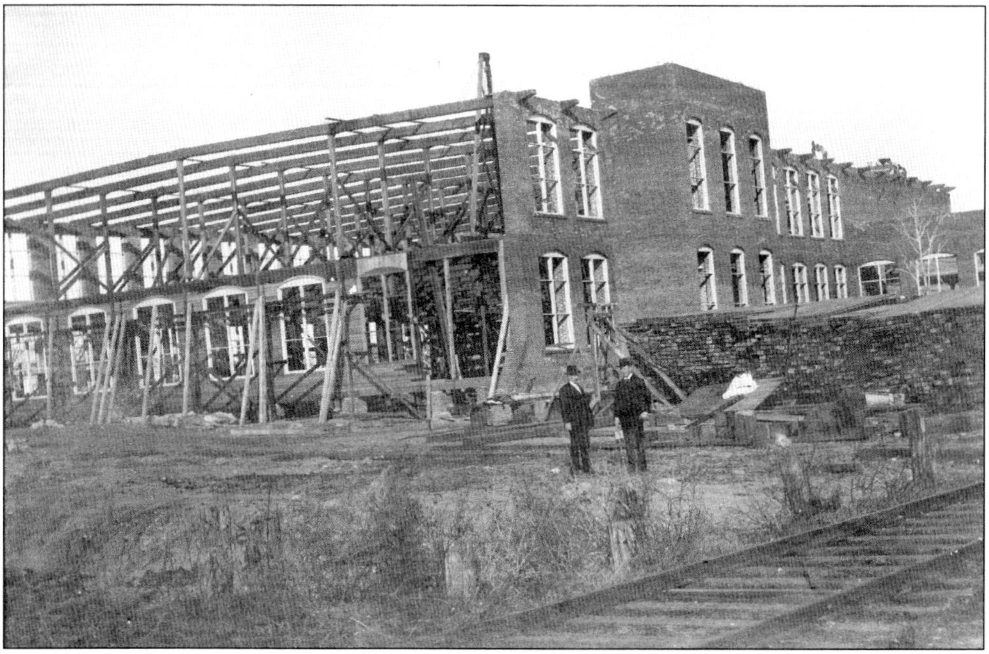

Construction on the Southwestern Cotton Mill took place east of downtown along the Houston & Texas Central tracks near the dawn of the 20th century. It reorganized multiple times and underwent name changes, but the large plant turned thousands of bales of cotton from the region into a variety of cloths, providing a few hundred jobs in the process.

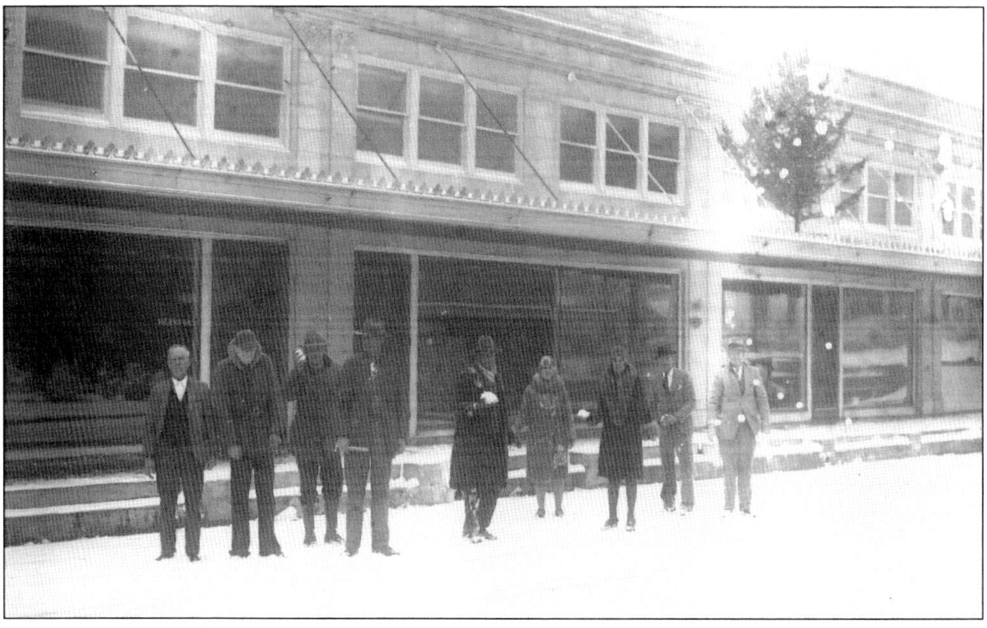

Coat-wearing Brenhamites gather in front of Hermann's Furniture on Alamo Street during a rare snow. Gottlieb Hermann, a German immigrant, started the business barely a decade after the Civil War. With a nose for people's tastes, the founder added finer furnishings. Eventually, seven Hermann Furniture stores opened around the region, but today only the original Brenham location remains, operated by the fifth generation of the Hermann family.

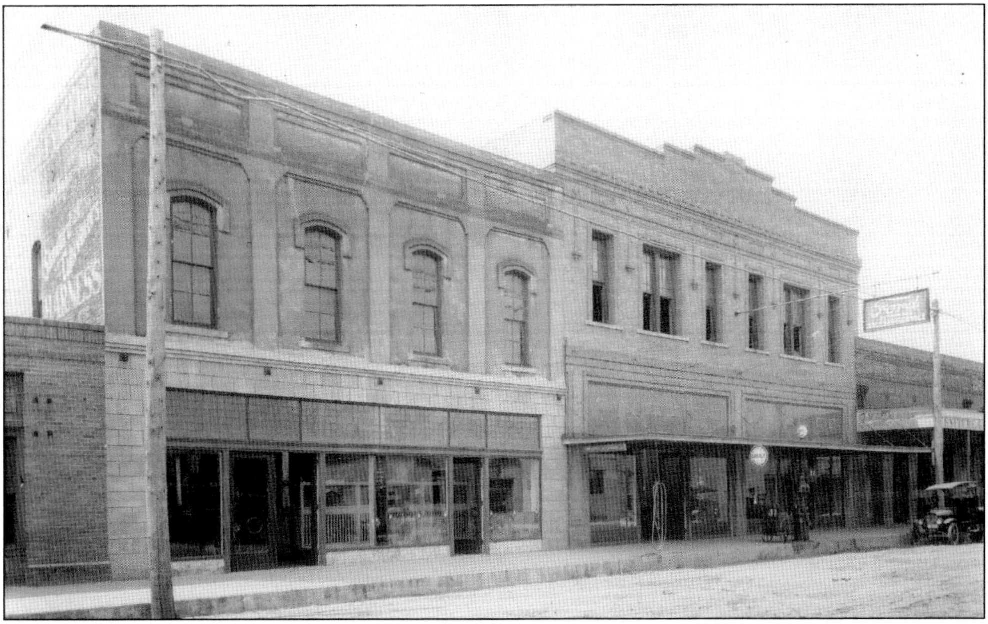

The Frederick William Schuerenberg company on Alamo Street dates to 1873. It began as a blacksmith operation and reached a peak selling animal-drawn farm implements under management of two Schuerenberg sons. After the advent of gasoline engines, the business remained for decades, augmented by side lines including auto painting and canvas car tops.

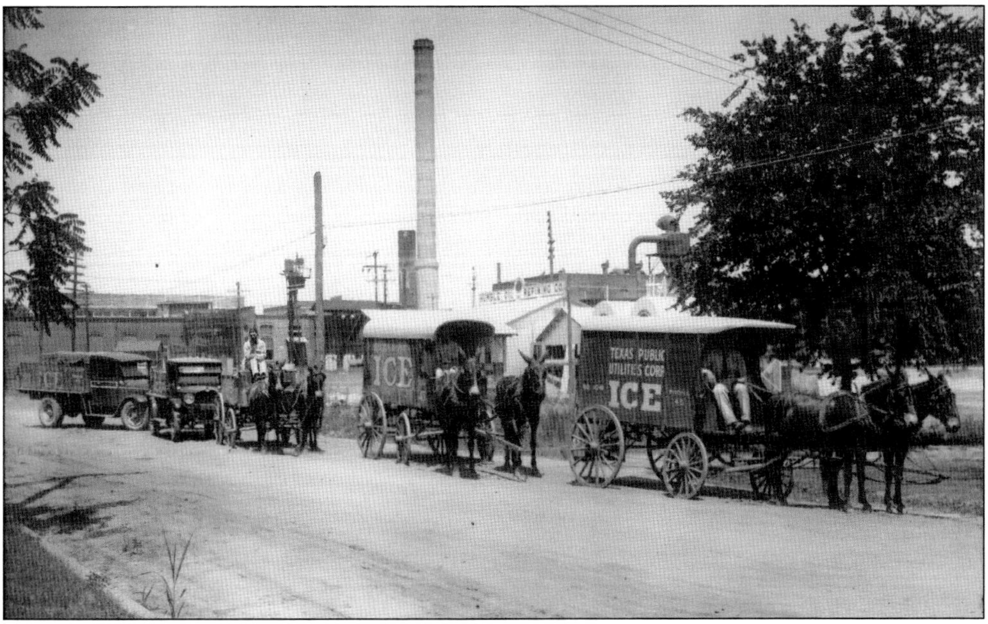

A Texas Public Utilities Corporation ice truck and wagons line up west of downtown. The smoke stack of the cotton oil mill rises in the background. In 1924, the cottonseed operation sold off the light, gas, and ice portion of the business, which included a great mechanical capability, and was rechartered as Texas Power & Light. The business did electrician work and supplied lighting to customers.

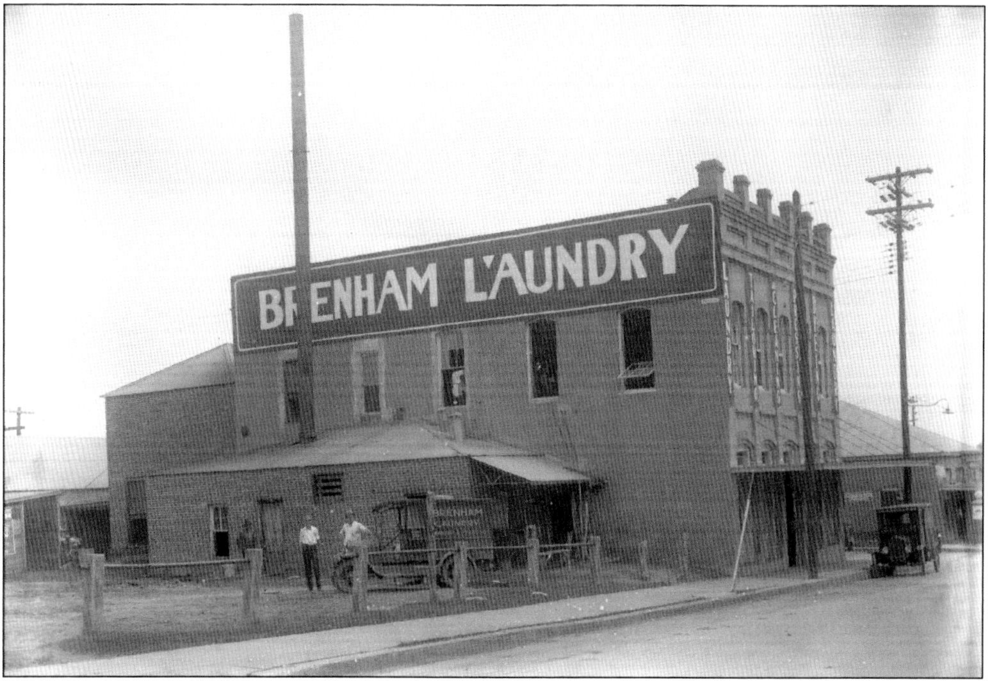

The Brenham Laundry on Market Street boasted modern steam equipment and promised on-time delivery of all orders. In 1915, Charles DeWare sold a half interest to George Derr and his wife, who moved from San Antonio to assume management. Across Commerce Street on the extreme right is a service station advertising Studebaker cars and Goodrich tires.

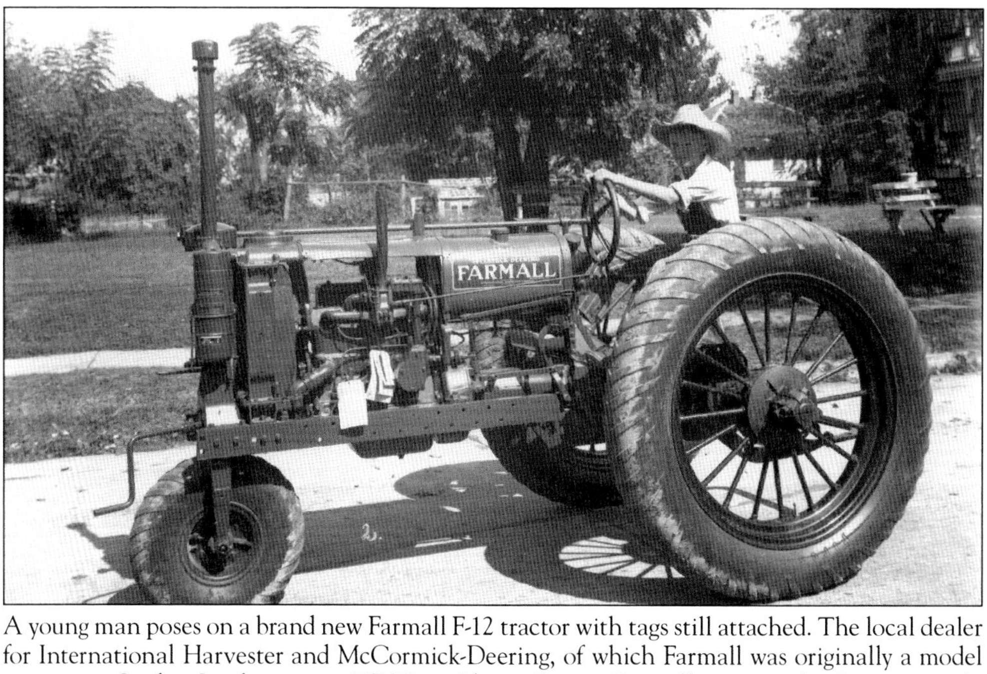

A young man poses on a brand new Farmall F-12 tractor with tags still attached. The local dealer for International Harvester and McCormick-Deering, of which Farmall was originally a model name, was Lurker Implement at 217 West Alamo Street. Farmall was popular for its tricycle configuration, good power, and low cost.

Five

PLAY

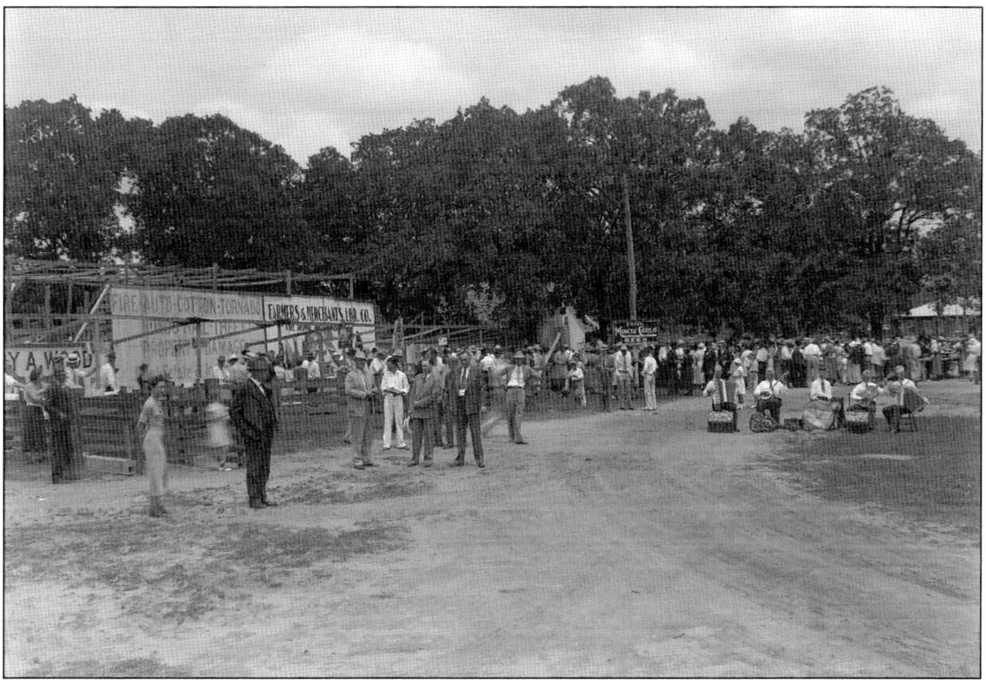

Fairs, festivals, and parties are always better with music. Longtime fairgoers in Washington County recall seeing rising stars of country music who added Brenham to their tour schedule, but in the early part of the 20th century, the music was likely to be either homegrown or from an adjoining county. It was also a good possibility that the tunes on tap were polkas and waltzes. (Washington County Fair.)

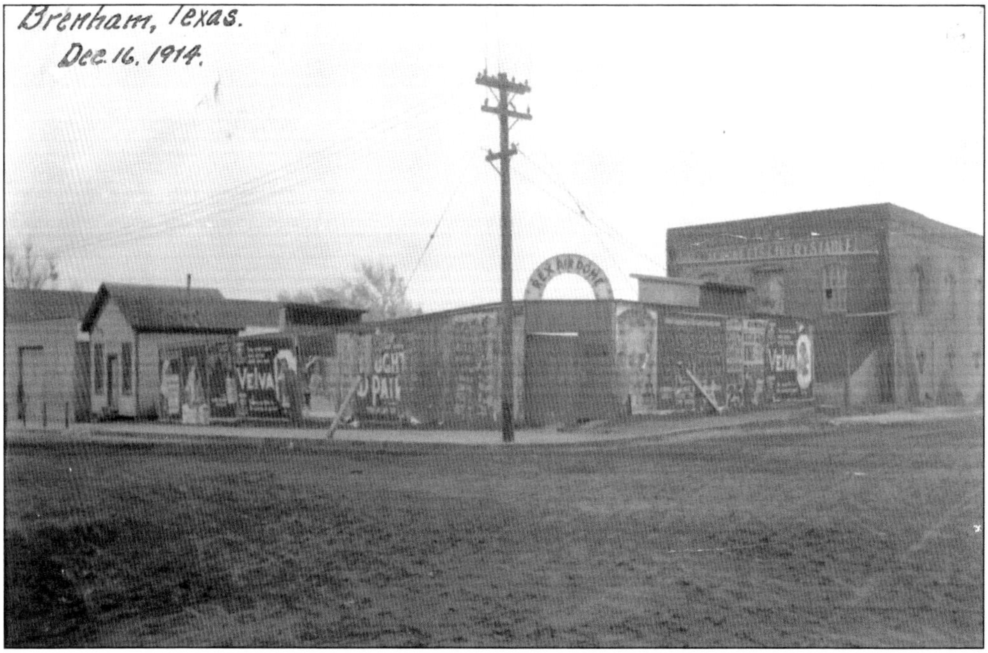

The Rex Air Dome movie theater sat at the southeast corner of Main and Market Streets. With no roof, shows were all after dark. It was a popular local attraction, and even the Methodist church held an evening service there coupled with the silent film *Honor Thy Father*. Within less than a year of this photograph, the Rex was razed for construction of the new post office building.

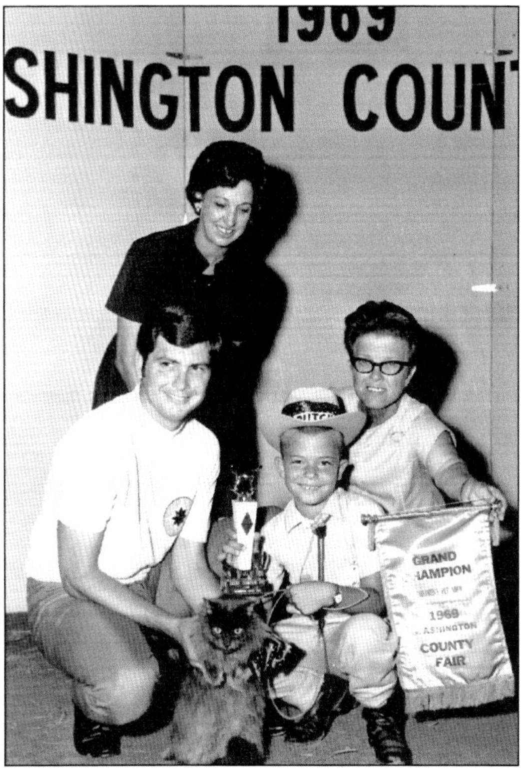

Always growing new ideas, the pet show was added to the Washington County Fair in the late 1960s. Celebrity judges were sometimes used, and the event was an instant hit. Though cute dogs and cats abounded, it was not uncommon for more exotic entrants such as raccoons, possums, or chinchillas to appear. (Washington County Fair.)

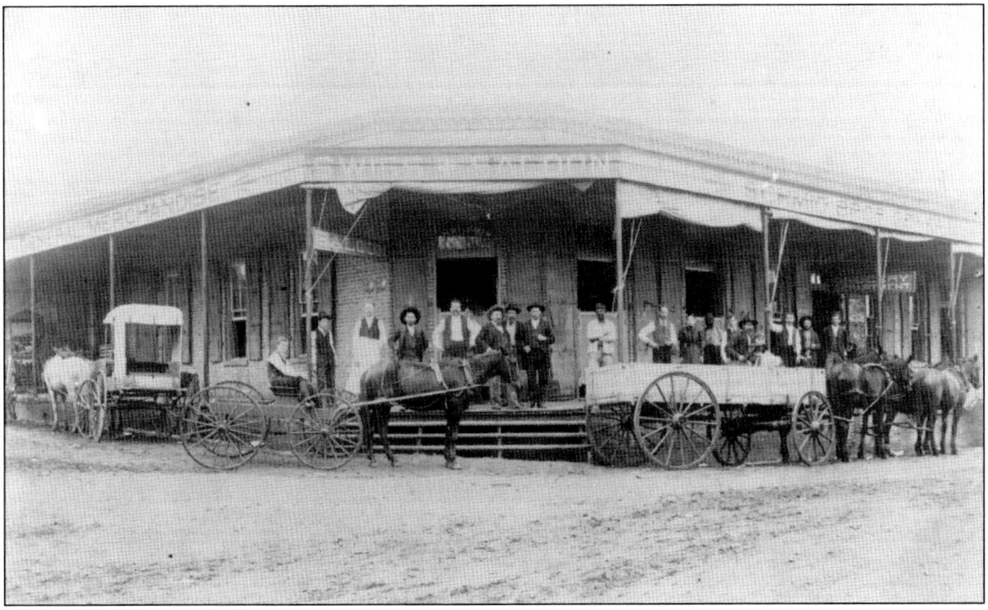

The Swiss Saloon boasted the corner spot next to Schmid Brothers Grocery at First and South Austin Streets. The Schmid brothers moved their grocery operation to Commerce Street about 1899. They were no stranger to beer themselves, advertising that they were the sole local distributor for the Lone Star Brewing Company.

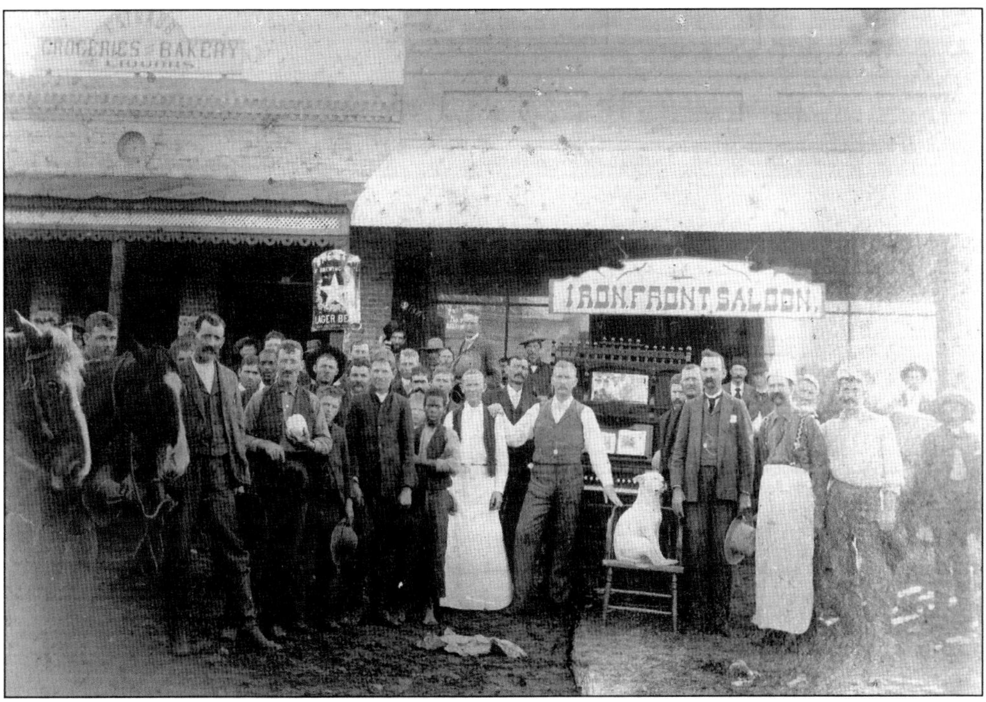

When the Iron Front Saloon got the chance to be photographed, it pulled out all the stops. It also pulled out the piano, two horses, a couple of bartenders, all the patrons, and a dog. Fritz Meyer was the owner during the 1890s before he sold out to a Mr. Heindenmann from Houston in early 1900.

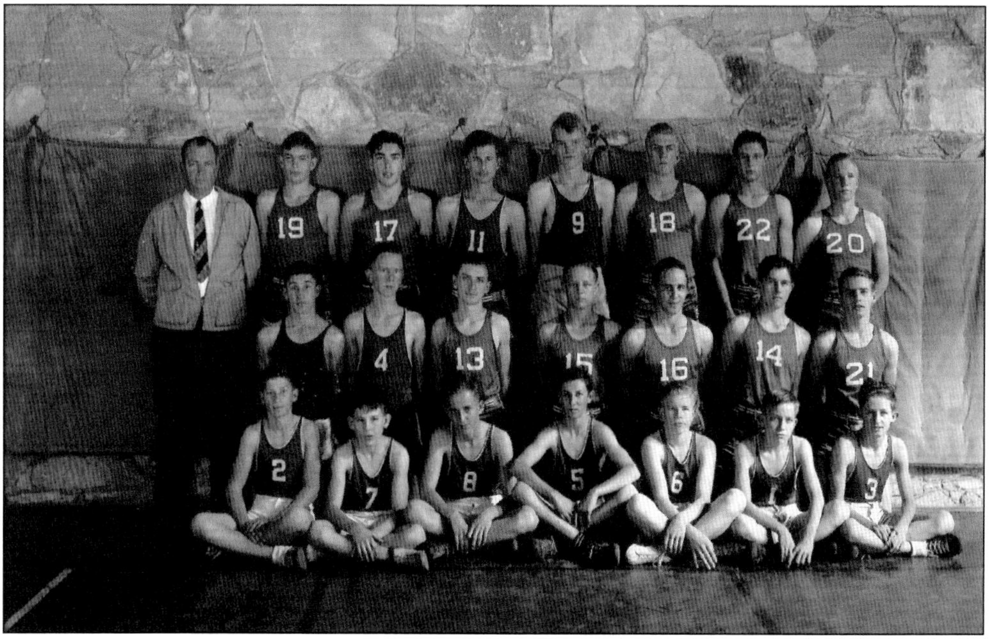

A Brenham Cubs basketball team poses inside the landmark rock gymnasium. Built with a local fieldstone veneer by the Works Progress Administration, a federal government New Deal program, the gym was similar to one built on the Blinn College campus about the same time. The Brenham High School version opened in 1940.

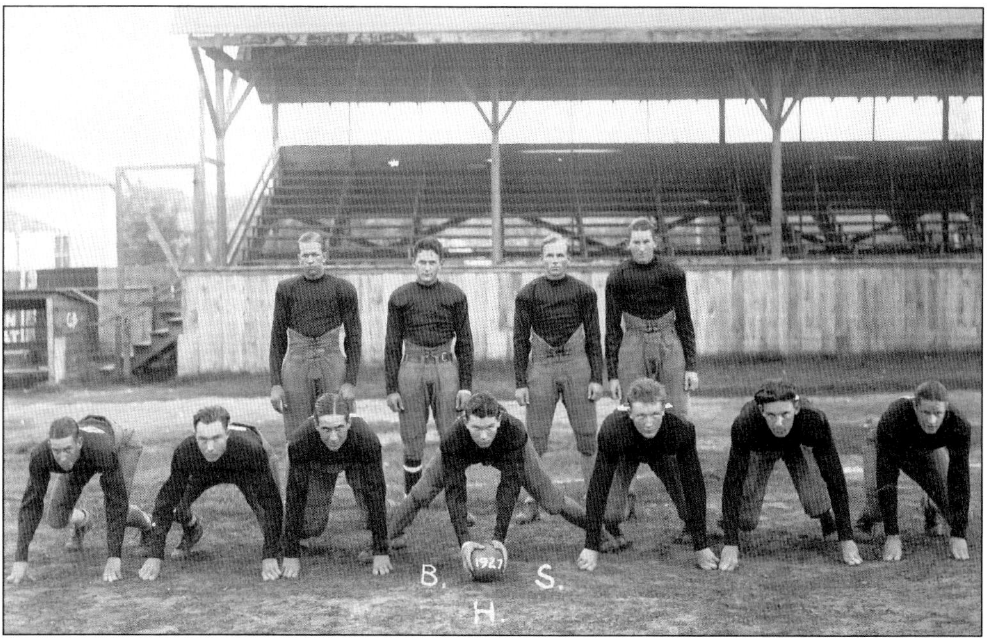

The Brenham High School football squad of 1927 played its games at Fireman's Park, where the starting 11 put on their fiercest game faces for this photograph. Under the guidance of coach Frank Allenson and captain and quarterback Vernon Wilkening, the Cubs went undefeated in regular season play, winning their first ever district and bi-district championships by beating powerhouses Caldwell and Georgetown.

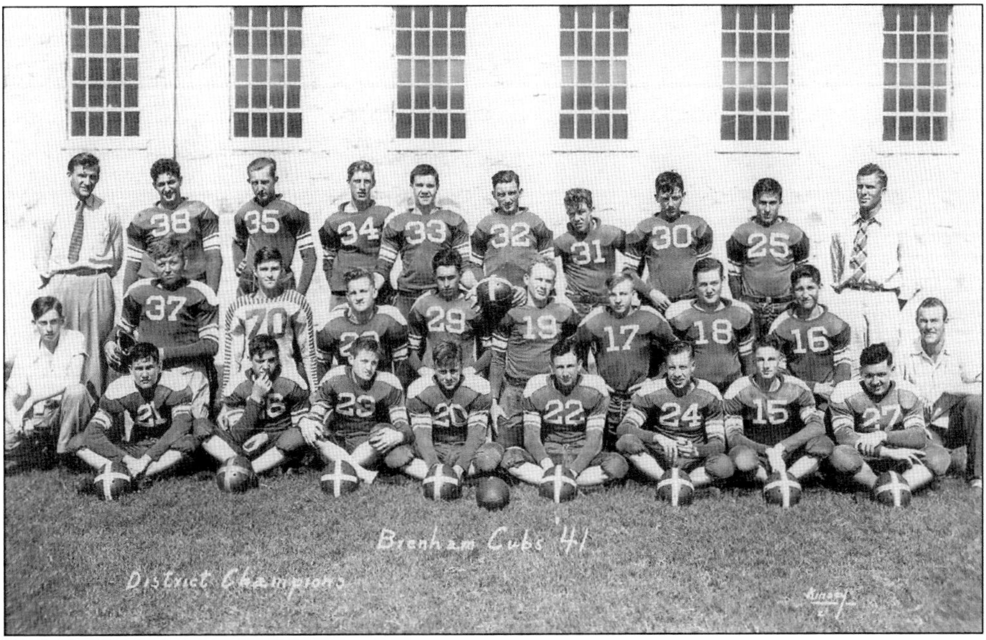

Brenham High's 1941 football team won the district championship. It was part of a strong run for the team that brought much local optimism. The following year marked the only undefeated gridiron squad in the school's history as the playoffs were canceled following regionals due to the country's involvement in World War II. (Susan Myers.)

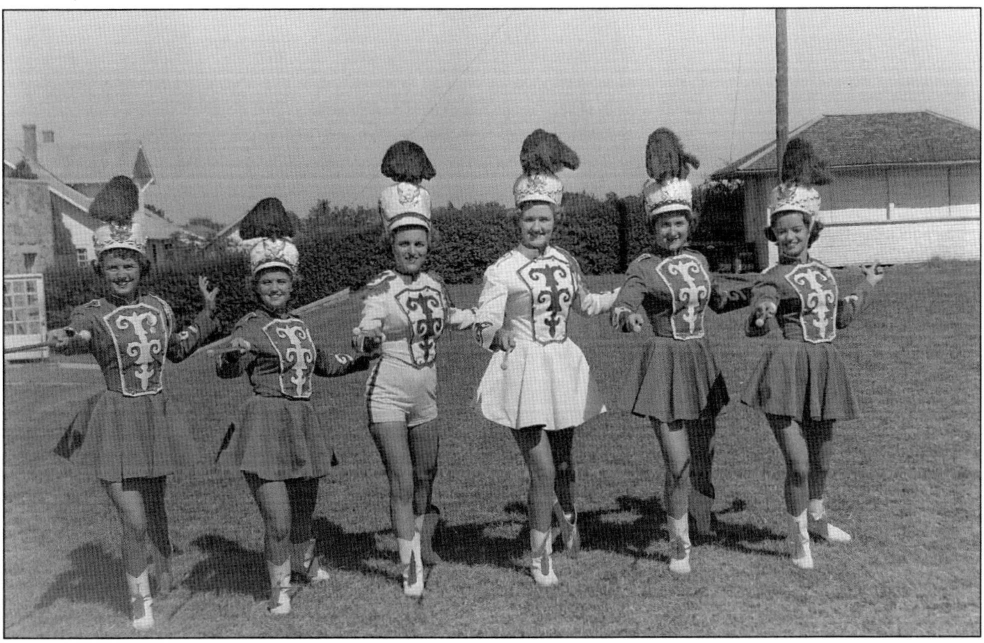
Brenham High School twirlers stand outside the rock-faced gymnasium in the early 1950s. It was a good time for Brenham Cubs athletics. The football teams were a relatively consistent district powerhouse in the post–World War II years, so the twirlers of the era could produce genuine smiles. The rock-faced gym was constructed with federal Works Progress Administration funds in 1939–1940.

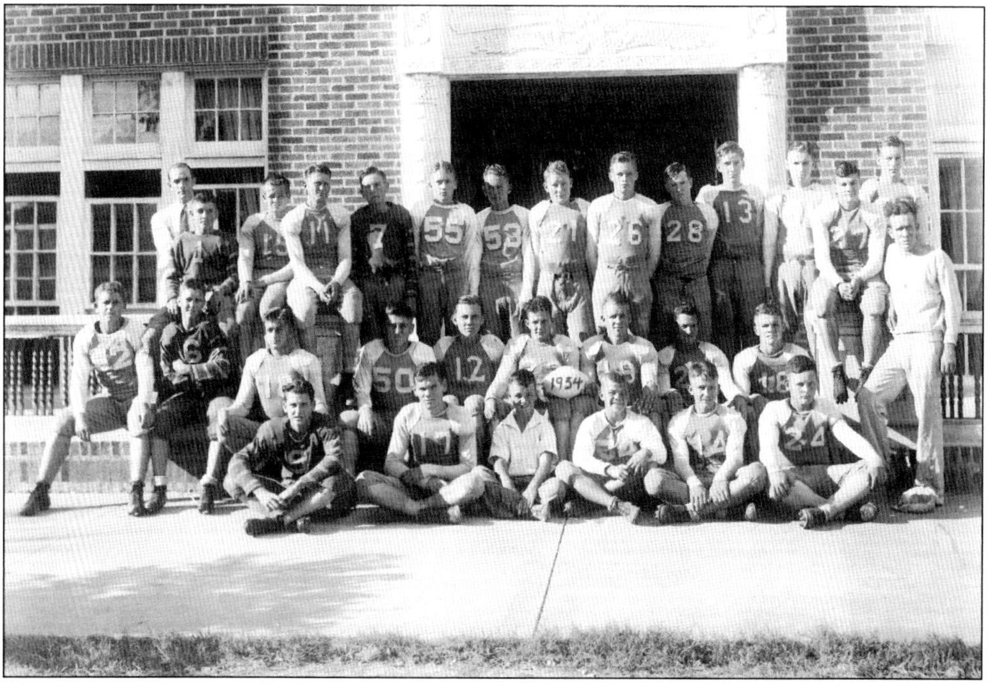

The 1934 Brenham High School football team poses on the school steps in practice jerseys. The official team photograph was under the goal posts, where the team did well. They did not quite live up to the regional finals team of the previous season, but coach Dan O'Neil led his Cubs squad to the district championship, where they lost a tough one to the Bryan Broncos.

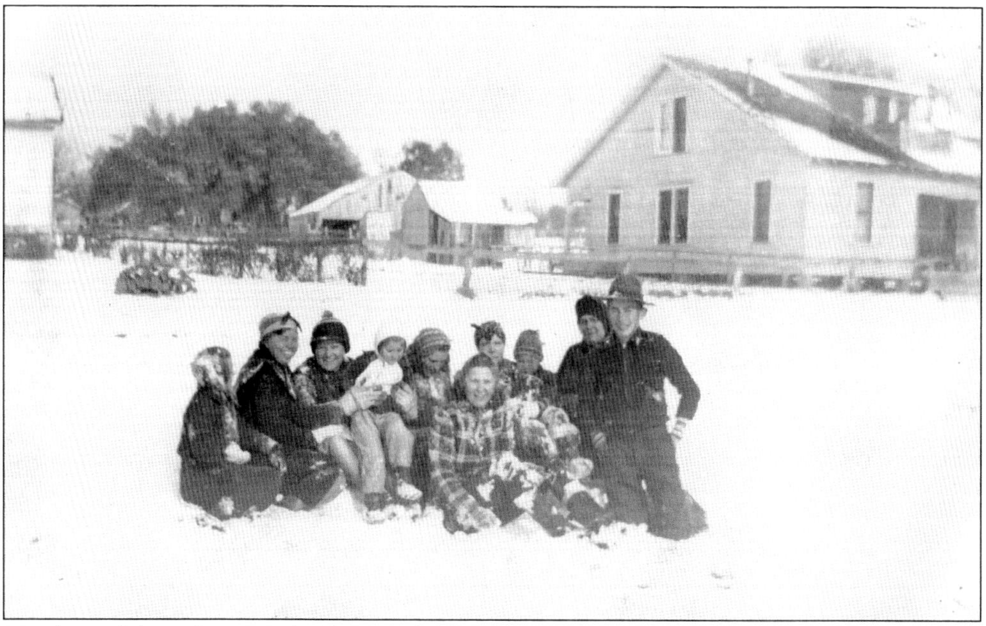

Members of the Lehrmann family and children from neighboring farms relished a rare snowfall in South Central Texas in 1937. Even more surprising was the fact that this winter storm arrived in November. Though Brenham itself saw only sleet and ice, the snowfall was heavy enough to stick all day in the northern portion of the county. (Debbie Lehrmann.)

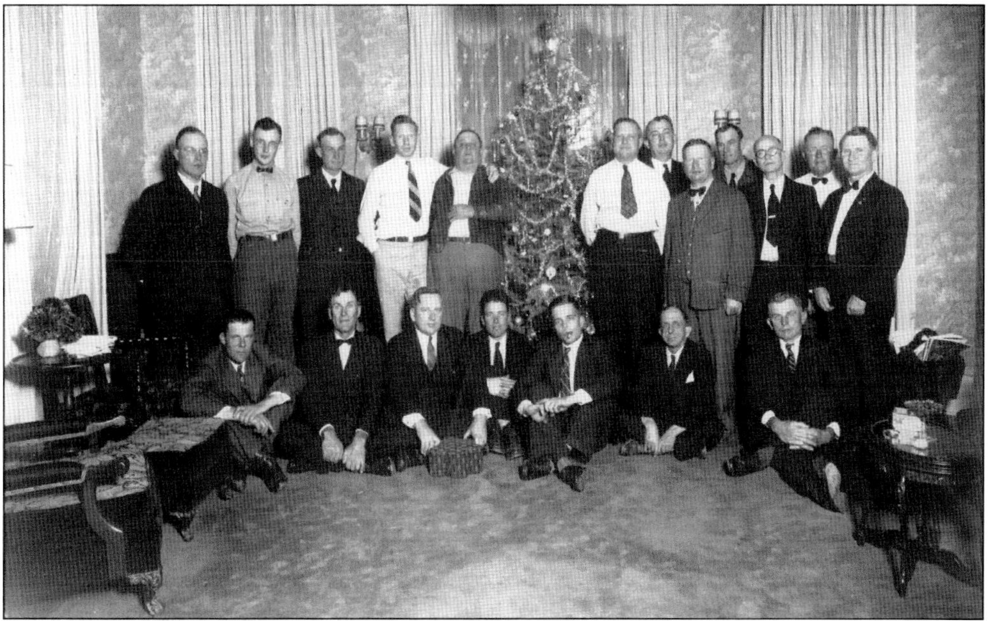

Employees of the Brenham Post Office gathered for a Christmas celebration at the home of postmaster T.A. Low Jr. He had taken over the top local postal job from Henrietta Fricke in 1934. On the eve of World War II, the Brenham Post Office oversaw six rural routes and also employed four city carriers and nine clerks in addition to custodians, who were not invited to the party.

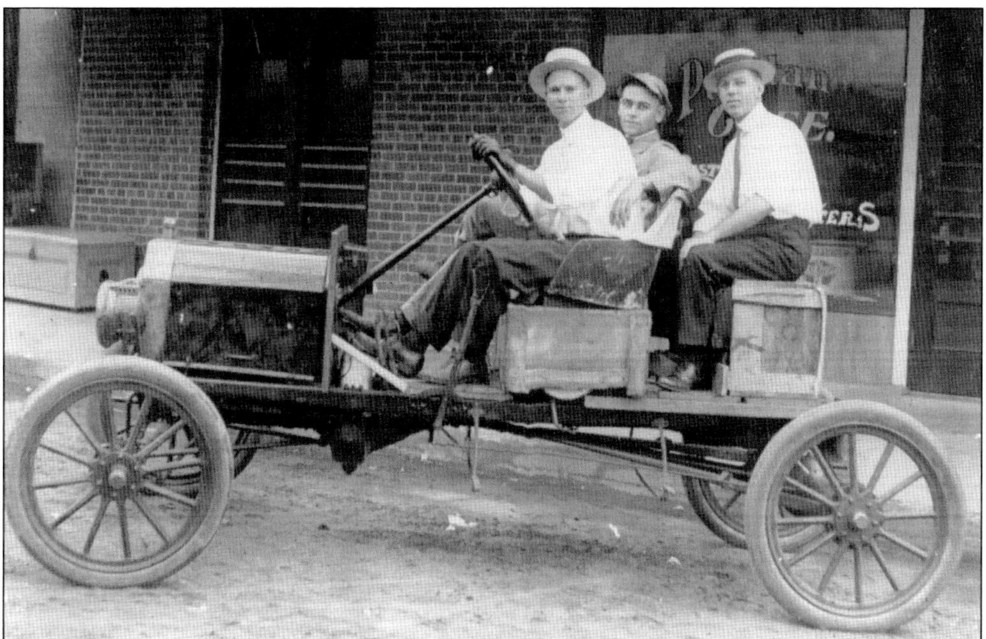

In the 1910s, automobile prices ranged from less than $400 for a Model T Ford to several thousand for high-end touring models. They were cheapest for enterprising souls who made their own by attaching wooden crate "seats" to the chassis. Behind this homemade vehicle is the Puritan Cafe, which closed in 1918 after the managers were called to military service and a fire destroyed the interior. (John Barnhill.)

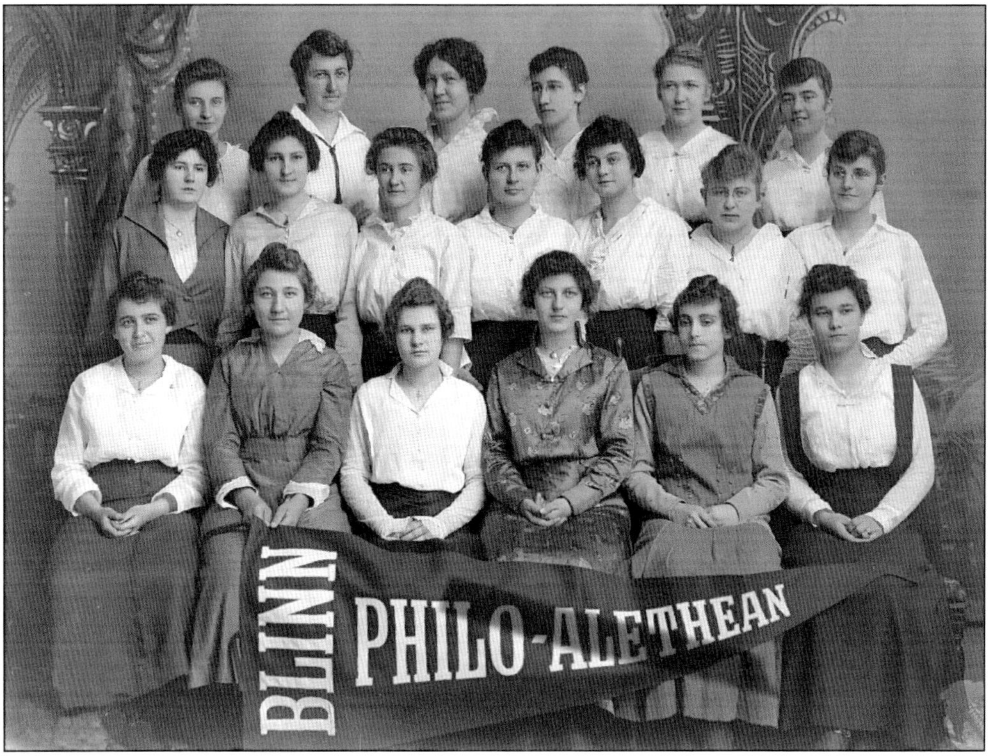

The Philo-Alethean Club at Blinn College was a women's organization that bridged the years on either side of World War I. The goal was the enjoyment of literary and artistic pursuits. A typical program in 1923 included a reading, two piano solos, a vocal duet, an original essay on "How I Spent my Vacation," and the presentation of riddles and jokes.

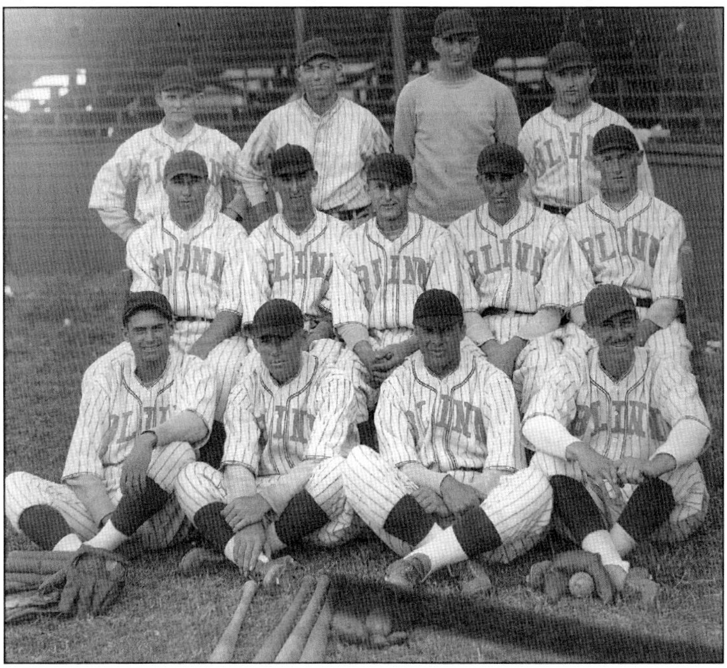

Blinn College's baseball team in 1928 was the first squad to move up to the junior college ranks. With so few Texas schools bearing that designation, competition came wherever it could be found, including regional high schools. Among those who came through that early Blinn program was Ernie Koy Sr., who starred at the University of Texas before going on to a long career in the National League. (Blinn College Library.)

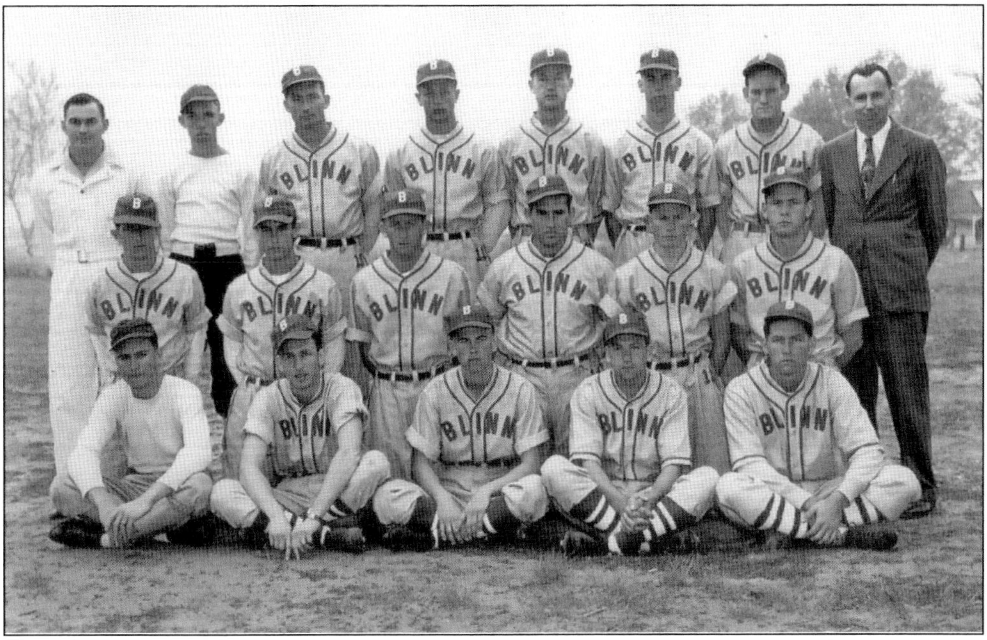

Blinn College wanted an intercollegiate baseball program in 1943 but needed a coach. The story is that the task fell to the campus professor who protested the least. Dr. Henry Boehm Sr., pictured at far right, was brought to campus to do the college's accounting and teach related courses. His previous baseball experience had been playing during high school in north central Texas. (Susan Myers.)

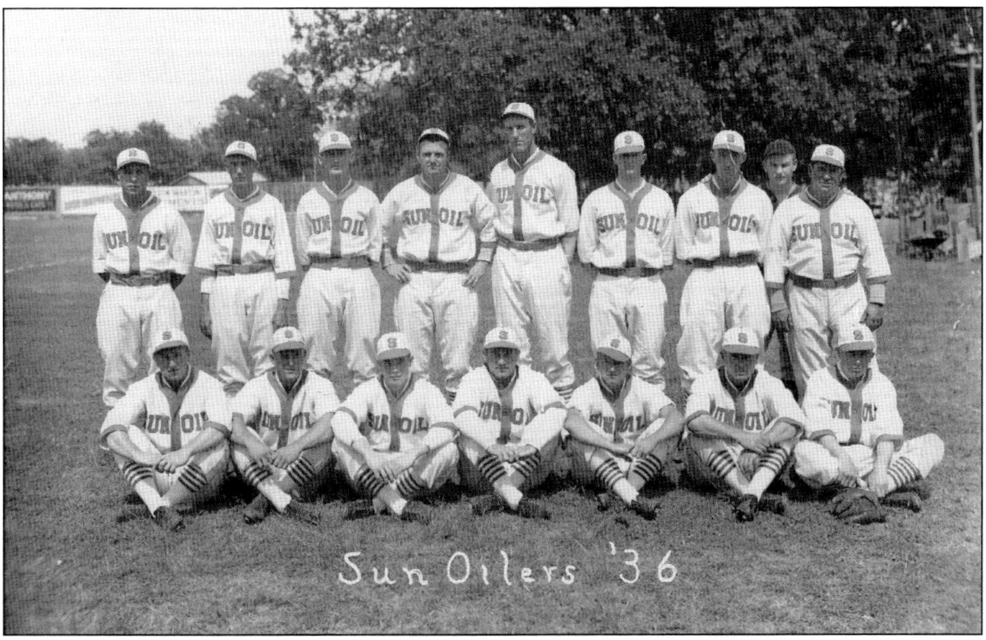

The Brenham Sun Oilers were a semiprofessional powerhouse in the 1930s. Though everyone was expected to be company employees, many ringers were on the payroll solely for their baseball prowess and to bring bragging rights to the company. The stars generally had at least college or minor league experience, and some even left the majors because the pay was higher in semiprofessional.

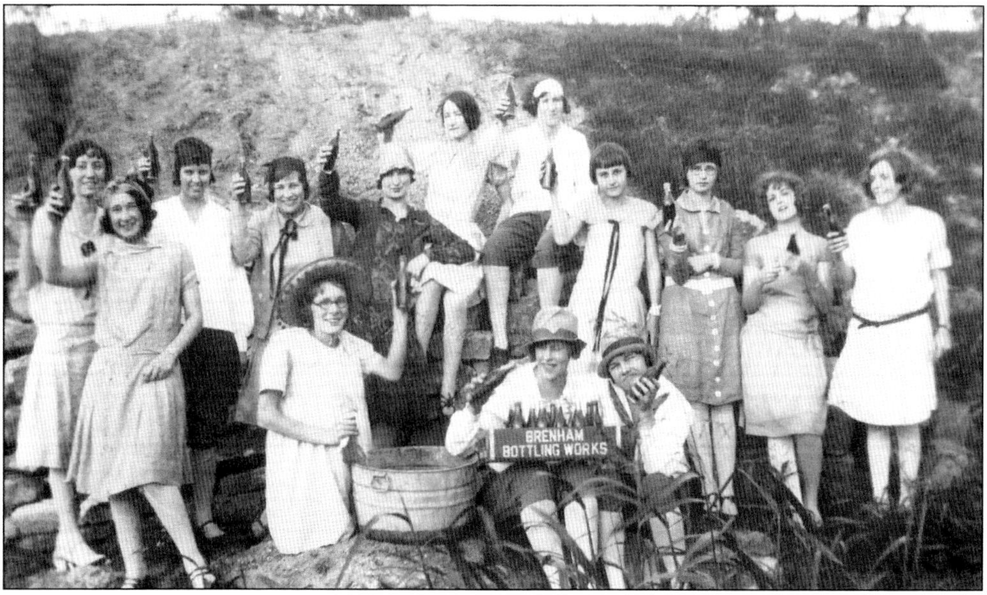

Brenham Bottling Works had the girls of Blinn College well supplied with sodas for this 1928 summertime outing. The company advertised that it was "bottlers of all kinds of soft drinks." As for the Blinn girls, they were enjoying one of the entertainment options open to them—socializing and talking. Late 1920s outdoor fashion had high hemlines, but stockings were still a must.

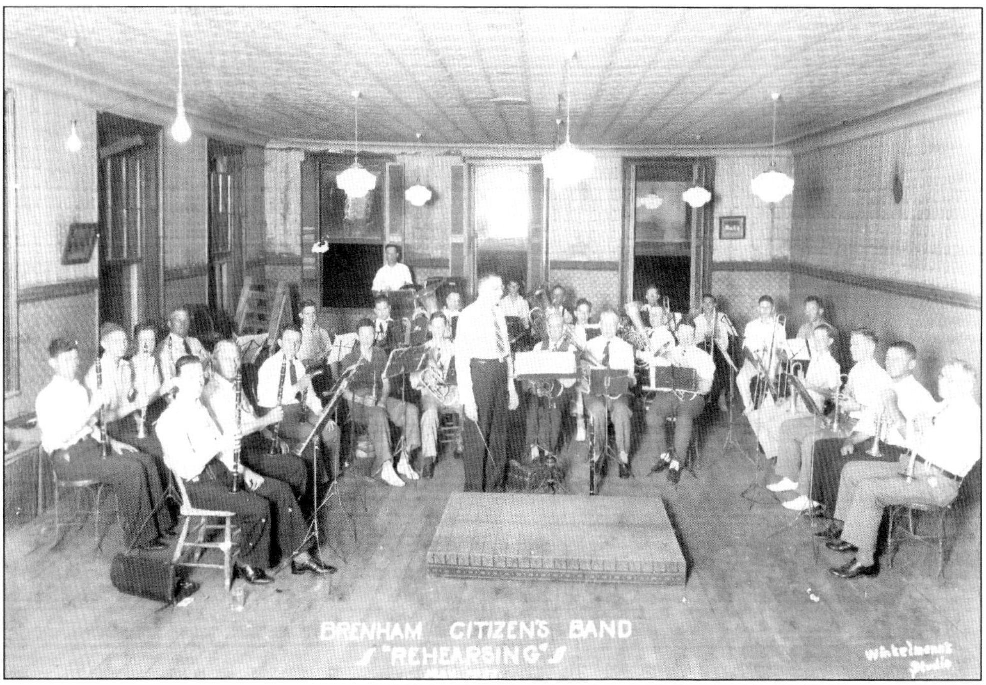

F.J. Navratil, as the orchestra leader, organized the Brenham Band in 1922. Over 300 local citizens and businesses gave money, from $50 down to a single dollar, to help buy instruments for the musicians. On nights that the band practiced above an Alamo Street business, locals often parked their cars to listen through the open windows. (Gloria Nix.)

Emmie Schlottmann was among the 1928 graduates of Blinn Memorial College. She and her friends spelled out the name of their alma mater on the bottoms of their shoes. Luckily, they lined up in the correct order. Their graduation year marked the first full year for Blinn as a junior college as opposed to the academy rank it previously held.

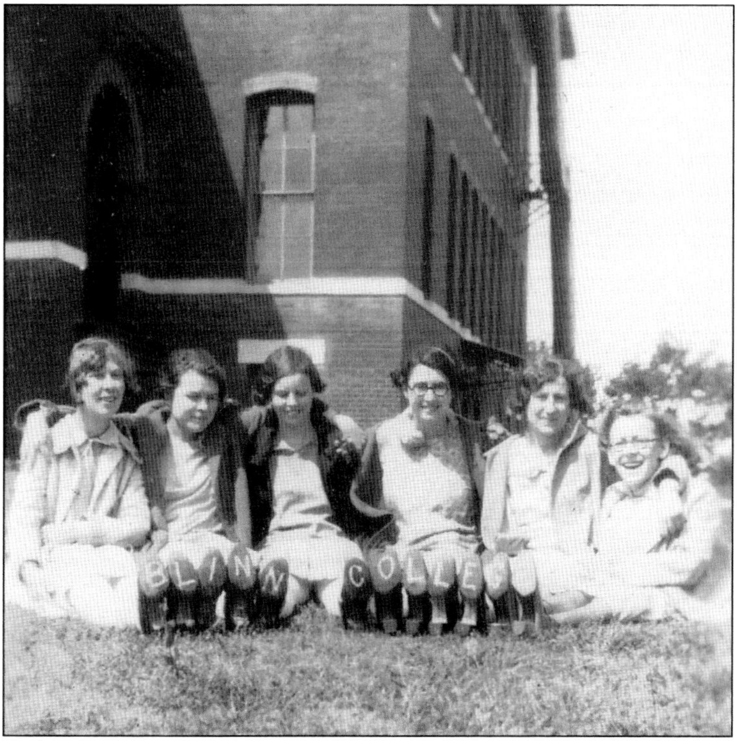

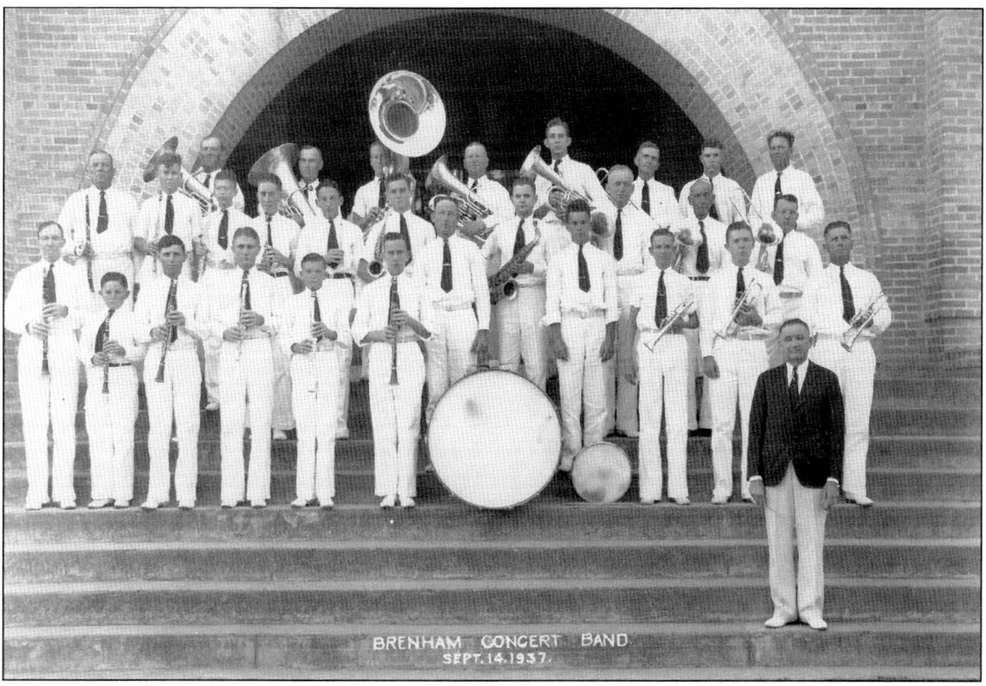

The Brenham concert band, comprised of men of all ages, poses in 1937. The band gave regular shows in the courthouse gazebo on warm summer nights. Citizens from around the county would come, with many adults remaining in their cars while children ran amok on the courthouse grounds. These concert nights meant a bonanza in ice cream sales for Barnhill's and Citizens Drugstores.

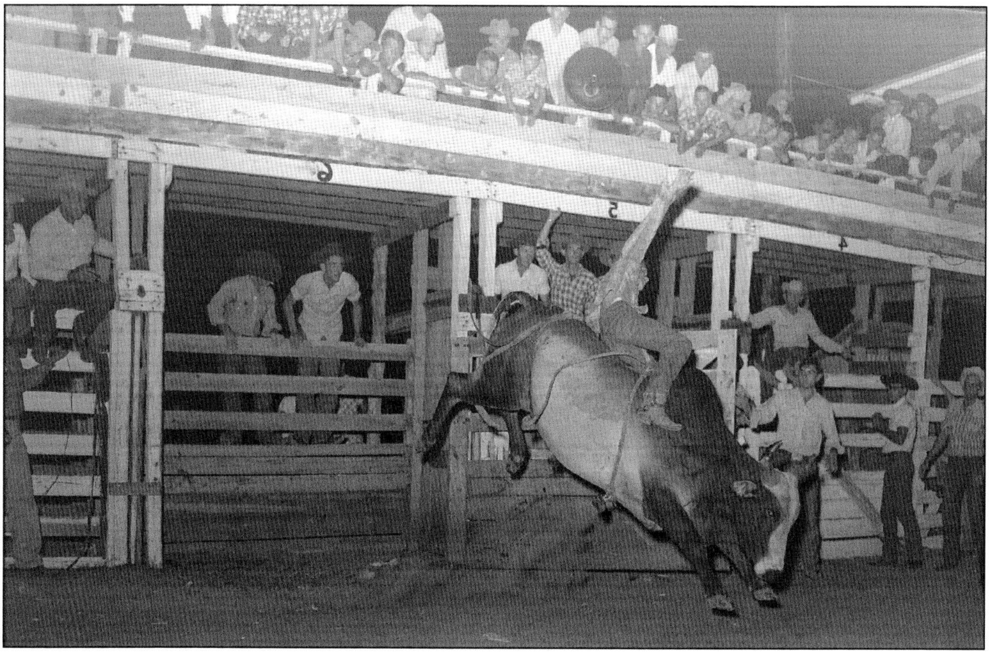

Rodeo man Reese Lockett introduced the sport to the Washington County Fair in 1932. By this rodeo in the early 1950s, a bigger and better arena was in place at the brand new fairgrounds, which opened in 1949 on the northeast side of town. The nightly rodeos drew large crowds from Washington and surrounding counties. (Washington County Fair.)

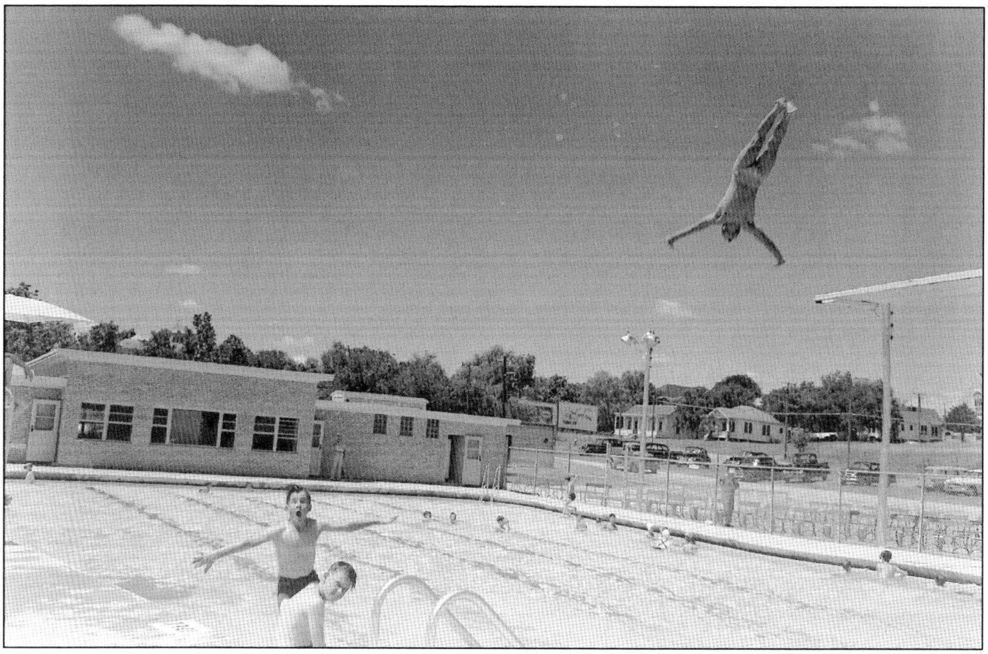

The Brenham pool opened in 1954, and two generations of local kids whose families did not belong to a private club spent summers there. The playground next to the Nancy Carol Roberts Library occupies the space today. The city pool remained until a new public aquatic center opened at the end of the 20th century.

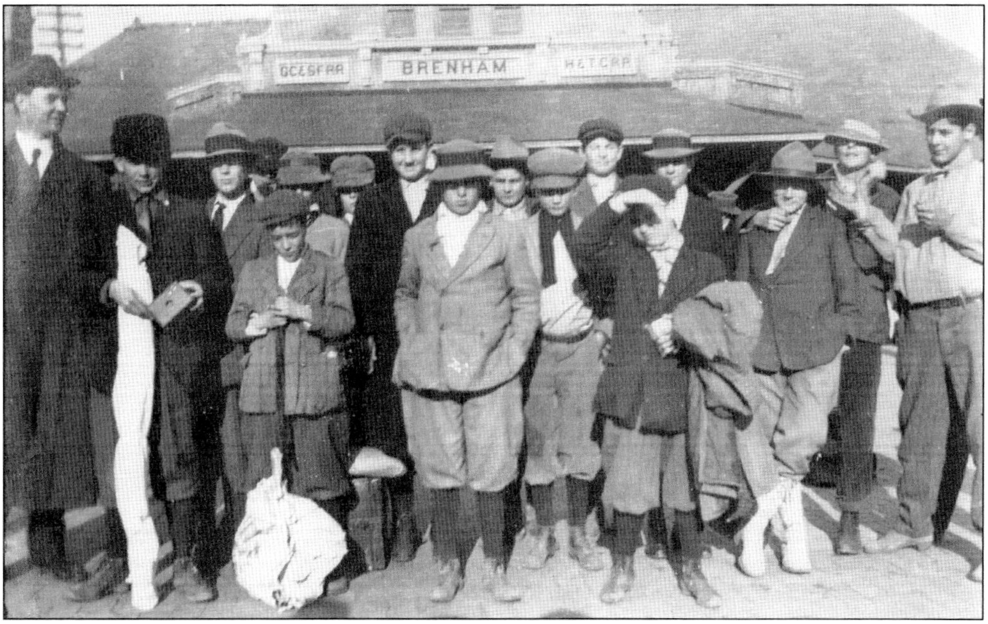

Young boys ready for a train ride on a cold day gather in front of the railroad depot that served both the Houston & Texas Central and the Gulf, Colorado & Santa Fe Railroads. The joint passenger depot was built in 1906 and lasted until 1957. It is now the site of the Washington County Chamber of Commerce.

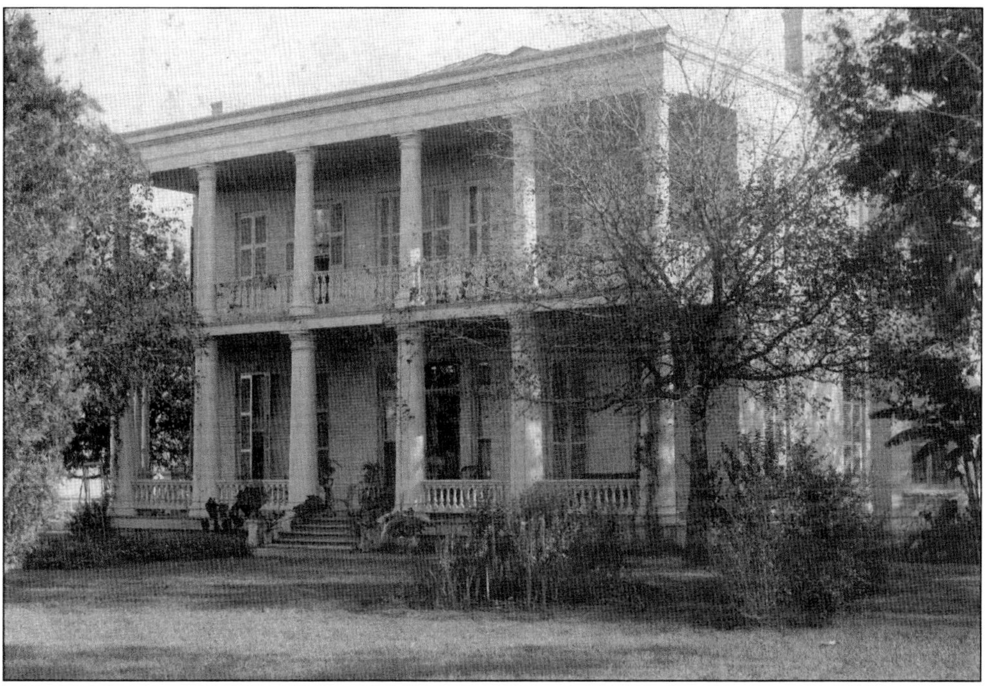

The Giddings-Stone Mansion was the grandest home in Brenham on the highest hill in town when it was completed in 1870. Local banker and attorney J.D. Giddings moved his family into the palatial home and later passed it on to his sole surviving daughter, Mary, and her husband, Heber Stone. Giddings descendants remained in the home for over a century.

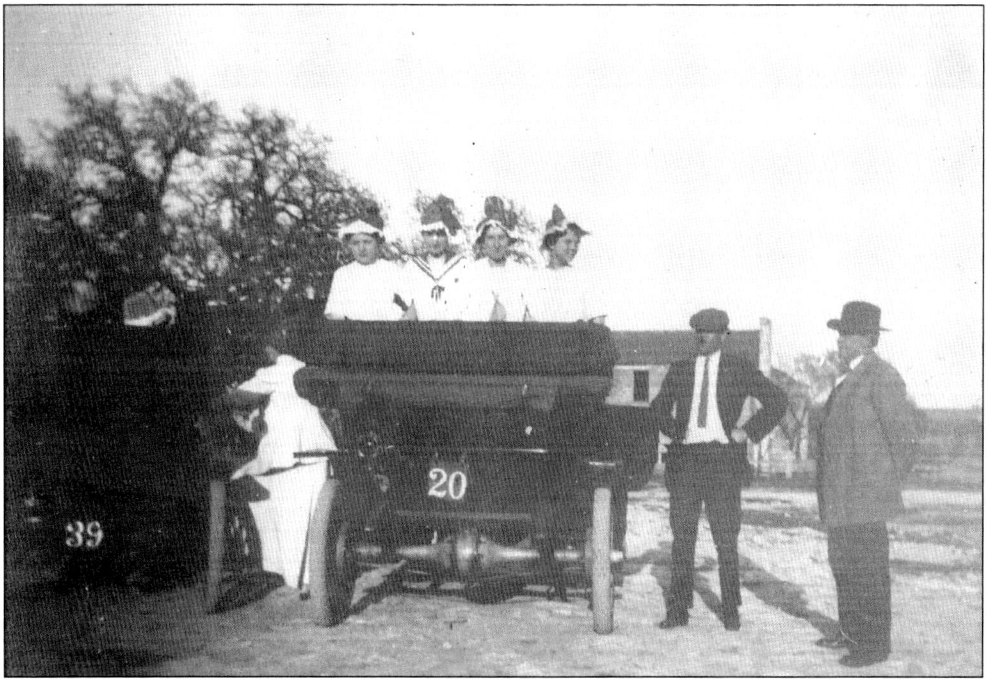

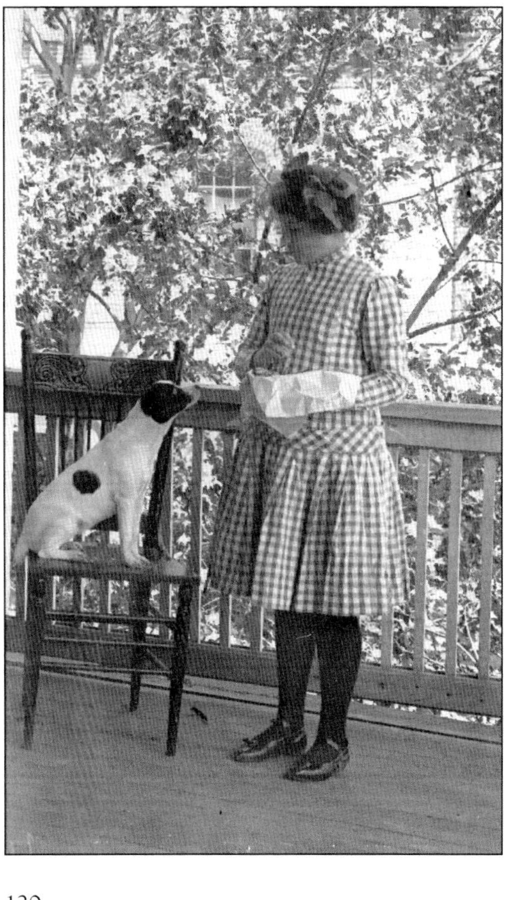

When Frank Wood Jr. captured these young ladies in the back of an early automobile, he probably did not realize that the biggest rarity would be the double-digit license plates issued not by the state but by Washington County. These were the 20th and 39th cars registered that year.

Frank Wood photographed his younger sister and her dog on the family's Academy Street porch in the 1910s. George Eastman, the pioneer of photographic film, had introduced the Kodak Brownie in 1900. That box camera brought photography to the masses, creating the snapshot and hundreds of thousands of photography enthusiasts like Wood.

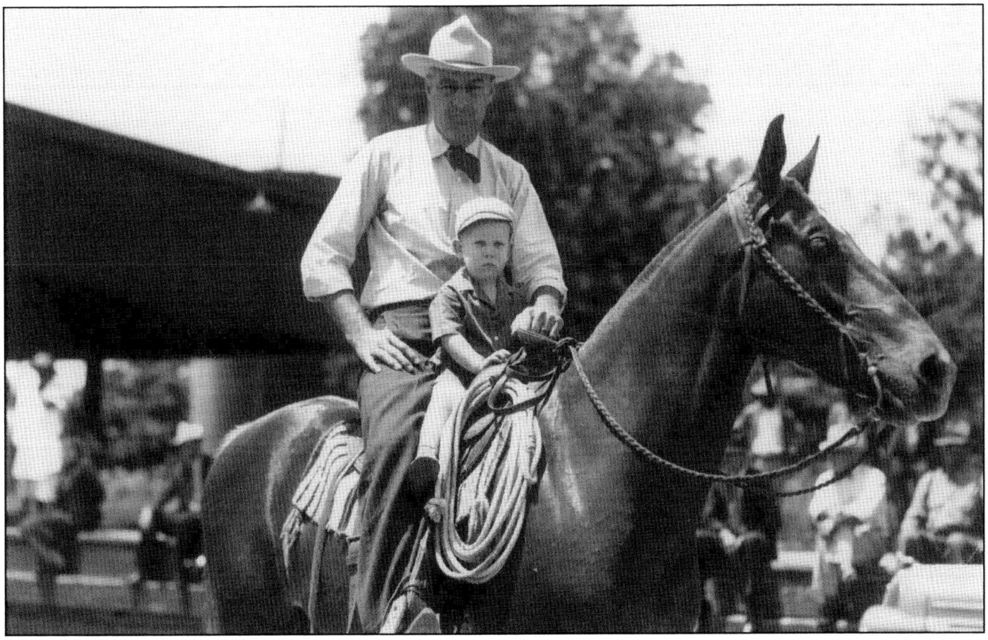

With his rodeo background, Reese Lockett was comfortable on horseback throughout his time as Brenham's mayor. His son Reese Jr. was introduced to horse riding early. Lockett Jr. served as one of the last of the Maifest Parade's sporadic grand marshals. On that downtown ride, he used a beautiful saddle inlaid with silver that had been presented to his father by the Houston Livestock Show and Rodeo.

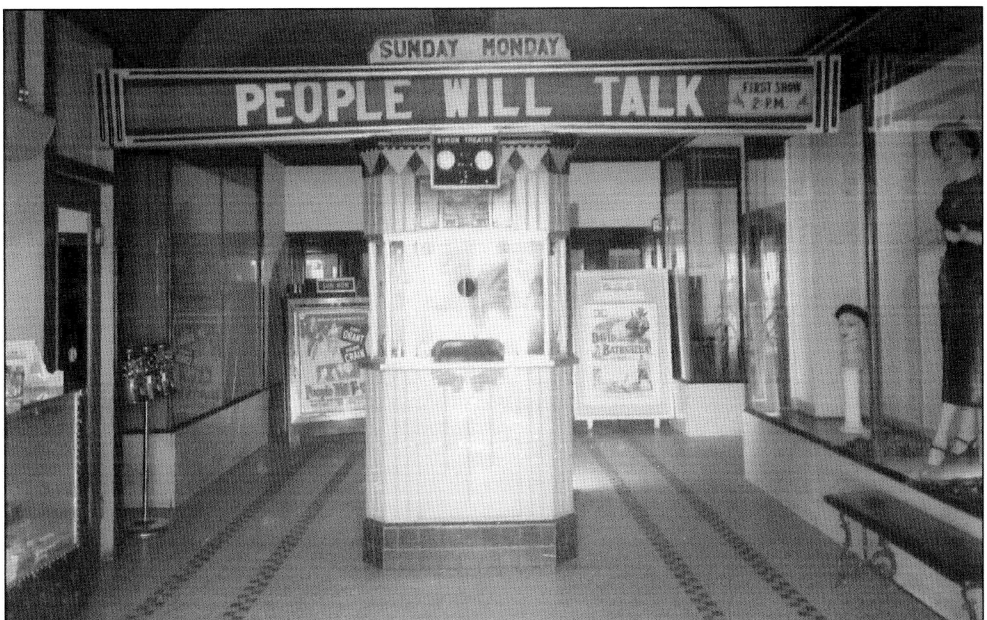

The 1951 20th Century Fox feature *People Will Talk* played at the Simon Theatre with Cary Grant and Jeanne Crain in the starring roles. At the start of this decade, the Simon was Brenham's upscale theater most likely to have popular new releases. The Rex operated a few blocks away, and the new Starlite Drive-In was rocking on the highway just east of town.

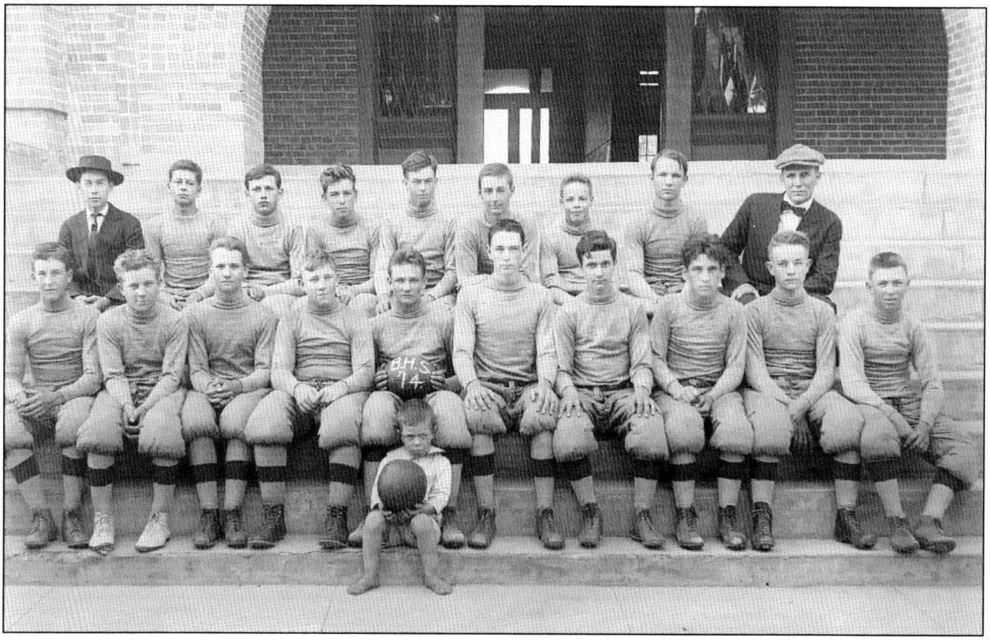

Padding was rather limited for the 1916 Brenham High School football team. The star that year was Wallace Buck, an underclassman who was described in the yearbook as a "demon on defense" and whose "plunges never failed to gain 3 or 4 yards on fourth down." The team did opine that they hoped the student body would show the football team greater support in the future.

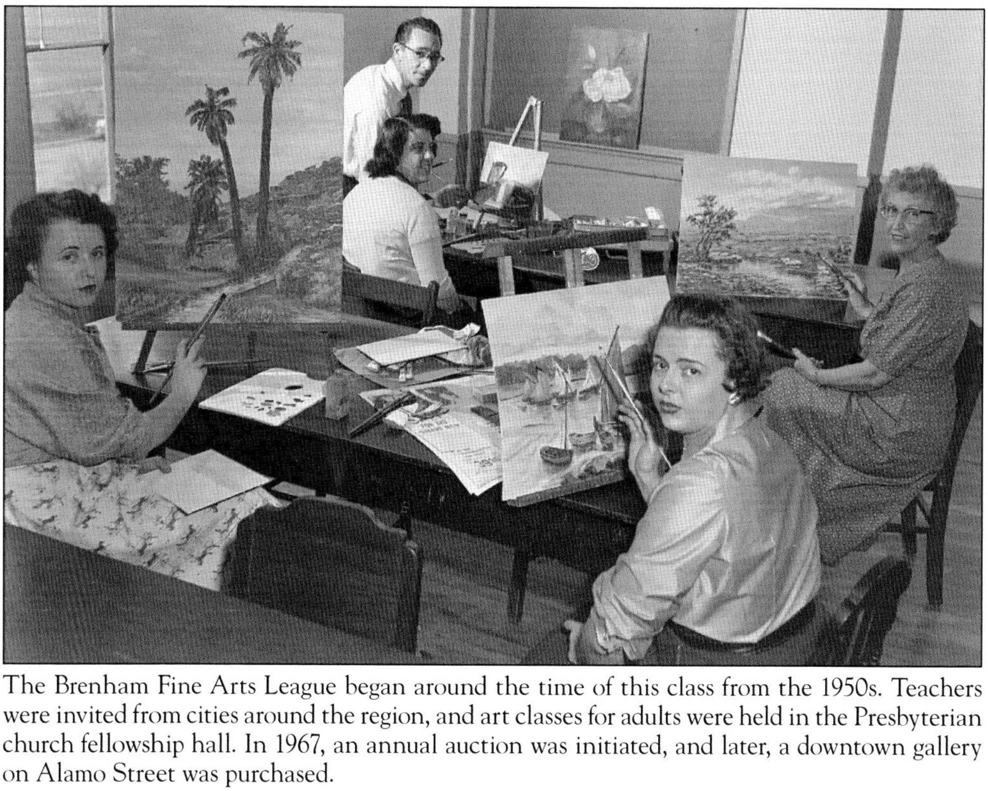

The Brenham Fine Arts League began around the time of this class from the 1950s. Teachers were invited from cities around the region, and art classes for adults were held in the Presbyterian church fellowship hall. In 1967, an annual auction was initiated, and later, a downtown gallery on Alamo Street was purchased.

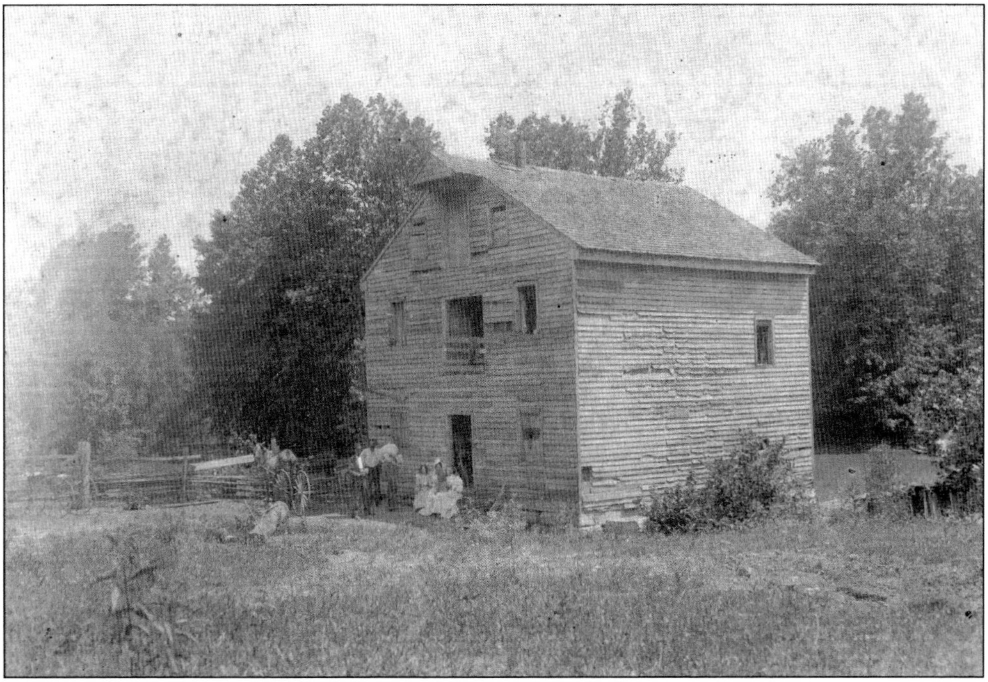

This unidentified old mill was a fine spot for a late-19th-century outing. A few decades earlier, mills were vital to improving the area. Sawmills produced boards for construction, and gristmills made the grain needed for breads and other baking. This mill, on a stream, was powered by water, but before 1830, Austin's Colony also had mills run by steam and some by oxen.

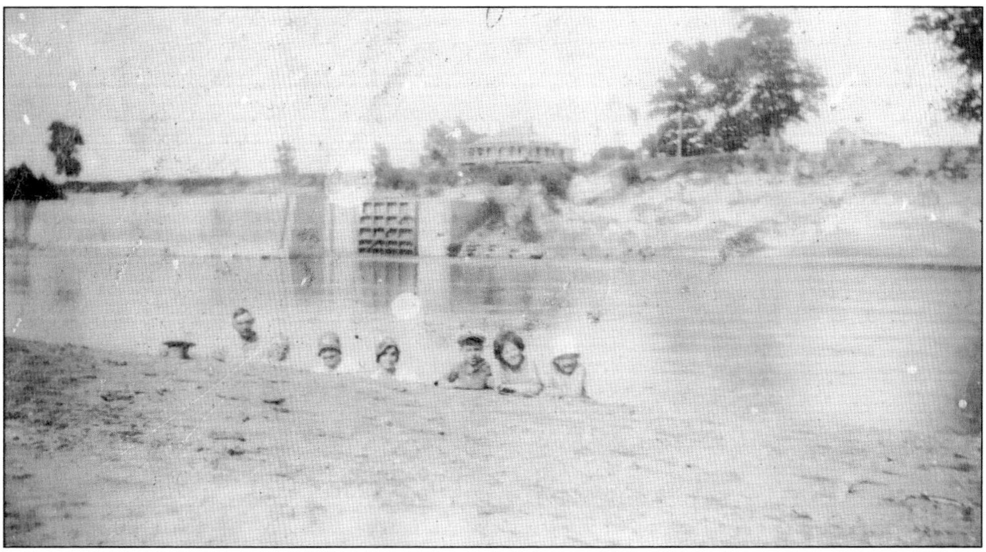

Hidalgo Falls remains a natural feature on the Brazos River near where Brazos and Grimes Counties meet on the east bank. It had been an impediment to the idea of riverboat traffic since Americans came to Austin's Colony in the 1820s. A river lock built about 1910 failed to solve the problem, but it did prove to be a popular swimming hole for residents of eastern Washington County. (Stanley Sommer.)

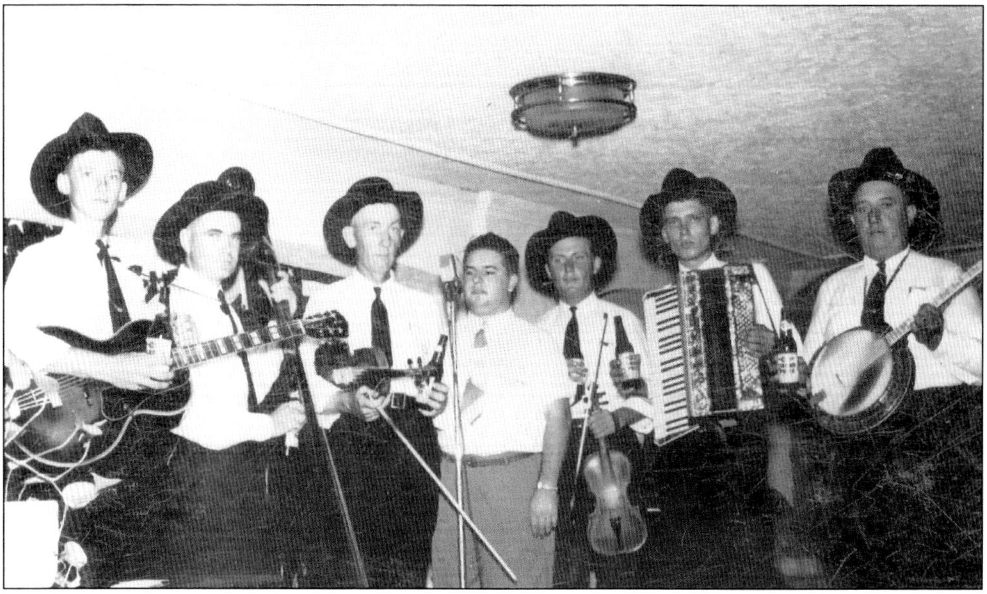

Brenham High grad Sonny Look, posing with the band, achieved restaurant fame in Houston, but started at the New York Café on Main Street as a busboy. He eventually bought the place. He sold it with a gentlemen's agreement to buy it back when he returned from World War II, but the new owner refused to uphold the handshake deal, so Look moved to the Bayou City in 1945.

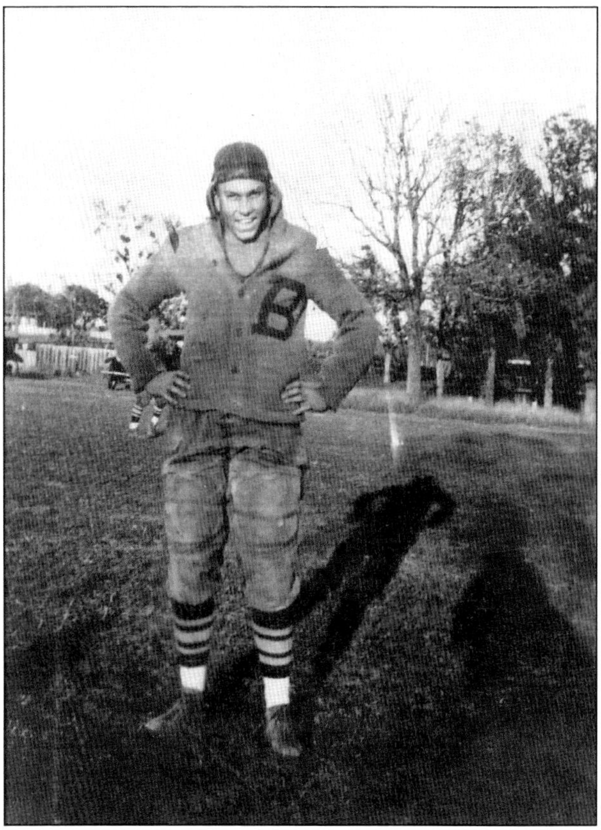

Lathe Morriss, son of the Washington County surveyor, played quarterback for Brenham High School in 1921 and also returned punts. It was a far cry from athletics a century later. The schedule was still being added to in late September, and the Brenham Rotary Club's gift of $150 was necessary to supply "football equipment."

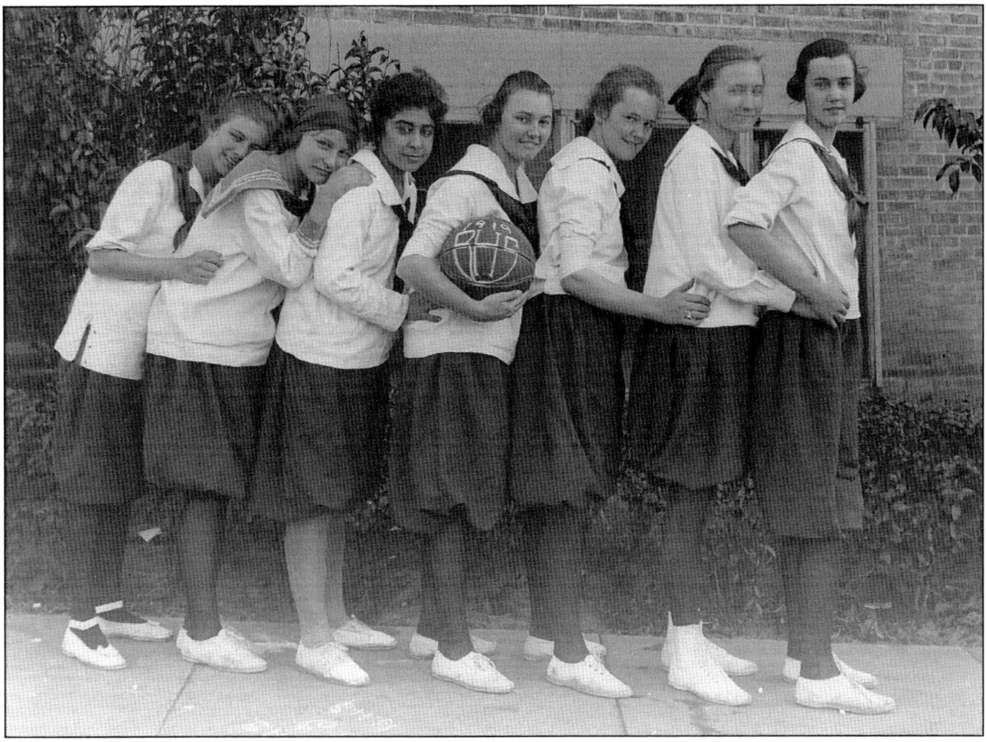

The Brenham High girls' basketball team in 1919 played in a rather ad hoc system. Though the University Interscholastic League formed in 1913, girls' basketball championships were not awarded until 1950. Outside competition in 1919 was arranged one-on-one with other schools or organizations. That same season, Temple High trumpeted itself as the best in the state after winning just two games.

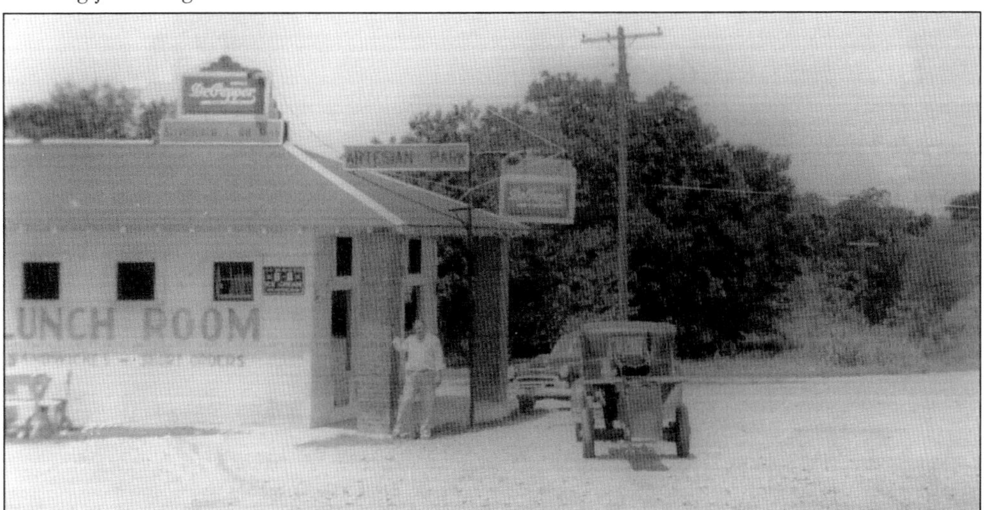

The Artesian Park Lunchroom opened in 1931 in a former Gulf gas station adjacent to the swimming pool constructed three years prior. The pool offered cold spring water. Johnnie Grabarschick was the manager-operator of the café and dance hall in the late 1940s when he posed outside. Though the name lives on, the once-popular pool was filled in long ago.

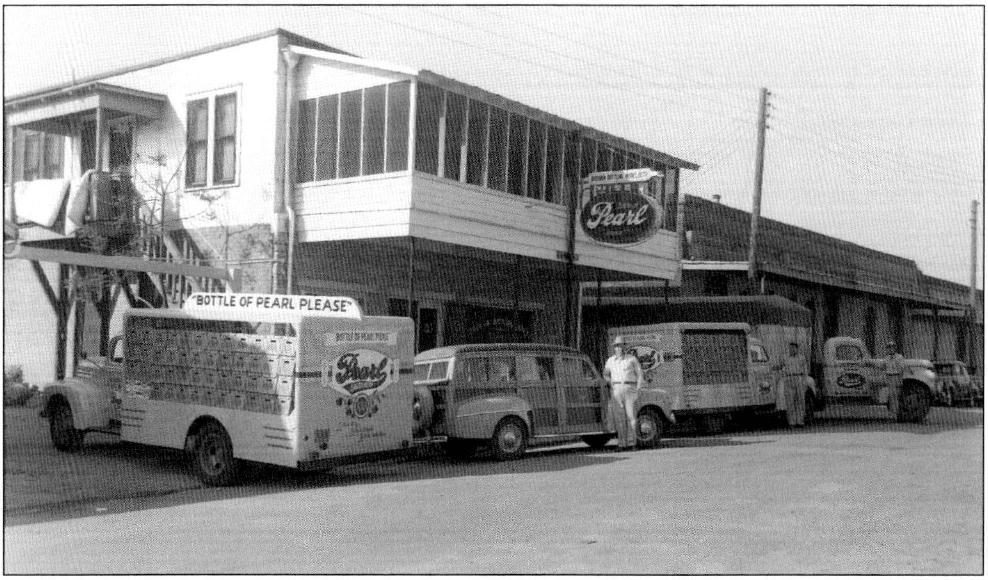

Pearl Beer distributor Manny Lehrmann had his bottling business in this space on First Street, which operated later as a taproom. An earlier Brenham, with a third of its current population, had as many as two dozen saloons operating at one time. Many of the establishments offered free food, and workers spent their lunch breaks enjoying a cold beer or three.

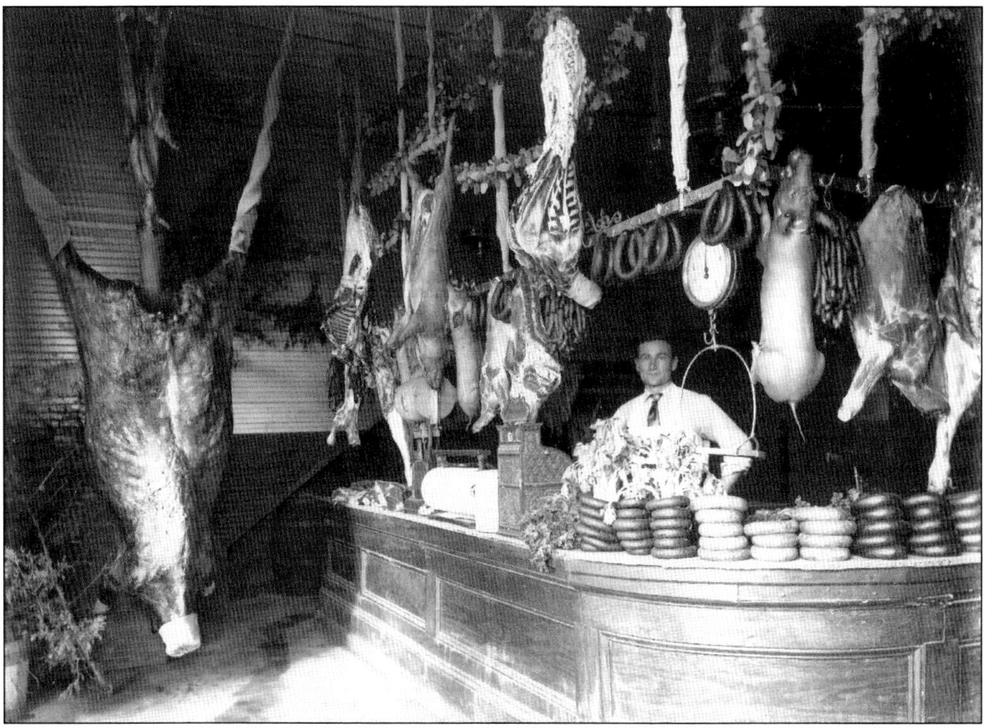

Meat markets abounded in Washington County. This one offered everything from a ring of sausage to whole turkeys or hogs. These German American–owned meat markets also often sold smoked meat by weight to hungry workers of all ethnicities. Those takeaway lunches wrapped in butcher paper started a legacy still enjoyed in central Texas today.

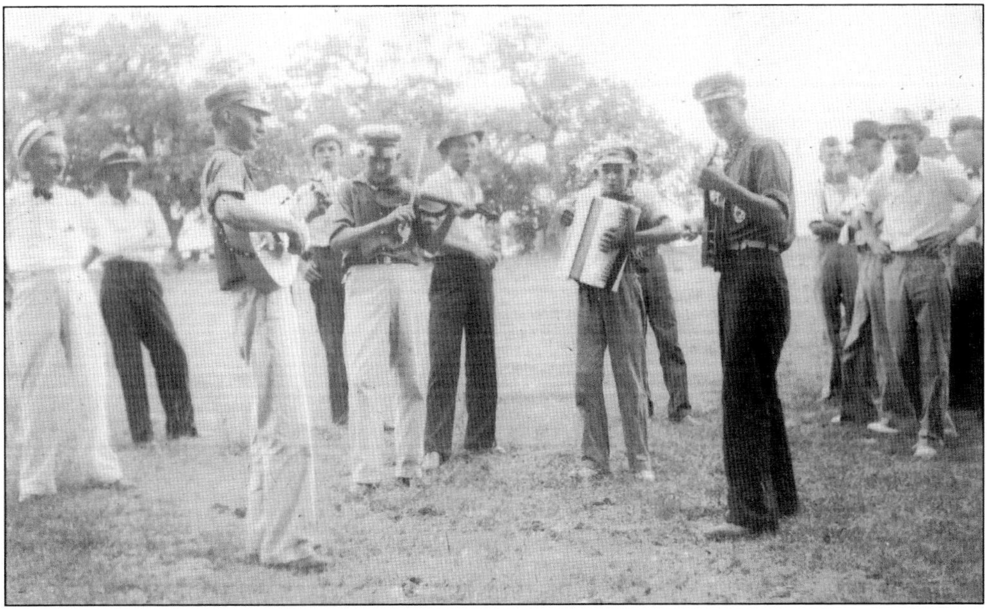

The 4 Square Boys regularly provided dance music at places like Maennerchor Hall in Welcome in the late 1930s. Sometimes they did not even require a hall, as evidenced by this outdoor gig at a Washington County ranch. At the time, dance halls dotted Southeast Central Texas and could be busy venues on the weekend or even midweek. (Stanley Sommer.)

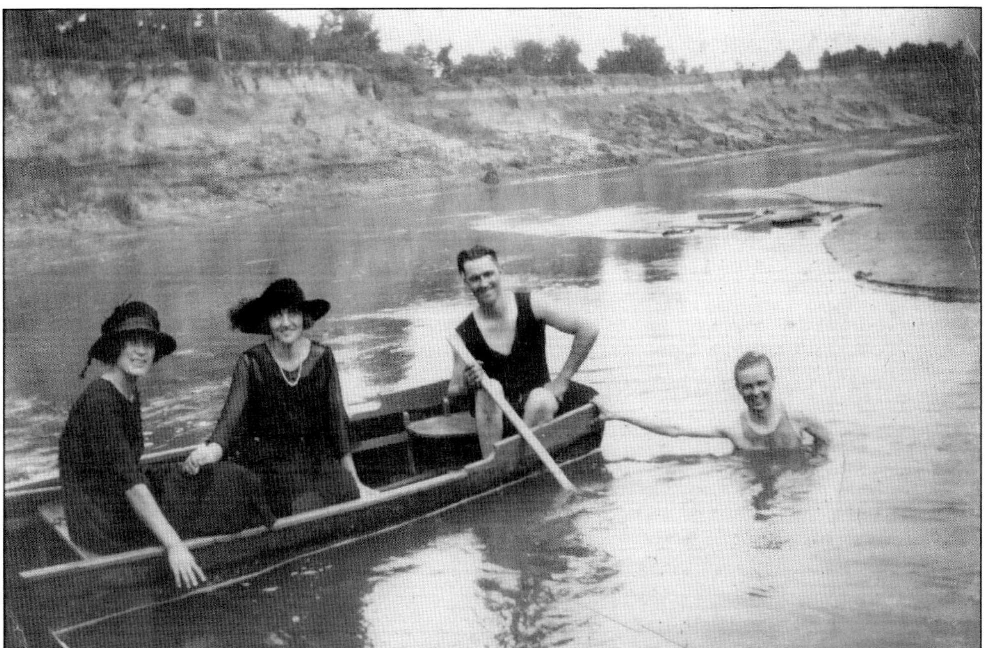

Today, most Texans, even those in Washington County, think of the Brazos River as merely a bridge on their travels or a potential flooding problem that impacts agriculture. For locals of an earlier era, the Brazos was a recreation spot. Motor boats were rare in the 1920s, but swimmers, fishermen from boats or banks, and canoeists of all stripes were plentiful. (Stanley Sommer.)

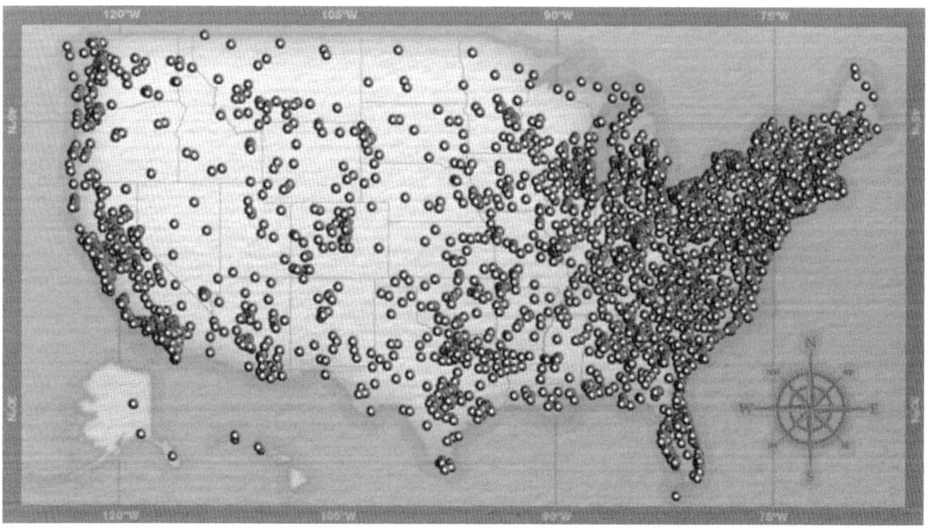